EX LIBRIS

Claude O. Winans
California Collection

CALIFORNIANA

OUTPOST OF EMPIRE
by Herbert Eugene Bolton

THE BARBARY COAST
by Herbert Asbury

LOS ANGELES
by Morrow Mayo

These are Borzoi Books,
published by ALFRED A. KNOPF

THE BIG FOUR

THE BIG FOUR

THE STORY OF HUNTINGTON, STANFORD, HOPKINS, AND CROCKER, AND OF THE BUILDING OF THE CENTRAL PACIFIC

BY

OSCAR LEWIS, *1893-*

1938

ALFRED A KNOPF

NEW YORK   LONDON

Part of this book appeared in The Atlantic Monthly
under the title
MEN AGAINST MOUNTAINS

FOREWORD

When the rails of the Central Pacific and Union Pacific Railroads were joined in Utah Territory in the spring of 1869, the pioneer era of the West drew to its official close. The building of the first transcontinental railroad profoundly influenced the social, economic, and political life of the Pacific Coast, bringing about its transition from an isolated and largely self-sustaining region to one with fortunes closely linked with those of the rest of the nation.

It was a period rich in significance and incident, and one not often touched on today. " California Annexes the United States," read one of the transparencies carried through San Francisco streets the night the driving of the last spike was celebrated; the sentiment signified the mood in which the Pacific Coast, half playful, half arrogant, prepared to shake off its enforced insularity and to take its place (near the head of the table) with the family of states.

Typical products of that period were the Central Pacific's Big Four: Huntington, Stanford, Crocker, and Hopkins — men who from places behind the counters of pioneer stores had, in far less than two decades, shouldered their way upward to places of national importance. The careers of these four, and of half a dozen of their associates, covered a long and colorful era of Pacific Coast history, beginning with Mark Hopkins's landing at San Francisco in '49 and ending with Huntington's death in 1900.

It should be pointed out that the attempt to trace the

rise of the Big Four, to judge their methods and motives, and to evaluate their accomplishments was beset by rather unusual difficulties. The group held the center of the stage in California for more than a third of a century, and during the entire period there was hardly an issue of a Pacific Coast newspaper or magazine that did not contain references to some phases of their varied activities. Almost none of this, however, is impartial comment. Enterprises controlled by the Big Four closely affected the interests of so large a part of the population that few commentators could, or wished to, write of them without bias. Consequently the mass of material written about " the railroad " falls naturally into one or another of two groups: that which emanated from papers controlled by the railroad or from individuals enjoying or hoping to enjoy favors at its hands, and, balancing this, the outpourings of the group of journals and individuals that made opposition to the Big Four their chief stock in trade.

In the present work the aim has been to steer a middle course through this mass of contradictory evidence and at the same time to select for emphasis those events that most clearly reveal the personalities and motives of the controlling group. For the book is primarily biographical; it is not intended to be a formal history of the Central Pacific Railroad. Readers will find, therefore, some phases of the road's story but sketchily presented, and others related in much fuller detail than a strict regard for historical proportion can justify. These pages attempt to throw into perspective the group brought into prominence by the railroad enterprises, to show them in relation to their general and specific backgrounds, and to trace how they influenced — and were in turn influenced by — the remarkable chain of events that drew them from their Sacramento shops and gave them a degree of wealth and power unprecedented in the West.

A list of the sources consulted, and acknowledgments to institutions and individuals, will be found at the end of the volume.

CONTENTS

ILLUSTRATIONS

Illustrations

THE BIG FOUR

JUDAH

"I HAVE ALWAYS HAD TO
PIT MY BRAINS . . . AGAINST OTHER
MEN'S MONEY. . . ."

1

THEODORE DEHONE JUDAH died in 1863, at the age of thirty-seven years and eight months, and he was forgotten almost at once. He was never considered an entirely normal man and there were times when he was a trial to his pretty wife, who had been Anna Pierce, a belle of Greenfield, Massachusetts. Miss Pierce was a daughter of a senior warden of the Greenfield Episcopal Church, and there is other evidence that she had not been raised to be the wife of an eccentric man whose condition was complicated by a touch of what may have been genius. Yet she made him a good wife, following him dutifully to places far removed from Greenfield and writing, after he was dead, some intelligent and forceful letters in his defense.

During his lifetime the word "fanatic" was not considered too strong to apply to him even by his friends. Within the last decade an old man, searching dim corridors of memory, recalled standing on a Sacramento sidewalk and hearing his companion remark in an excited undertone: "Here comes Crazy Judah!" The crazy man stopped to talk and the youth, who had never before seen

3

an insane person, mastered his apprehension and remained to stare and listen. The episode had an unsatisfactory ending. No violence ensued and the handsomely
bearded young man's remarks seemed abnormal only because they were uncommonly temperate. When he was
gone the boy voiced his incredulity. He learned then that
Crazy Judah was crazy only on the subject of a transcontinental railroad.

" But he didn't even mention it! " he protested.

The other spat into the powdered dust of the street.
" That's because I've forbidden him to approach me on
the subject again."

The boy spun about and his eyes followed the bobbing
head of the railroad builder as long as it remained in
sight.

He was born on March 4, 1826, at Bridgeport, Connecticut. His father, an Episcopal minister, moved from
Bridgeport to Troy, New York, where he presently died,
and the boy Theodore gave up the expectation of a career
in the navy — his brother Henry, later a brigadier general, was already at West Point. Theodore began the study
of engineering at a local technical school. A railroad was
being built from Troy to Schenectady, and Theodore,
his pronounced talent already becoming known, stepped
from the classroom into the practical business of construction. He continued industriously to build railroads and
to discuss railroads and to dream railroads as long as he
lived.

When he was twenty-two, he lived in a cottage he had

built for his bride at the edge of the Niagara River, " between the falls and Suspension Bridge . . . with a beautiful view of both the falls and the whirlpool rapids below." He was then planning and building the Niagara Gorge Railroad, one of the engineering marvels of the '40s. Earlier, he had helped build bridges in Vermont, surveyed railroads in Massachusetts and Connecticut, and overseen the construction of a section of the Erie Canal. A year or two later, in 1854, he was at Buffalo building part of what later became the Erie system, and an urgent telegram summoned him to New York.

In his absence his wife, who had moved twenty times in half a dozen years, wondered where the next jump would take them. On the afternoon of the third day a telegram informed her: " Be home tonight; we sail for California April second."

" You can imagine my consternation . . ." she wrote.

Judah was twenty-seven. He was studious, industrious, resourceful, opinionated, humorless, and extraordinarily competent. The New York message took him to the office of Governor Horatio Seymour, where he was introduced to C. L. Wilson, president of an unbuilt railroad that was expected some day to operate between Sacramento and a placer-mining district in the Sierra foothills. Wilson had come east to engage a chief engineer.

For once Judah was not enthusiastic. California was not unknown to him; a brother, Charles, had been practicing law in San Francisco's new Montgomery Block since 1850, and his letters home had told something of the uncertainty and harshness of life on the far coast. Besides, the Atlantic states just then were a hive of railroad-building activity. The hard-working young man was already known in his profession, and progressively more important works were being thrust upon him. Nonetheless, he remained in Seymour's office while Colonel Wilson enlarged on his plan and detailed its possibilities. The Westerner talked so well that two nights later Judah was pacing the parlor of his home in Buffalo, trying to awaken a spark of enthusiasm in his awed and hesitant wife. " Anna, I'm going to California to be the pioneer railroad engineer of the Pacific Coast! "

But to her it was a journey full of unknown dangers, with a raw and probably barbarous land at its end, and three weeks were far too little time to shop and pack and say good-by. Judah ignored these details. But he had once told her that she always had the right pair of gaiters on; she must continue to deserve the compliment. So the impossible was accomplished, and when water widened between the ship and the New York dock, the two were on board, the breathless wife tearfully answering salutes from her young brothers, Charles and John, down from Greenfield for the momentous farewell.

2

FIVE weeks ensued of experiences completely new, for life in the vibrating steamer had no precedent. State-rooms were crowded to capacity and narrow decks and companionways swarmed with men whose daylong conversations, still untouched by disillusion, revolved about the wealth to be made in the quartz mines or in the awakening industrial life of the Coast. Judah was affable in his serious way and interested in positively everything. A sprinkling of seasoned Westerners were on board; their conversations, heard at mealtimes above the churn of the paddle-wheels, were filled with names that sounded legendary to his ears: Meiggs' Wharf, Mormon Island, Whisky Bar, Jimtown, Columbia Bluff. . . .

Young enough to be fascinated by its novelty and color, the two endured the smells and heat and delays of the crossing at Nicaragua and boarded a crowded Pacific Mail steamer on the Pacific side. They were deposited at last in San Francisco, with its brilliant sunshine and cold winds, alien and teeming and expensive. A day or two of homesickness followed, then a noisy riverboat, ablaze with lights, pounding through the night up the Sacramento, and almost immediately a return to the familiar work of railroad planning, with its talk of profiles and cuts and fills and all that went with a normal environment.

But it was not quite normal. At Sacramento Judah found that he was no longer practicing a familiar profession in a country where railroads were already a commonplace. The screech of a locomotive was yet to be heard west of the Rockies. Not a length of rail had been laid and from Monterey to Shasta the Iron Horse meant novelty and excitement quite as much as mere transportation. In 1854, Californians believed in the economic value of railroads with a faith that had been entirely unshaken by experience, but what they chiefly wanted was an exciting show. Miner and merchant, farmer and cowboy and clerk waited impatiently for the time when they could watch a locomotive streak across the landscape, belching steam and fire, and feel the unparalleled exhilaration of a ride, at twenty-five miles an hour, in the swaying, smoke-filled coaches.

It was not the normal atmosphere and Judah, whose profession filled him with a perennial wonder, found it exactly to his liking. Railroad building was fast becoming a business in the East; here it remained sheer romance. He was no longer expected to keep his enthusiasm in check. Dozens of bearded and homesick young men were eager to share his belief in the limitless future of railroads. Oil lamps burned late each evening in the upstairs office in the Hastings Building while groups of new friends hung on the words of this intense, argumentative Easterner who had come out to be chief engineer of the Sacramento Valley line.

Inevitably all such discussions swung round to the most exciting possibility of all, to the ultimate railroad that would span the continent. Here was a project young Judah found completely fascinating. Periodically the magnificence of the scheme would engage his thoughts so completely as to wipe all other considerations from his mind. He was then a man bewitched and hypnotized, dazzled by the magnitude of the conception. Even before he had left the East, the possibility of spanning the continent with bands of railroad iron had been insistently present in his thoughts; it had remained close to the surface during the years while he was gaining experience and testing his capabilities on minor projects. " He had always read, talked and studied the problem," wrote Anna Judah years later. He had been ready to argue the feasibility of a Pacific railroad with anyone who would listen. During these early years his calm wife had borne the brunt of his monologues. One prophecy was repeated so often that thirty years later it remained in her memory: " It will be built, and I'm going to have something to do with it."

His words then had been inspired by unsupported hope; the prediction was based on nothing more substantial than the wish that it might be so. His coming to California brought the goal a long step nearer. It was still remote, well beyond his grasp, but here at least men discussed the possibility seriously and listened without boredom to his gaudy prophecies.

They were not bored because California's isolation was seldom absent from their thoughts. Insufficient transportation, the slowness and hardship and cost of communication with the Atlantic Coast, this was the almost insuperable barrier retarding the growth of the new state. Stronger still was the personal side. The average Californian of the middle '50s felt that he was a long way from anywhere, and much time that might have been better occupied was wasted in daydreams of impossible holidays at home. For the American resident of that day was not of the quality of those who had come out before '49. The latter were natural pioneers, men of backwoods training and preferences, independent, resourceful, born wanderers. They were free agents, unfettered by sentimental attachments that caused others to call certain localities home. To them home was where they chanced to be, and homesickness was a word without meaning. The thousands who had been drawn west by the discovery of gold were another variety of pioneer. Life on the remote frontiers had no natural attractions. Not love of pioneering but the hope of gain had drawn them from their normal settings. The mountain solitudes, the raw mining camps and valley towns formed an alien and unfriendly environment, and home was still the farm or store or office stool beyond the Mississippi. It was these who climbed the stairs at Second and J streets, nightly crowding the office of the Sacramento Valley Railroad while young Judah pursued his obsession, holding forth the promise of fast, easy, cheap communication with home.

3

THERE was little new about his promises. Others had been discussing a railroad to the Pacific for years, some before Judah was born. Since the discovery of gold, pledges to support the project had become stock planks in all political platforms, an inevitable part of the harangues of office-seekers from Maine to Sacramento. " No candidate for Congress," wrote California's veteran journalist " Old Block " in 1869, " could be popular unless he endorsed the Pacific Railroad." But a third of a century of rhetorical support had accomplished nothing. In 1852

Congress had authorized the Secretary of War to conduct surveys to locate " the most economical and practical route for a railroad to the Pacific from the Mississippi." The resulting official reports were embodied in seven quarto volumes, as handsomely made as any ever to issue from the Government Printing Office. But their publication brought no comfort to those who wished to see the railroad become a reality. " The Government," wrote John C. Burch, a California Congressman and friend of Judah, " had expended hundreds of thousands of dollars in explorations, and elaborate reports thereof had been made and published in immense volumes, containing beautiful and expensive engravings showing the most picturesque and wonderful scenery in the world on the route of the exploration; highly colored pictures of the topography, accompanied by exact representations of the animals, birds, fishes, reptiles, shrubs and flowers found on the route . . . yet all this did not demonstrate the practicability of a route, nor show the surveys, elevations, profiles, grades or estimates of the cost of constructing the road over the route finally adopted."

These handsome but immaterial volumes were not yet published when Judah reached California. Later he was to have an opportunity to examine them, and to comment with nicely controlled irony on their beauty and uselessness. Meantime he set himself with energy to the work at hand. He arrived in mid-May 1854, and on May 30 his report and preliminary survey for the proposed Sacramento Valley line were in the hands of his employers. His estimate of the business of the road — a matter diffi-

cult to compute in a country without railroads — had
been arrived at by placing men on wagon roads paralleling
the proposed route. Day and night for a week they had
kept count of the number of passengers on stages and
estimated the tonnage of the freight-carrying wagon-trains.
Judah considered the prospects of the line uncommonly
good, and he thus concluded his report: " With such a
road and such a business, it is difficult to conceive of a
more profitable undertaking." Events proved that any
number of more profitable undertakings might have been
conceived, but the engineer was an optimist born and the
first railroad on the Pacific got under way with enthusiasm.

Soon after his arrival the optimist formed a friendship
with the editor of the Sacramento *Union,* then the great
journal of the Coast. Through its columns he was able
to pursue his obsession before vastly larger audiences.
Each step in the progress of the twenty-one-mile road was
religiously recorded in the pages of the *Union.* By the
middle of February 1855 a hundred men were engaged in
the unfamiliar work of grading the roadbed, and the clipper ship *Wingèd Racer* was completing a five months' run
to the Golden Gate with the first cargo of iron rails ever
to round the Horn. Two weeks later Judah, in town for
the day from the head of construction, stopped to see his
friend Upson, and the *Union* next day contained this
paragraph: " On yesterday was exhibited to us by Mr.
Judah a handsome ring, manufactured from gold found
in the direct line of the railroad now in construction between this city and Negro Bar." Inside its band was a
crowded legend: " Sacramento Valley Railroad, March 4,

THEODORE DEHONE JUDAH
Courtesy of the California State Library

THE JUDAH MONUMENT AT SACRAMENTO
Erected 1930 by employees of the Southern Pacific Company,
J. MacQuarrie, sculptor.
Courtesy of the California State Library

1855. First gold ever taken from earth in making Railroad bank." March 4 was Judah's birthday. He was twenty-nine; he had eight years to live.

Five months later occurred a memorable event. Four officials of the new line — Judah, Morse, Carroll, and Robinson — bent in unison and lifted a newly assembled handcar on the newly laid track. The car was pushed a hundred yards and stopped and the four descended. They were the first to travel on a Pacific Coast railroad. The stunt was probably arranged by Judah, in whom the instinct to dramatize railroads was always strong. A few days later, crowds of loafers congregated on the Sacramento levee while winches strained and a fifteen-ton locomotive was lifted from the deck of a riverboat and eased over the side. On August 19 a delegation of San Franciscans crowded on two tiny flatcars and, escorted by clouds of dust from the unballasted roadbed, were drawn thrilled and half-suffocated across the hot valley to the head of construction fifteen miles away. The next year, on Washington's Birthday, an excursion and grand ball celebrated the triumphant completion of the road.

To Judah, as to everyone else, this seemed the auspicious dawn of an era of railroad building on the Coast. The line to Folsom cut a full day from the long haul between Sacramento and the mines. Passenger stages and freight trains shifted their western termini, and another of California's mushroom towns miraculously appeared at the railhead. Within a few weeks passengers arriving by train from Sacramento confronted a battalion of twenty-one stages drawn up on the muddy main street, each soon to careen off on as many routes, some bound for villages in the neighboring foothills, others to follow fantastic roads into the mountain canyons, and still others, the aristocrats of the assemblage, to pass over the distant crest of the Sierra on the long ordeal of the Overland Trail.

But receipts from the placer mines fell off and the population of the canyon towns diminished alarmingly. Hard times, long in eclipse, returned. The Sacramento Valley Railroad, planned to cover the state, lost its ambition and remained to the end a feeble strip of iron that meandered eastward from Sacramento. Out of a job, the pioneer railroad engineer of the West turned his hand successively to a series of other projected roads, none of which got beyond the paper stage, and for all of which Judah, who saw a pot of gold at the end of every railroad rainbow, predicted brilliant success, and handsome profits for anyone bold enough to push them to completion.

While he argued for these purely local schemes, Judah's mind was ever visualizing a larger picture. Every length of rail laid or projected became in his secret hope a unit in the road that was to link the oceans. He was hired to run a preliminary line for a railroad someone hoped to build from Sacramento to Benicia, a growing village on the upper bay. He began his report — and was presently harping on his major enthusiasm: " There is still another light in which your Road may be viewed." Readers knew what was coming. " It is in connection with the great Pacific Railroad. . . ." A little later, inevitably: " Your Road will be a grand avenue of approach to the metropolis of the Pacific."

A few months later he was engaged to explore the passes of the Sierra to locate a feasible route for a new wagon road to the growing silver towns of Nevada. Again it was Pacific Railroad problems and not the job at hand that held his attention during the long summer in the mountains. He returned fired with enthusiasm for what he conceived to be a practical passage for the iron rails, and his obliging friend of the *Union* published glowing descriptions of the Dutch Flat route. The wagon road, of course, was forgotten; his employers, who did not share his railroad obsession, looked elsewhere for a man to locate their road. Judah was unconcerned. Of what consequence were wagon roads? Already he heard the shrill blasts of a locomotive — loveliest of sounds — rending the solitude of the Sierra canyons.

He was not the type of enthusiast who is content to expend all his energy in mere talk. Talk he did, with surprising persistence and volubility. But it presently began to be recognized that his talk had sanity as well as conviction, and each week saw a number of adherents won over from the ranks of the scoffers. Of course, it was never a question of convincing Californians of the desirability of a railroad to the East; they were a unit in their desire to see the line built. Judah's problem was to persuade them that the thing was possible, to crystallize a demand that something be done toward making a start. To this task he had set himself with such singleness of purpose as to arouse in some minds perfectly sincere doubts of his sanity. But those who called the enthusiast " Crazy Judah " overlooked the fact that he was also a gifted and experienced engineer with facts at his fingertips and solid earth beneath his feet.

Tireless harping on his single theme slowly strengthened his position and widened his following. After four years talk began to be accompanied — it was never supplanted — by action.

4

'THE SCENE shifted to San Francisco. An even hundred delegates met in the town's largest hall and on September 20 the Pacific Railroad Convention of 1859 got under way.

Judah, a delegate from Sacramento, was tirelessly active, presenting resolutions, arguing about routes, lining up support of this and opposition to that, writing heated and inconveniently long letters to the press. The result of the convention was the sifting of ten years of discussion into a definite statement of what the Coast would do toward the construction of a railroad to the East, and of what it expected in the way of help from the federal government. The first necessity was to get its recommendations before, and through, Congress. On October 11 Judah was entrusted with the task. He waited nine impatient days before the *Sonora*, Captain Baby, left for Panama.

While the ship was still in the bay, the enthusiast was introduced to a fellow passenger, also Washington bound: Congressman-elect John C. Burch. Recalling the meet-

ing, Burch later wrote: " Our introduction was immediately followed by a statement to me in detail of the objects
and purposes of his mission." One can believe it; detailed
statements of his objects and purposes were Judah's stock
in trade. " I have always had to pit my brains and will
against other men's money," he once told his patient wife.
Of course he won the embryo Congressman over to his
views. The two became, in the latter's words, " immediate
and intimate friends." Burch continued: " No day passed
on the voyage to New York that we did not discuss the
subject, lay plans for its success, and indulge pleasant
anticipations of those wonderful benefits so certain to
follow that success."

Like others, his new friend found the engineer a singularly well-posted madman. Not only did he have the
technical features of the proposed railroad clearly in
mind; the involved problems of finance and legislation
had likewise received study. And of course his unquench-
able optimism followed him into these fields. " On the
various provisions of a proper bill to invite the introduction of capital into the work," stated Burch, " and, in short,
on every conceivable point he was armed with arguments,
facts and figures, and so thoroughly so that all questions
of political economy involved were of easy solution to his
mind."

Loaded to the brim with his facts, the voluble engineer
became a familiar figure on Washington streets and in
Washington committee-rooms during the following winter and spring. On the Coast his arguments had been
worn thin from much repetition; here the story was new

and he repeated it wherever it might do any good: to members of the House and Senate, to editors and newspaper correspondents, to cabinet members and heads of departments, to seventy-year-old James Buchanan in the White House. " His knowledge of his subject was so thorough," continued Burch, " his manners so gentle and insinuating, his conversation on the subject so entertaining, that few resisted his appeals." That winter he somehow found time to make hurried trips through the East to awaken further interest in the project or to collect data on recent developments in his profession. Between times he wrote letters to the newspapers and prepared and distributed circulars and maps.

One of those who lent a particularly willing ear to Judah's eloquence was John A. Logan, then a Congressman from Illinois and chairman of the House committee on contingent expenses. By Logan's influence he was granted the use of a room in the Capitol. There he established what became known as the Pacific Railroad Museum, drawing on the archives of the various departments for maps, surveys, reports, whatever he could lay his hands on that might explain, illustrate, or dramatize the necessity for a transcontinental railroad. The room became his Washington headquarters; scores of members of both houses, officials of the departments and bureaus, and droves of plain citizens passed through its open door, spent a few minutes — or an hour — listening to the grave young man's cunning arguments, and passed out again knowing more of the Pacific Railroad than they had learned in a lifetime before. Judah nightly returned to his boarding-house on Fourteenth Street only after the last stragglers had left the Capitol.

As a dispenser of Pacific Railroad information the engineer proved a great success. But the attainment of the object that had brought him east remained as remote as ever. His attempts to get a Pacific Railroad bill before Congress were uniformly blocked, for that body had a larger problem on its hands. Eventually, like almost everything else unrelated to slavery, his bill was shoved ahead to the next session. Regretfully Judah wrote a report to the San Francisco convention and appended his expense account. The latter made no references to his living or other expenses and no charge for nearly a year of his time. It contained but two items:

For printing bill and circular in New York $20.00
For printing bill and circular in Washington $20.00
$40.00

Thrifty New England ancestors turned in their graves and Anna Judah pondered the possibility that the amiable lunatic might some day grow violent.

Failure at Washington dimmed his enthusiasm only temporarily. What was needed, he decided, was still more facts. " With facts and figures they cannot gainsay my honest convictions. . . ." He must be able to say to harassed and skeptical politicians, not merely: " There is a practical route over the mountains," but: " Here are the maps, profiles, and estimates of such a route."

His thoughts settled on this new phase of his obsession, and on the return west the uninterrupted flow of his conversation centered on the mountain survey. In their hot stateroom his wife listened mildly. Nearly thirty years later she wrote: " Oh how we used to talk it all over and over on the steamer en route to California in July. . . ." The boat docked at San Francisco and Judah set off at once on the trail of his facts. A friend accompanied him. " No one knew what they were doing," wrote Mrs. Judah. " The ' engineer ' was in the mountains." She added, a bit plaintively: " I remained in San Francisco and Sacramento among friends."

The engineer and his companion remained in the high Sierra so long that winter surprised them and they had to fight their way down snowy canyons to the lowlands. Back at the foothill town of Dutch Flat, Judah's perennial enthusiasm soared to new heights: he had found his feasible route over the mountains. On the counter of Dr. Strong's drug store he triumphantly checked over his field notes and profiles. Then he spread out a fresh sheet of paper and wrote the Articles of Association of the Central Pacific Railroad of California. At the bottom of the sheet he and Strong signed for more stock than they could afford, and all the next day the paper was circulated among the solvent citizens of Dutch Flat.

The California law then required that capital stock in the amount of one thousand dollars for each mile of railroad must be subscribed before the company could be incorporated. The distance from Sacramento to the state line was estimated at 115 miles; subscriptions for $115,-000 of stock were therefore necessary. In three days Dutch Flat and a few neighboring villages had pledged $46,500.

Judah set off with confidence to raise the balance in Sacramento and San Francisco. A week later Strong received a letter with a San Francisco postmark. " I have struck a lucky streak, and shall fill up the list without further trouble. I have got one of the richest concerns in California into it."

A meeting of the capitalists was arranged. With his facts and figures under his arm, Judah stepped from the Russ House and strode up the resounding board sidewalks of Montgomery Street to conclude the deal. His wife waited in their hotel room. ". . . On his return from the meeting his words of me were these: ' Anna, if you want to see your friends in the morning you must pack your bag and trot around to see them, for I am going up to Sacramento on the boat tomorrow afternoon. Remember what I say to you tonight, so you can tell me sometime: not two years will go over the heads of these gentlemen . . . but they will give up all they hope to have from their present enterprises to have what they put away tonight! " It was the prophecy of an angry and disappointed man. Curiously, it proved to be true in every detail.

The next morning Anna Judah dutifully visited her friends, and the afternoon boat carried the pair up the river to Sacramento. He started his campaign all over again: more conferences, more bringing forth of facts, and fluent repetition of arguments; finally a meeting in the St. Charles Hotel on K Street, poorly attended; a second meeting with fewer still, this time in a room above a hardware store.

It was not a promising setting in which to launch by far the greatest engineering enterprise ever projected in the West. About a dozen men were present. At a table was Judah with his bundle of data, distributing his pamphlets, showing his profiles and estimates, unrolling his maps and tracing the route of his railroad with a confident forefinger, painting a gaudy picture of profits for its builders. In the room were Dr. Strong, the Dutch Flat druggist; a surveyor named Leete; James Bailey, a Sacramento jeweler; two railroad promoters, brothers, named Robinson; Lucius A. Booth; and Cornelius Cole, who later became a United States Senator and was to look back after half a century and write a time-fogged account of the meeting.

Four other men were present, grouped loosely as merchants. One was a wholesale grocer with a liking for politics. His name was Leland Stanford. Another was Charles Crocker, who dealt in drygoods. The other two were the hosts of the evening, for they were proprietors of the hardware store downstairs. One was a tall, frail man of nearly fifty, Mark Hopkins; the other, broader, solidly built, and a full ten years younger, was Collis P. Huntington. A druggist, a jeweler, a lawyer, the owner of a drygoods store, two hardware merchants: this hardly seemed promising timber to carry out the vast scheme Judah had envisioned. Nor did the four storekeepers, Huntington, Stanford, Crocker, and Hopkins, seem likely founders of dynasties of wealth so impressive that a lifetime later their names would continue to command deference throughout the West.

The fact that Judah did that evening what he had failed to do in San Francisco was due to a simple circumstance. He was dealing, not with metropolitan capitalists, but with a group of shopkeepers in a town of moderate size. Sacramento had been his headquarters for nearly six years. He knew the town and he knew with exactness the nature of the appeal he must make to win support from its businessmen. The kerosene lamps burned late in the upstairs room at 54 K Street while Judah regarded his audience and prudently clipped the wings of his plan. What he proposed was no fantastic scheme for a railroad across the continent. Deliberately and with skill he reduced his conception to a point within easy comprehension of the men whose money he needed. In later life four of his listeners accepted easily the roles of men of vision, who had perceived a matchless opportunity and grasped it with courage. It was a role none of them deserved.

Judah eliminated all but the purely local features from his plan. He did not repeat his earlier mistake of trying to convert storekeepers into idealists. Instead he told them what they as merchants most wanted to know: how to sell more of their goods, how to make their property more valuable, how to expand their businesses and stifle competition. Help me, he asked, to run my survey over the mountains. With this we can get government support for the company — and you can control the company. If you get control of the traffic to the Nevada mines, you, and you alone, will control that market. " Why, you can have a *wagon road* if not a railroad."

23

5

CONTROL of the business with the new towns beyond the Sierra was a possibility his listeners found pleasant to contemplate. Nevada's decade of tremendously reckless buying was already under way. The discovery of the silver bonanzas had provided a series of sensations that had shaken the Coast and sent the mining fever to heights unknown since the early '50s. For the second time in a dozen years normal life was suspended while citizens by the thousands abandoned their usual pursuits and hurried eastward in the sure expectation of wealth. This time the horde passed completely over the Sierra to the floor of the plains beyond, penetrating thousands of waterless canyons from Tahoe to the edge of Salt Lake. Reports of startling discoveries seeped back daily to California, their purported richness limited only by the imagination of the narrators.

Not all the bonanzas were chimerical, but even those that were, promised a gambler's chance at easy wealth, and to half the population of the Coast that was sufficient. A heavy migration was soon under way and within a few months dozens of parched mountainsides had been staked out in claims, chiefly by veterans of the California placer and quartz mines.

California furnished not only the men for these roaring new towns, but everything else. From San Francisco and Sacramento — particularly the latter — came food and clothing and other necessaries of a large population in a completely unproductive country — and many other things besides. For mining in Nevada was not of the early California variety that had required only pick and shovel and homemade sluice-box. Here the complicated machinery of quartz mining was necessary: drilling and tunneling and hoisting equipment, stamp mills, reduction plants.

The result was that a tremendous volume of freight, at extremely high rates, was presently leaving Sacramento and crawling along snake-like roads over the lofty hump of the Sierra. The mines proved shockingly rich; dividends of leading companies presently reached a million a month. Equipment and supplies were ordered recklessly at prices that taxed credulity, and were paid for promptly, in bright, newly minted silver.

The prospect of gaining control of this almost fabulous market naturally received close attention from Judah's group of merchants. With skill the enthusiast led up to the matter for which the meeting had been called: would his listeners subscribe for enough additional stock to allow the company to incorporate? The result was less disappointing than that of the San Francisco meeting a week earlier. Several of the men who were present later put on paper accounts of what had happened — for this gathering above the hardware store presently became known as a historic occasion. " I think every one present," wrote Cornelius Cole, ". . . agreed to take stock in the concern. Several subscribed for fifty shares each, but no one for more that that. I took fifteen shares . . . and subsequently acquired ten more." This is inaccurate in one detail; not everyone present agreed to take shares.

There was at least one exception. Nevertheless, the minimum required for incorporation was reached that night and the Central Pacific Railroad Company of California — but by no means the railroad itself — became a reality soon after.

The exception noted above was C. P. Huntington. He, too, later recorded his version of what had taken place. He told of Judah's appeal for subscriptions and of the response of the others. He added: " I did not give anything. When the meeting was about to break up, one or two said to me: ' Huntington, you are the man to give to this enterprise.' " But, as always, Huntington had plans of his own. " I told Mr. Judah as I left: ' If you want to come to my office some evening, I will talk to you about this railroad. . . .' "

Judah was at his office the following evening. " He sat down and talked with me," continued Huntington. Judah talked and Huntington weighed the possibilities. There was little to lose by going in: a subscription for a few shares of stock, on which only a ten-per-cent deposit was required, and the thing could always be dropped if the government failed to be liberal in the matter of subsidies. The engineer knew the ropes at Washington — he seemed confident that adequate help would be forthcoming, and he was convinced that the road over the Sierra would eventually be built. Huntington was no prophet, but he knew how to look ahead. If the road should be built, it would be unpleasant to have it controlled by his competitors. The hardware merchant considered this possibility and thought of the crowded stages and lines of freight wagons that daily rolled out of Sacramento and Folsom bound for Nevada.

He decided to go in — but cautiously. " I told him I would furnish six men that would pay for a thorough instrumental survey across the mountains . . . I did not expect to do it myself altogether." The six proved to be, besides himself, his partner Hopkins, Stanford, James Bailey, Charles Crocker, and Lucius Booth. All were Sacramento merchants with goods to sell beyond the mountains; the group contained no philanthropists. The six subscribed to a total of only 800 of the 85,000 shares, but when the company was incorporated their interests were protected. Stanford was made president, Huntington vice-president, Bailey secretary, and Hopkins treasurer. The remaining two became members of the board of directors.

But Judah, for the moment, was content. He was chief engineer of a railroad that might some day, if his good luck held, become the first part of his hoped-for transcontinental road. Moreover, there was practical work to be done and — pleasant novelty — money in the treasury to pay for it. In their rooms at the Vernon House he directed another jubilant monologue at his wife: " If you want to see the first work done on the Pacific Railroad, look out of your bedroom window; I am going to work there this afternoon, and I am going to have these men pay for it." It was the final remark that she found chiefly interesting. She thought again of the forty-dollar expense account, and her reply was characteristic of the wives of all enthusiasts: " It's about time somebody else helped."

6

THE FIRST work duly commenced that afternoon. Judah and a few helpers with chains and stakes and heavy brass instruments ran their lines down the muddy street under the eyes of skeptical spectators. By early summer the survey had crossed the foothills to the base of the mountains; there operations had to be suspended until the party could follow the retreating snowline up the mountainside.

To the railroad engineer of the early '60s the Sierra Nevada offered an unprecedented problem. The western slope of the mountains is rugged in the extreme; the rise from base to summit, a matter of seven thousand feet, is made in less than twenty miles. To locate a railroad in such terrane, to keep grades and curves moderate enough for practical operation, and this without so much bridging and tunneling as to make the cost prohibitive, were a sufficient tax even on Judah's unquestioned technical skill.

In his preliminary report, rendered toward the end of the summer, the optimist did not minimize the problems presented by the towering barrier of the Sierra. He listed the chief obstacles: the abrupt rise of the western slope, the narrow, deep canyons cut by snow-fed streams, the difficulty of running cuts and tunnels through miles of solid granite on the upper ridges, the problem of how to build — and to keep the completed line open — in the face of winter snowfalls that sometimes reached thirty feet. Nonetheless, he was able to point out how each obstacle could be overcome. This first thorough survey, with a second made the following summer, later came to be recognized as a technical accomplishment of a very high order. With minor changes, it was along the route then laid out that the road was built; it remains to this day, in the opinion of competent engineers, the most practical route for a crossing of the Sierra Nevada.

Like everything else Judah wrote on this subject that fascinated him, the first report bears the mark of his unconquerable optimism. This time, however, it was necessary for him to draw a rosy picture; the continued existence of the company depended on his findings and recommendations. That fact was not absent from his thought when he added his " Summary of the Prominent Features of the Line." A few typical sentences are quoted: " It crosses no deep river canyons or gorges. The longest tunnel will not exceed 1,350 feet. . . ." Then, of particular interest to Sacramento storekeepers: " It commands, and will perform, the entire business of Nevada Territory, Washoe, and the silver mineral region. It will also command the business of the newly discovered Humboldt mineral district, Pyramid Lake, Esmeralda, and Mono mineral districts. Reduces the time of passenger transit to and from the Washoe (center of the greatest mines) to $8\frac{1}{2}$ hours. . . ." He stated his conviction that citizens of the mining region would save a million dollars a year on their freight bills by using the new railroad, and that it would provide a means by which the low-grade ore then heaped uselessly about three thousand tunnel-heads could profitably be shipped to Europe for reduction. The list ended of course with a return to the major theme: " The line over the mountains," he wrote, " completes the first Western link of the Pacific Railroad, overcoming its greatest difficulties."

Copies of this and of subsequent reports may be encountered today in many collections of Western railroad material, the pamphlets often having the inscription: " Respects of T. D. Judah," in the engineer's slanting hand. An examination of them reveals anew his persistent, thoroughgoing optimism. The staking out of a mining claim anywhere near the projected railroad became in his mind the beginning of a city of thousands, its inhabitants all eager to do business with the road. The company presently came into possession of large tracts of timberland; at once his nimble imagination and pencil came into play and his next report contained this paragraph:

" The fact cannot be controverted that your Company possesses . . . timberland which will by the construction of your road through it, become . . . largely enhanced in value; and if we allow that 300,000 acres, or two-thirds of this land, contains only *ten trees per acre,* from which can be cut six logs twelve feet long per tree, averaging twenty-four inches square, this gives 3,400 feet board measure per tree, and the total quantity amounts to ten thousand million feet of lumber, which delivered at Sacramento at, say $15 per thousand, amounts to one hundred and fifty millions of dollars. . . ."

Rose-tinted calculations of this sort fascinated him. Like a lover seeking new ways to describe his lady's charms, he covered page after page, piling up theoretical millions:

"It is known that the sugar pine of these lands often runs 125 feet high without a limb, and often measures eight feet through at the base — while a tree is seldom found measuring less than three and a half feet at the base. Cut but one tree per acre per year, and it gives an annual yield of 1,000 million feet of lumber — three million feet per day, equal to 5,000 tons per day, or say 1,750,000 tons per year."

Again:

"Allowing 500,000 acres . . . to yield fifty cords per acre (a very low estimate) and it amounts to twenty-five million cords of wood, which, if delivered at Sacramento at $6 per cord, would amount to 150 millions of dollars, and pay the road about 100 millions of dollars freight. . . ."

Such glittering fantasies were perhaps helpful in keeping up the courage of the stockholders, but in 1860 the main obstacle had still to be overcome. Six years of unremitting work, exploring mountain passes, lobbying in Washington, writing reports and pamphlets and numberless letters; most of all in talking about the project in California and the East — all this had impaired Judah's health and wrecked his finances. But a beginning had been made, and he was more than content.

It was no more than a beginning. In California, or elsewhere, not one man in fifty believed that the road controlled by the Sacramento group would ever lay rails over the mountains. The history of too many projected railroads, begun with just such a flourish and forgotten in a few months, was too clearly in mind to permit optimism for the future of this vastly larger undertaking.

31

All such roads, and in particular this costly line over the mountains, could be financed only with substantial government help, and, notwithstanding Judah's hopes, the prospect of a liberal federal subsidy seemed remote.

Appeals to the national government for help in constructing a transcontinental railroad had been made to Congress with clock-like regularity for over a decade. No action had been taken, and none was likely to be taken, for the ample reason that the Pacific Railroad had become inseparably a part of the slavery question. To suggest a northern route was to win the instant antagonism of every Congressman and Senator from south of the Potomac; mention of a southern line caused the Northerners to act as a unit in opposing it. In the beginning of the '60s there seemed less possibility than ever of breaking the deadlock.

Yet it was to attempt this feat that Judah sailed again for Washington in October 1860. His wife as usual " had the right gaiters on " and went along with him. They parted at New York, however, she returning, a much traveled young woman, to her family at Greenfield while the engineer pushed on to Washington. This time Anna Judah felt she was not unrepresented at the Capitol, for when Judah reopened his museum he was able to decorate its walls with certain of her sketches of the Sierra scenery, made on a visit to the mountains the previous summer. More, two of her drawings, of Donner Lake and Donner Pass, had been copied by the engraver and used to embellish the company's stock certificates. Yet another of her sketches, suitably framed, hung in the office of the company's president, who was then a candidate for Governor of California and thought to have an excellent chance of election.

The story of Judah's new attempt to tap the federal treasury for the benefit of his company may be briefly told. Washington was not the city it had been on his last visit two years earlier; the temper of Congress had undergone tremendous changes. On April 12, guns had blazed at Sumter and the location of a route for the Pacific Railroad promptly ceased to be a sectional question. Judah reached the capital three months after Bull Run, two weeks after McClellan had been given command of the Union army, and when Washington had at length realized that it had more than a ninety-day war on its hands. For the first time since its inception the project of a railroad to the Pacific Coast could be brought up for debate without immediately becoming involved with the slavery question.

Judah and his Sacramento associates recognized that events had given them a matchless opportunity. What before had been the rashest of gambles had been transformed overnight into a sound and conservative enterprise. Had the South not seceded, the transcontinental road might have been delayed for a decade or longer. It might have had to be constructed entirely without federal help; certainly government assistance, if it came at all, would have been on a less liberal scale.

Judah's first days in Washington were devoted to altering his campaign to meet the new circumstances; arguments were overhauled, strategy simplified. The project was put forward primarily as a war measure. The railroad, it was argued, would help hold California and

Nevada Territory in the Union, and California and Nevada were producing in volume two commodities highly necessary to a nation at war: gold and silver.

But all was not yet plain sailing. Judah and the California delegation faced the problem of getting their railroad bill to the attention of the lawmakers. Congress had been jarred from its routine by the formation, in February, of the Southern Confederacy. The absence of the contingent from the South was still evident in the unoccupied desks and disorganized committees, and those who remained were struggling to dispose of large accumulations of emergency measures.

Judah had taken passage from San Francisco on the same boat with Aaron Sargent, newly elected California Congressman. Sargent had agreed to sponsor the Pacific Railroad bill in the House. But a new Congressman was not expected to introduce important legislation, particularly with the calendar overloaded with war measures, and Judah watched the weeks slip by with no prospect of action. He and Sargent had become close friends; the latter found their waiting as distasteful as did the engineer, and the two agreed on a drastic move. A few days later, during a debate on an unrelated matter, the new member mildly astonished the House by obtaining the floor and delivering a lengthy speech on the railroad bill. The chairman disposed of the interruption in the usual way — by appointing a subcommittee to consider the matter — and the House resumed its regular business. A similar committee had already been appointed by the Senate.

Judah, no longer an amateur in Washington politics, had meantime been pulling wires to such advantage as to get himself appointed secretary of the Senate committee. Sargent then made him clerk of the House subcommittee, and he presently consolidated his position by becoming clerk of the main House committee on railroads. He then had close official connection with the three committees through which the bill must pass on its way toward enactment. This gave him a voice in all committee hearings, as well as the privilege of the floor of the House, and the documents and records of all three committees were in his keeping. For a man whose one desire was the passage of the Pacific Railroad bill (which he had helped write) it is hard to picture a more satisfactory arrangement. Whatever may be said for the ethics of such appointments — which would hardly have been made had not Congress been depleted in membership and overburdened with work — there can be no doubt that had Judah remained on the outside, the bill would never have come to a vote that session.

As it was, the debate was prolonged and the opposition strong in both the House and the Senate. It was not until midsummer of 1862 that the bill was eventually passed and, on July 1, received President Lincoln's signature.

Judah was already looking ahead to new tasks. Promptly a message sped west over the recently strung wires of the Pacific Telegraph:

" We have drawn the elephant. Now let us see if we can harness him up."

7

WHAT was the nature of the elephant Judah had drawn for the amateur railroad men of Sacramento? The bill designated two companies to build and operate a railroad between Sacramento and the Missouri River. In the way of federal aid it granted a strip of land for right-of-way purposes and made further grants of ten alternate sections per mile of public domain (with unimportant exceptions) on both sides of the line over the entire distance. Further, it provided for a government loan to the companies, in the form of thirty-year bonds at six-per-cent interest, in amounts ranging from $16,000 to $48,000 per mile, depending on the nature of the territory over which the road would pass.

The elephant was, hence, a full-grown, adult beast, even a giant. What had been a gambler's chance had become overnight a sure thing, a legitimate enterprise of limitless possibilities. The passage of the act marked the real beginning of a stream of easy profits that was to raise the four storekeepers from the semi-obscurity of their Sacramento shops and provide them with more wealth than they had dreamed of owning.

But the elephant had first to be broken and put to work. With this in mind, Judah resigned from his Congressional committees, closed the museum, and caught the first steamer out of New York for Panama. In Sacramento again, his mild wife observed that the engineer's standing with substantial citizens seemed far higher than it had been a few months before. Crazy Judah, the sponsor of a fantastic scheme for a cross-country railroad, had passed permanently from the picture. He had become chief engineer of the Central Pacific Railroad of California, and the Central Pacific, thanks to the liberality it had encountered at Washington, was already gathering unto itself the enormous prestige it was to maintain for a generation.

Judah abruptly found himself a man of consequence. Acquaintances no longer turned down convenient alleys at his approach. It became unnecessary for his wife to warn him against wasting his thunder on small-town capitalists, who had listened to his arguments with absent-minded smiles and put him down as an idealistic nonentity. The story of how he had got himself appointed to the railroad committees in Washington got abroad. This was shrewdness of a type then particularly admired; more than anything else it enhanced his popularity by demonstrating that the dreamer had a practical side. Citizens on the Coast read with respect the latest of his voluminous and rose-tinted reports, the composition of which had occupied his time on the westward voyage.

The preliminaries were over. Surveying parties remained in the field through the fall of 1862, making the working survey for the initial unit of the line, and before the year was out the Charles Crocker Company had received a contract to grade the first thirty-two miles of roadbed. The holidays passed. On January 8, 1863 a throng, no longer skeptical, followed lines of flag-draped carriages through Sacramento's muddy streets to a deco-

rated platform beside the levee, where actual construction
was to begin. Frock-coated notables ascended the platform and, at the stroke of twelve, Crocker, red-faced and
jovial, called the crowd to order. Leland Stanford, by
then Governor of the state as well as president of the
company, delivered an address in which he predicted
that his listeners would presently observe passing through
Sacramento " the busy denizens of two hemispheres, in
their constant travel over the great highway of nations."
Six other speeches, of much the same tenor, followed.
Stanford then descended to the base of the platform, lifted
a shovelful of damp earth, and tossed it into the bed
of a flag-draped wagon — performing the feat with such
zeal as to prove, according to one newspaper scribe, " that
his muscles were in the right place." The crowd cheered.
The band played its loudest and liveliest tune. Crocker
called for nine rousing cheers, and when they were given,
added that even while they celebrated, a pile-driver was
working near by on the foundations of the American
River bridge.

Judah made no speech. He had been talking for eight
years. He may have been a bit preoccupied as he heard
others repeating his familiar prophecies; possibly he
glanced eastward across the valley to where the granite
ridge of the Sierra Nevada cut a silhouette high into the
skyline. As he well knew, seven speeches and a shovelful
of earth do not build a transcontinental railroad.

But if Judah then looked forward to a period when he
could devote himself unhampered to the work of construction, he must soon have been disillusioned. Hardly

had the voices of the speakers died away when the engineer and the four merchants were ranged on opposite sides of a variety of questions. By the terms of the Railroad Act, the government bonds were not to become available until after the first forty miles of the line had been completed. To raise capital for this initial unit, two methods were adopted: Huntington went east and tried, with varying success, to sell stock, and Stanford, aided by his prestige as Governor, induced the state and a number of counties and cities to make substantial subscriptions. Money began to flow into the methodical hands of Treasurer Hopkins at an encouraging rate.

With financial prospects brightening daily, Judah prepared to leave the question of further money-raising to his associates and to devote himself to the more congenial pursuit of judiciously expending it. The plan failed to work out, for it presently developed that he and the Sacramento group regarded these first forty miles of the road from widely different viewpoints. The engineer saw them as the western end of the longest and potentially the most important railroad ever built. Huntington and his three associates looked on the section merely as an inconvenient hurdle that must be surmounted before the government subsidy would become available. Judah wished to build rapidly, but well; the others also wanted speed, but they wished to shave costs in every possible way. The engineer saw the traffic of the nation, and the Orient, passing over the line for generations in the future. The four speculators were looking toward the moment when the rails would be laid far enough into the foothills to enable them to underbid competition for the freight and passenger business with Nevada Territory.

8

THIS clash of interests and viewpoint had of course been inevitable from the beginning. Judah might have foreseen it had he not been blind to every consideration except that of getting the project organized and under way.

It was another skirmish in the traditional battle between the builder and the speculator; between men whose aim was to create and those whose sole purpose was to make a profit — as large a profit as possible as quickly as possible. In his railroad-building activities in the East, Judah must have encountered some manifestations of these opposed viewpoints; but in California circumstances had conspired to sharpen the contest. For a dozen years business on the Coast had been speculative to a degree unknown in older communities. The Sacramento four were well schooled in this hothouse atmosphere, where prices changed so rapidly that a few days, even a few hours, often meant the difference between a large profit and a heavy loss. A quick turnover and a quick profit were consequently the cardinal rule of business in the early days, and the habit was not at once outgrown. In the '60s no local businessman was interested in a conservative, long-term investment. Judah had got support from the merchants because they regarded the project as another likely speculation, with possibilities of a large and quick return. Judah, too, believed the railroad would yield a handsome profit, but he looked to the future, not the immediate present. With luck, he argued, the road would be opened to through traffic in five years. The Sacramento group smiled. To wait five years, or one year, before profits would begin to flow in seemed to them contrary to all sense. They proceeded to show the theorist that the affairs of resourceful men were not so conducted in California.

From the beginning others on the Coast doubted the intentions of the Sacramento four. The latter were known in business and financial circles in California; nothing in their previous activities encouraged the hope that they might be seriously embarking on a semi-public enterprise of vast proportions, from which in the normal course of events no substantial return might be expected for years. Shrewdness and a well-developed trading sense, the ability to turn a quick and profitable deal, these were the qualities that had characterized them in the past; the claim that they had abruptly become men of constructive imagination and long vision aroused natural skepticism. Particularly in San Francisco the contention that the four were actually planning to build the western half of the great Pacific Railroad was not taken seriously. There must be some catch in it.

The doubters presently thought they had discovered what the catch was. The conviction grew that Huntington and his partners were planning a roadbed over the mountains for other purposes than those announced. Predic-

tions were made that no rails would ever be laid beyond
the foothill town of Dutch Flat; that the famous route
over the Sierra would become and remain a mere wagon
road, by means of which the four would control the
California-Nevada traffic. Judah's difficulties with the
board of directors lent point to the theory, notably
the fact that his efforts to extend the railroad survey beyond the California line (a matter that needed early
attention if the road were to be finished within the time
specified by Congress) were consistently opposed.

Long-smoldering suspicion eventually flared into open
scandal. Thousands of Californians grew convinced that
their hopes for a railroad connection with the East had
again been disappointed. Many California newspapers,
originally favorable to the project, became reserved, then
openly hostile, and those who had subscribed for stock
began to ask if they had been tricked. Public confidence
which Judah had been building up for years slipped rapidly away. In the minds of thousands the Central Pacific
became " the Dutch Flat Swindle " — a scheme for building at public expense a monopolistic wagon road. The
engineer shared with other officials the resentment of
an angry and disappointed public.

The situation did not promote confidence within the
company, and other developments made matters worse.
The four merchants were by then in virtually complete
control; they so dominated the program that Marsh and
Strong, two of the original directors, soon retired. Judah,
however, held on. Not only did he hold on; he waged
effective counter-warfare. He was chief engineer of the

Central Pacific and chief engineer he persisted in remaining, regardless of who was ranged against him.

As the man mainly responsible for the company's existence, and as the only trained engineer of the group, Judah continued to insist that his be the deciding voice in all matters pertaining to construction. This the others refused to concede. Since, they argued, they were investing their money in the speculation and since the loss or profit would be chiefly theirs, their control must extend to every aspect of the work. All Judah's persuasive powers, his admitted force in argument, were expended in attempts to win the group over to his viewpoint. For a time one of the four, Stanford, was convinced and gave the engineer tentative support. But Huntington returned to the Coast, Stanford promptly shifted his position again, and Judah presently wrote to Dr. Strong, his Grass Valley friend, that the four were opposing him as a unit.

" I had a blowout about two weeks ago and freed my mind, so much so that I looked for instant decapitation. I called things by their right name and invited war; but counsel of peace prevailed and my head is still on; my hands are tied, however. We have no meetings of the board nowadays; except the regular monthly meeting, which, however, was not had this month; but there have been any quantity of private conferences to which I have not been invited."

One method by which the four tried to bring the rebel to terms was by demanding payment in cash for the initial ten-per-cent deposit on the Central Pacific stock Judah had bought, although the engineer contended it had previously been agreed that his services in organizing the

43

company would be counted as such payment. Failing in this, the group disregarded his recommendations as chief engineer, made decisions affecting construction without consulting him, and made it clear that he was to have no further voice in the management of the corporation.

"I cannot tell you," Judah wrote Dr. Strong in the letter quoted above, ". . . all that is going on . . . suffice it to say that I have had a pretty hard row to hoe." He had. But he had no intention of standing by while his project was wrecked. He was forced to give way, but he gave way slowly, and he managed to deliver some telling blows. The resourceful four had already hit on the money-making device that was soon to make them multimillionaires. The plan was a simple one: their control of the company gave them, of course, the power to grant contracts for the construction of the railroad. Rather than let the profits from construction go to other contractors, the group organized a construction company of their own, which, however, was quite independent of the railroad. The next step was for them, as directors of the Central Pacific, to award contracts to themselves as railroad builders, and on terms liberal enough to assure very large profits.

This was not Judah's idea of how the Central Pacific should be built. When the contract for the first section of the road was awarded to a newly formed company nominally headed by Charles Crocker, Judah fought the move with a persistence that must have surprised the Sacramento group, and to such good effect that he was able to inform Dr. Strong: "I have had a big row and

AN EARLY CENTRAL PACIFIC CHECK, SIGNED BY JUDAH AND HOPKINS

Courtesy of the California State Library

ADVERTISEMENT OF THE
SACRAMENTO VALLEY
RAILROAD
from the State Register and Year Book,
*1857. Courtesy of the California State
Library*

COVER OF "CLEAR
THE WAY," A SONG BY
STEPHEN C. MASSETT
*urging the building of
the transcontinental
railroad, published in
San Francisco in 1856.*
Courtesy of
Edwin Grabhorn

fight on the contract question, and although I had to fight alone, carried my point and prevented a certain gentleman from becoming a further contractor on the Central Pacific Railroad at present."

On another occasion Judah was able to put a temporary check on the group's rapidly growing talent for thinking up ways of reaping extra profits. By the terms of the federal act the amount of the subsidy was to be increased from $16,000 per mile in the valley to $32,000 when the road reached the foothills. As a commentator expressed it at the time, the four undertook the Herculean task of " moving the foothills down into the middle of the valley." Judah was asked to join others in stating that the foothills began many miles distant from the spot where in his opinion they actually did begin. He refused, and by so doing ended the possibility of further friendly relations with the Sacramento financiers.

It became a question of who should retire, and it was Judah who went. The exact terms under which he withdrew are not certainly known, but it appears that he was offered, and accepted, $100,000 for his share, and besides received options to purchase the interests of the other four for the same amount each. With his options, the engineer prepared to leave again for New York, certain he could find men who would take them up and proceed with the building of the road. There are indications that he had intended approaching the Vanderbilt group, which was known to be planning to increase its interests on the Pacific Coast. Letters had been exchanged and a meeting arranged. Years later Judah's widow wrote: " He had secured the right and had the power to buy out the men opposed to him and the true interests of the Pacific railroad at that time. Everything was arranged for a meeting in New York City on his arrival. Gentlemen from New York and Boston were ready to take their places."

Judah viewed the outcome with characteristic optimism. In his cabin on the *St. Louis*, before the steamer left its San Francisco dock, he wrote a final letter to Strong:

" I have a feeling of relief in being away from the scenes of contention and strife which it has been my lot to experience for the past year, and to know that the responsibilities of events, so far as regards the Pacific Railroad, do not rest on my shoulders. If the parties who now manage hold the same opinion three months hence that they do now, there will be a radical change in the management of the Pacific Railroad, and it will pass into the hands of men of experience and capital. If they do not, they may hold the reins for a while, but they will rue the day that they ever embarked in the Pacific Railroad.

" If they treat me well they may expect a similar treatment at my hands. If not, I am able to play my hand.

" If I succeed in inducing the parties I expect to see to return with me to California, I shall likely return the latter part of December."

The *St. Louis* left San Francisco in early October 1863. Judah's last word to the Sacramento group was a confident prediction of a radical change in the management of the company. What the outcome might have been must be left to conjecture. At Panama he encountered adversaries more inexorable than the four he had left behind. Yellow fever, contracted at the Isthmus, made rapid inroads. In their guarded stateroom his wife watched over him during the delirious eight days of the run to New York. His case was hopeless when he was carried from the steamer. He lived a week longer, and died November 2, 1863. His thirty-eighth birthday was four months distant.

The engineer's body was shipped to Greenfield for burial, and on one of her later unobtrusive visits to California the widow was pleased to discover that the monument she had provided for his grave was very like that of Starr King, San Francisco's noted preacher of Civil War days.

Anna Judah lived quietly for many years in her native Massachusetts town. On the day in 1869 when the road was completed, which chanced to be her wedding anniversary, she denied herself to callers, determined to have no part in a celebration in which praise was heaped on the Sacramento four, and few recalled to whom credit for the road's inception was due. But she remained moderate in her judgment of her husband's ex-partners. In later years she could be aroused to something approaching resentment only when she read statements that Judah had resigned from the enterprise. She wished it understood that the engineer had died in the belief that he was to return to the Coast and push the line through to completion.

That his services should have been so quickly forgotten seemed to her an inexplicable bit of carelessness. There is no record, however, that she ever reproached the partners for their failure to do anything to perpetuate his memory, even to the extent of naming a crossroads station after him, although that mark of recognition was given to many relatives of the Sacramento four and to dozens of members of the company's administrative and legal staff. But even her generosity had limits. The millions reaped from the enterprise presently gave the wives of the four partners great social prestige. With mild irony Mrs. Judah once reminded a Sacramento acquaintance that she enjoyed none of the perquisites of a " Railroad Queen " — that she was merely the widow of the man who had made the " Railroad Kings " possible.

In the dead man's place, the four appointed a chief engineer less critical of their methods, and at their next meeting the board of directors passed a resolution of sympathy for the widow. For many years this remained the corporation's only mark of recognition of Judah's services. When at length a new station was erected at Sacramento, a bust of the engineer was set up in the plaza before the structure, with funds raised by Southern Pacific employees. Thus recognition came, but it had not come hastily. The Judah bust was unveiled more than sixty years after its subject's death.

CROCKER

1

IN a moment of exasperation Huntington once remarked that Stanford's share in the building of the railroad had consisted in turning the first shovelful of earth and driving the last spike. Stanford on the other hand was convinced that his political influence and personal popularity had been mainly responsible for the success of the enterprise. Uncle Mark Hopkins, close-mouthed and cautious, seldom stated his opinions, but there is evidence that he regarded himself as the balance-wheel that enabled the machine to function. Two of the four, Huntington and Stanford, definitely claimed credit for creating the railroad, and Hopkins in one or two oblique references indicated that the honor belonged to him. " Charley " Crocker never bothered to argue the point. To his mind the thing was not open to question. He merely stated: " I built the Central Pacific " — and let it go at that.

He normally weighed over two hundred and fifty pounds. Like most very large men he had periods of extreme activity, of seemingly limitless energy, and others when he refused to move at all. Crocker's passive spells were not frequent, but they were sometimes inconveniently prolonged. Years after the event, one of Superintendent Strobridge's riding bosses recalled an incident in the epic race up the Humboldt Valley, when the Central Pacific construction crews, five thousand strong, were straining to wrest as many miles as possible from the Union Pacific. Crocker, noisy and cocky and energetic, had been storming up and down the line for weeks, bellowing, in his own words, " like a bull," his large face caked with sweat and alkali dust, his sorrel mare covered with lather. Then he vanished. Foremen, waiting for orders, finally found him in his car at the railhead, prone on his bunk, his Chinese servant, Ah Ling, standing above him waving a palm-leaf. He refused to get up, refused to issue orders, or to O. K. requisitions or sign dispatches. Then toward the middle of the next afternoon he miraculously appeared again, teeming with energy, active, loud, and profane.

He was boastful, stubborn, tactless, vain, and completely lacking in the quality then described as low cunning. At a banquet celebrating the completion, in 1876, of the Southern Pacific's branch to Los Angeles he slouched in his chair while his obsequious shadow, Dave Colton, told two hundred guests that " no man living or dead had superintended the construction of so many miles of railroad on the face of the earth as Charley Crocker." Crocker got ponderously to his feet and with protruding jaw announced that all his life he had been a doer, not a talker. Among the railroad's officials, he continued, were some whose talents definitely ran to talking — whereupon he introduced Stanford. The latter stood up, glared indignantly at Crocker, and made one of the worst speeches of his career.

Modesty, like diplomacy, was never an outstanding characteristic, but few accused him of giving himself airs. Men with requests they would never have taken to Huntington or Stanford descended on him in droves at his office or, more often, buttonholed him on the street or in the lobby or bar of the Palace Hotel. Sometimes the number and variety of these requests got under his skin and he complained bitterly that he had to listen to more cranks than any other man in California. But the task was one he could have avoided, and the only possible explanation is that he preferred to spend his days thus rather than attending the routine business of operating a railroad.

By temperament he was entirely unfitted for confining work. Sitting behind a desk was a form of self-discipline to which he consistently refused to submit. In later years in San Francisco those who wished to find him knew the futility of looking in at his office at Fourth and Townsend streets. " I'm at my desk twelve hours every day of the week," Huntington used to admonish his partners on trips out from the East. Crocker listened with a large, mild interest, and did nothing. After the active work of building was over, his lazy spells came more frequently and lasted longer. There were periods when he seldom put in twelve hours a month, possibly because he realized he had no talent for administrative routine. " His feet," wrote a San Francisco editor, " are more often on his desk than under it." Questioned later about financial or administrative details of the company during the construction period, Crocker had a stock reply: " I knew nothing about that. I was building the road."

After the Central Pacific was completed, in 1869, the prospect of ending his days in an administrative job so depressed him that he insisted on selling out. Travel satisfied him for a time, but after a few months of wandering over Europe he was back in San Francisco apparently quite willing to return to harness. He resumed his title of first vice-president, put on weight, and spent the next fifteen years in a more than moderately successful attempt to avoid becoming a slave to his job. Of all the railroad officials, he was ever the hardest to locate; fortunately his presence was not often required. Much of his time was spent wandering about the Coast, inspecting property — coal and gold mines, cattle ranches, irrigation projects — which he was always considering buying and sometimes did buy. Often he was to be found at the railhead of whatever lines the extending Southern Pacific was currently constructing. One of his favorite haunts when he was in town was the bar of the Palace, where his hulking figure, then not far below three hundred pounds, was frequently pointed out to visitors.

But there was nothing of the poseur about him. Although he had overseen the construction of thousands of miles of railroad, he freely admitted that he knew nothing about engineering. " I could not have measured a cut any more than I could have flown." Later he was to make a more surprising admission. Showing a friend through the picture gallery in his redwood mansion on Nob Hill, he remarked: " I don't know much about art." Among American millionaires of the '80s, frankness could go no further. In his later years he, like Stanford, was quite willing to supply newspaper advice to those who wished to become multimillionaires. But whereas Stanford sprinkled such interviews with references to the solid virtues: industry, sobriety, thrift, piety, Crocker's approach was more realistic. " One man works hard all his life and ends up a pauper. Another man, no smarter, makes twenty million dollars. Luck has a hell of a lot to do with it."

2

LUCK had a lot to do with Crocker's success, but not everything. Except during periods when he chose to indulge his weakness for inactivity, he was not only capable of hard physical labor, he actively enjoyed it. Like all his associates, the habit of industry had been drilled into him from early boyhood. " I never had a nursery period," he once announced with pride. " It was my habit to work day and night." Crocker was born in Troy, New York, on September 16, 1822. He had earned — and saved — money since he was ten. By his own later and perhaps romanticized account, he quit school at twelve, went two hundred dollars in debt to purchase the agency for a New York newspaper in Troy, and with his earnings supported his mother and sister. Meantime his father, having failed in the liquor business in Troy, had gone out to Indiana with his remaining four sons and settled on a block of virgin woodland. A year or two later, in 1836, young Crocker sold his newspaper agency, pocketed a hundred-dollar profit on the transaction, and took his dependents west.

On the Marshall County farm the reunited family endured the slavery common to life on the agricultural frontier a century ago. Charles, then fourteen and big for his age, helped clear the land for the plow and put in the first crops, finding time to hire out to neighbors during the harvest season. Possibly the memory of the remunerative business career in Troy dampened his enthusiasm for splitting oak logs and digging out tree stumps, for his father presently grew convinced that the youth was not heading for success as a farmer. When he was seventeen the elder man expressed this conviction in such unmistakable terms that Charles demanded:

" Father, do you want me to leave home? "

" Yes and no," said Isaac Crocker. " Yes, because you are no use here. No, because I am afraid you would starve among strangers."

Young Crocker chose to leave — and he did not starve. Later, in his self-dramatizing way, he was to comment: " All I had in the world was a pair of woolen socks, a cotton shirt, and a linen dickey, tied up in a cotton handkerchief." He helped on a neighbor's farm until spring, then got work, at eleven dollars a month and board, at a crossroads sawmill. True to tradition, he was to return

CHARLES CROCKER
from a photograph by Taber, San Francisco.

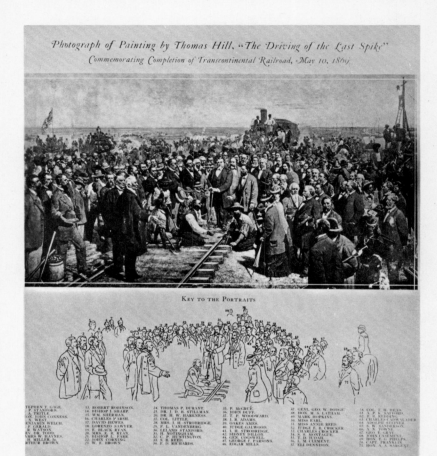

Photograph of Painting by Thomas Hill, "The Driving of the Last Spike"
Commemorating Completion of Transcontinental Railroad, May 10, 1869

KEY TO THE PORTRAITS

STEPHEN T. GAGE.
P. STANFORD.
A. TRITLE.
HON. JOHN CONNESS.
N. WEST
BENJAMIN WELCH.
E GERALD
F. WATSON
EX DR. TODD.
JAMES W. HAYNES.
H. MILLER, Jr.
ARTHUR BROWN.

13. ROBERT ROBINSON.
14. BISHOP I. SHARP.
15. WM. SHERMAN.
16. CHARLES PARSH.
17. DAVID HEWES.
18. LORENZO SAWYER.
19. E. BLACK RYAN.
20. MRS. E. B. RYAN.
21. BISHOP E. FARR.
22. JOHN CORNING.
23. W. F. BROWN.

24. THOMAS P. DURANT.
25. DR. J. D. B. STILLMAN.
26. DR. H. W. HARKNESS.
27. COL. LITTLE.
28. MRS. J. H. STROBRIDGE.
29. F. L. VANDENBERG.
30. LELAND STANFORD.
31. H. NOTTINGHAM.
32. C. P. HUNTINGTON.
33. S. B. REED.
34. F. D. RICHARDS.

35. P. McGRUE.
36. JOHN DUFF.
37. T. P. WOODWARD.
38. J. R. ADAMS.
39. OAKES AMES.
40. JUDGE GALWOOD.
41. J. H. STROBRIDGE.
42. SIDNEY DILLON.
43. GEN. COGSWELL.
44. GEORGE P. PARSONS.
45. EDGAR MILLS.

47. GENL. GEO. W. DODGE.
48. HON. M. S. LATHAM.
49. MARK HOPKINS.
50. MISS EARL.
51. MISS ANNIE REED.
52. JUDGE F. B. CROCKER.
53. CHARLES CROCKER.
54. S. S. MONTAGUE.
55. T. D. JUDAH.
56. L. M. CLEMENT.
57. ELI DENNISON.

58. COL. T. H. HEAD.
61. A. P. K. SAFFORD.
62. E. B. REDDING.
63. CHARLES CLOWVLADER.
64. ADOLPH STEINER.
65. A. S. HALLIDSON.
66. N. N. TOWNE.
67. GEO. E. GRAY.
68. JOHN CASEMENT.
69. HON. T. G. PHELPS.
70. CAPT. FRANKLIN.
71. HON. A. A. SARGENT.

HILL'S "THE DRIVING OF THE LAST SPIKE"
The original is now in the historical collection of the Wells
Fargo Bank, San Francisco
Photograph courtesy of the California State Library

later and marry his employer's daughter, Mary Denning, and take her to California to share his improbable millions.

But nine years had still to pass before James Marshall's discovery in the Coloma millrace was to draw expectant thousands to the far rim of the continent. Meantime Crocker found a deposit of iron ore on an Indiana hillside and set up one of the crude furnaces then common on the western frontier, combination iron foundries and smithies. The venture barely supported him. In 1849 he willingly gave it up to join a group of the neighborhood young men — two of his four brothers among them — to hunt a more valuable metal in the foothills of California.

In later life Crocker looked on his crossing of the plains as a high point in his career. In his memoirs, dictated in the early '80s to Hubert H. Bancroft, he returned constantly to that period, always with a sort of mild wonder at the way he had conducted himself. For on the journey he first realized that if one boldly assumed leadership others were willing to accept the role of subordinates. The discovery permanently delighted him, as it has delighted others. His memoirs are studded with such remarks as these: " They would all gather around me and want to know what to do." " I grew up as a sort of leader and was always inclined to lead." " I had always been the one to swim a river and carry a rope across."

His experiences on the overland trek paralleled those of tens of thousands of others. The main body of his company left the home base first, carrying only such supplies as were needed to take the party to Fort Kearny, where the real crossing would begin. Charles and a few others gathered at Quincy, Illinois, with the bulk of the freight; this was to be shipped down the river to St. Louis, then on one of the Missouri steamers to Council Bluffs. This part of the journey was not without incident. At St. Louis they learned that because of insufficient water the Missouri River boats were operating only as far as St. Jo. To Crocker and his party the situation was serious; the delay would make it impossible to join the main group in time to begin the California passage that year. While they lamented their bad luck another steamer, the *Tuscumbia,* tied up at the St. Louis levee. Crocker, in his new role of leader, went aboard and found the captain. On the latter's coat the young blacksmith saw an emblem of a fraternal order. "As I was considerable of an Odd Fellow in those times I went up to him and gave him the grip and soon was on good terms with him."

The connection proved fortunate, for the captain agreed to attempt the passage to Council Bluffs provided Crocker and his group could supply fifteen deck passengers and two hundred and fifty tons of freight for that point — a condition they were able to meet. All went well until the vessel reached St. Jo and a few miles beyond. Then the *Tuscumbia* unexpectedly nosed in to shore and Crocker's brother Odd Fellow ordered passengers and freight landed.

"I of course was a prominent man among the passengers and they all looked up to me," Crocker recalled; and of course he was spokesman in this emergency. The captain's argument that there was not enough water in the river to go higher failed to convince his passengers, who took positions beside their piles of freight and insisted that the steamer go on. The captain regarded the group, saw that their firearms were prominently displayed, and came round to their viewpoint. The *Tuscumbia* threaded her way past the sandy bars of the upper river and safely reached Council Bluffs. To show there were no hard feelings, the captain produced a bottle of champagne and the party drank a toast to their success in the gold fields. Recounting the exploit later, Crocker did not fail to point out the moral: " This incident shows my determination not to allow anything to stand in my way when I have made up my mind to do anything."

3

THE PARTY reached California in March 1850. Like the great majority of those who arrived that year and later, Crocker failed to support himself as a prospector. Here his luck entered the picture. Instead of returning to blacksmithing he, in partnership with a brother, opened a store in one of the Eldorado County camps. At first his share of the work consisted in driving a team that hauled supplies from Sacramento. The store prospered moderately; the owners presently started a branch in a neighboring town; then, in 1852, another at Sacramento. Their prosperity continued and in the fall of that year Charles made a hurried trip east and married the daughter of the Indiana sawmill-owner. The two hastened to New York and took a boat for California, for the bridegroom was anxious to return to his flourishing business. They reached Sacramento a few days after the Crocker store and its contents had vanished in one of the town's periodical holocausts. Crocker, however, had brought new stock with him and he and his brothers raised enough capital to rebuild, this time with fireproof materials. In a few weeks their doors were open again.

Crocker lacked the flair for trade that distinguished, for instance, his future partner Huntington, but Sacramento was the supply center for scores of active mining communities, and business was booming. The Crocker store shared the general prosperity. By then the branches had been abandoned. The Sacramento establishment, dealing mainly in drygoods and with a growing wholesale department, easily survived the slack period of the middle '50s. By 1860 it was one of the substantial business houses of the town. Young Charles had no reason to regret that he had chosen to put himself behind, not a forge, but a drygoods counter. The picture of the former blacksmith measuring out yards of calico for the pioneer ladies of Sacramento was ironically evoked in later years, but it was just that step that made later triumphs possible.

Meantime the lessons he had learned on the trip west were not forgotten. In 1856 he joined the new Republican party; his name was put on the ticket in a local election and he unexpectedly found himself elected an alderman. Another member of the board was a fellow merchant, a thin, bearded man, Mark Hopkins, who, with

a partner named Huntington, did a thriving business in
shovels and axes and kegs of nails from their establishment on lower K Street. Leland Stanford, of Stanford
Brothers, wholesale grocers at Front and L streets, was
also active in the new party. Stanford became a candidate
for state treasurer in the election of 1857, and Crocker
ran on the same ticket for the assembly. Both were defeated, but these political alliances first made the four
storekeepers well acquainted.

It was, thus, not their common occupation but a common desire to see John C. Fremont elected president
that brought the group together. With the exception of
Huntington, whose dislike for politics seems to have dated
from the cradle, all became prominent in the counsels
of the new party. Their espousal of the cause of the
abolitionists brought them no local popularity, for state
politics were still firmly in the control of the Southern
Democrats. "A convention of Negro Worshippers assembled yesterday in this city," began a newspaper account
of the Republicans' first state convention at Sacramento
in 1856, and such phrases as " dangerous fanaticism " and
" spectacle of political degradation " were sprinkled
through the text. Yet by climbing thus early on the
Republican bandwagon, the four gained an advantage
that was later to prove invaluable. Stanford, Crocker,
his elder brother E. B. Crocker, and Mark Hopkins, all
learned practical politics as they went along, and time
worked to their advantage.

" Freedom, Fremont, and the Railroad," was the new
party's slogan in California in 1856. Six years later, so

rapidly had public sentiment shifted to the " Negro-worshippers " that Stanford was elected Governor and the four political amateurs were in control of the company that hoped to build the western half of the railroad. When ground was broken on the morning of January 8, 1863, Crocker was conspicuous on the flag-draped platform beside the levee, supervising Stanford's turning of the symbolical shovelful of earth, leading cheers for the success of the venture, turning upon the crowd to shout dramatically: " It is going right on, gentlemen, I assure you! "

The drygoods store had been sold. Crocker's resignation from the board of directors of the new company had already been turned in, for he had in his pocket a contract to build the first eighteen miles. He knew nothing of engineering, nothing of the practical aspects of railroad construction; but he had found a job exactly to his liking. Here was movement and excitement, a continuous pleasant uproar. It was almost like another trip across the plains, for again he was the one who roared the orders and kept things moving. He was later to boast that during the next six years he never slept in his Sacramento bed more than three consecutive nights. His home was one end of a battered day coach that shuttled back and forth over the line so continuously that he could awake in the middle of the night and tell by the car's vibration and sway exactly where he was.

4

ON the damp January morning when the project was officially inaugurated, pile-drivers were already pounding bridge supports into the silt-choked channel of the American River. The Pacific Railroad after forty-six years of discussion was under way. For weeks earlier, while Judah's transit men were completing the working survey, Crocker had been assembling men and equipment, establishing road camps and commissary, and preparing to tackle the first major job: the making of a long fill needed to keep the riverside track above water during the flood season. Huntington, the recognized trader of the group, had gone to New York, where he was already bringing his talents to bear on manufacturers of iron rails and spikes, making the first purchases of locomotives and rolling stock, driving hard bargains with shipowners to transport his supplies thirteen thousand miles round the Horn.

Through the spring and summer of 1863 the construction gang, not yet an efficiently organized unit, crept eastward from Sacramento, Crocker, as he later confessed, literally learning as he went. The lesson proved expensive. Costs exceeded estimates, and long before the easy eighteen miles to Junction (now Roseville) were finished, his cash was gone and weekly payrolls were being met out of the Central Pacific treasury. This, however, was immaterial, a mere bookkeeping detail, for Stanford, Huntington, and Hopkins were silent partners in Crocker & Company and were sharing its profits. For the building of this first section, Crocker & Company received $425,-000 — $275,000 in cash and the rest in Central Pacific bonds. It was the partners' first taste of easy money.

By the time Junction was reached, Judah, who disapproved of this polite form of embezzlement, had died, and one of his helpers, S. S. Montague, had become chief engineer. Crocker's superintendent was J. H. Strobridge, a burly, domineering gang foreman of the slave-driving type, willing and capable of enforcing authority with his ham-like fists. Both Montague and Strobridge remained with the Central Pacific, and later the Southern Pacific (which the partners organized in 1865) for many years. With Strobridge, Crocker quickly became intimate, adopting his viewpoint and supporting his methods whenever they came in conflict with those of the Stanford-Hopkins group. In later life Crocker was to quote with approval Strobridge's opinion that " the men were as near brutes as they can get."

There was perhaps ample basis for dissatisfaction with the workmen Crocker and Strobridge were able to find, for by the '60s labor on the west coast had attained a dignity that might have been mistaken for hauteur. Not the current War of the Rebellion but the Nevada mines had depleted surplus manpower. Entering a field already raked and reraked by dozens of harassed employers, Crocker & Company had meager pickings. Their agents daily harangued skeptical groups in San Francisco and other Coast towns, but the men who were collected and forwarded to the railhead proved — when they arrived at all — of a quality designed to incite Irish riding bosses to new heights of profanity. Agents who sometimes found the collection of a gang of pick and shovel men easy later learned that these had used their passes to the end of the line merely as an inexpensive means of making the first stage of their journey to the current boom town beyond the Sierra. Such duplicity hastened a decision a year or two later to try to build the road with Chinese — a betrayal of American labor that was not to enhance the popularity of the railroad or its owners on the Coast.

As a matter of fact, the road from the beginning had but a limited popular following. Play-going Californians looked on this attempt to scale the Sierra as an interesting show, but the production never had the support of the gallery. Largely because of this the new company found itself in a variety of difficulties before it was well started. During 1863 the rails had been laid to Junction, eighteen miles out. The next objective was Newcastle, a dozen miles farther into the foothills. Judah's objections and Crocker's inexperience and labor troubles prevented the latter from becoming the sole contractor here; Crocker & Company in fact undertook to build only two miles. The rest was let out in short sections to a variety of other amateur contractors. The result was altogether unsatisfactory. During most of 1864, these contractors struggled to complete their mile or two of road; then, short of equipment, short of men, and finally short of cash, all gave up in disgust. Crocker & Company, backed by the Central Pacific, resumed where the luckless independents left off.

Somehow the line was completed to Newcastle.

Twenty-ton locomotives newly sent out from the East were assembled at Sacramento and put to work hauling toy-like trains piled high with freight over the thirty-one-mile railroad. But funds grew progressively scarcer and work came to a virtual standstill. The partners borrowed some money on their personal credit and would have borrowed more had not Huntington objected. " If we can't pay a thousand men, we'll hire only five hundred — if we can't pay five hundred we'll hire ten." There were times when even ten was inadvisable. Stanford later told of a two-week period when there was not a dollar of cash in the treasury. As the last of the construction crews was withdrawn from the woods beyond Newcastle, public confidence dropped to nothing. Even the road's supporters grew convinced that the line would lose itself in its Sierra canyon, and not very far up the canyon. The partners had trouble getting credit to operate their prosperous Sacramento stores; their connection with the railroad made them poor business risks.

Much of the opposition, of course, was deliberately manufactured, for a completed railroad to the East would step on a variety of toes. The monopolistic Wells, Fargo Express Company, the huge companies controlling the stage lines of the Coast — the California, the Pioneer, Ben Holliday's powerful Overland — the Pacific Mail and other steamship lines, rival local railroads, telegraph companies, private toll roads — all these saw themselves endangered should the Central Pacific ever be completed. Even a San Francisco company that brought down boatloads of ice from Alaska saw possible competition from the snowy summit of the Sierra and joined the campaign. San Francisco saw Sacramento gathering in a progressively larger share of the Nevada trade and opposed the road on the sufficient ground that local capital was taking no hand in its building. The general gloom surrounding the company's promoters during this period reached even the normally optimistic Crocker. He later reported that he would have been glad to pocket the loss of everything he had put into it, " take a clean shirt, and get out." Huntington had a similar tale to tell: a friend with a gift for romantic phrases had warned him, he recalled, that he would " bury his fortune in the snow of the Sierras."

The picture was dark at this period, but hardly so dark as later accounts painted it. Difficulties were later magnified in Congress and before investigating committees to help justify the ultimate enormous profits, for the theory was propounded that great risks justify great rewards. Even during the first year or two, attempts to raise capital had not been altogether fruitless. By June 1863, above $200,000 had been paid in on stock subscriptions; the state and various California counties had bought stock to the amount of $1,500,000 and had agreed to pay interest on a like amount of the company's bonds. Even San Francisco, although it regretted its early generosity in voting a stock subscription, ended by being forced to make the company an outright gift of $400,000.

These amounts, plus the original federal subsidy, represented no minor feats in money-raising. But the promoters were already on the trail of bigger game. At Washington, Huntington, working for once in co-operation with the Union Pacific promoters, was urging on Congress the necessity of greater liberality, through a far-reaching amendment to the Railroad Act of 1862. This measure, again put forth as a wartime necessity — one of the arguments being that only thus could California be held in the Union — received President Lincoln's signature on July 2, 1864. It doubled the amount of land-grants, made the government bonds a second mortgage on the railroad, permitting the issuing of first-mortgage company bonds of the same amount, increased federal subsidies in the mountain region, and permitted these to be issued before the line was completed. More, the time limit was liberally extended; four years were allowed to reach the state line, and public lands outside the grants might be drawn on for natural resources — lumber, fuel, coal — needed in construction and operation.

These were some of the provisions of what even Huntington called " an extraordinarily generous act." Meantime the railroad group had been at work on another plan to increase the government's bounty. At intervals since 1862, wartime business had been put aside while Congress considered such weighty matters as the color of the soil on the east and west banks of Arcade Creek, a tiny, normally dry stream seven miles from Sacramento. The point was important because half a million dollars in subsidy bonds hinged on the result. If Congress could be convinced that the reddish soil of the east bank was characteristic of the mountains, and the darker soil three feet opposite was that of the valley, then it might be argued that there the valley ended and the mountains began. The fact that for miles beyond the creek the red soil was as level as a floor was beside the point. Geologists were ready to testify for the company that soil, not contours, determined the point where the valley left off and mountains began. If government experts accepted the theory, then the federal treasury was obliged to pay the company an additional $32,000 for every mile of road east of Arcade Creek for a distance of 150 miles, for the revised Railroad Act fixed the subsidy at $16,000 per mile on level sections and $48,000 in the mountains. The government considered the grave reports pro and con and, in January 1864, announced that the Sierra Nevadas officially began at Arcade Creek. When news of the ruling reached California a roar of amazement shook the state. Sacramento's four shopkeepers began to command closer attention, a grudging respect. Any group who could move the base of the Sierra Nevadas twenty-five miles westward into the center of the valley and could net a half-million dollars by the exploit would bear watching.

5

EIGHTEEN months had been consumed building the thirty-one-mile road to Newcastle, and the real test was still ahead. During most of 1864, Crocker's construction crews had melted away while the promoters, before courts, in Congress, and in the legislatures of California and Nevada, fought to win further concessions and to preserve what had already been granted. All this had required methods of persuasion more substantial than unsupported eloquence, and for months the company's till was never far from empty.

But as the year closed, the chief points at issue had one by one been decided, nearly all in a way favorable to the company. With ample financing assured and profits no longer theoretical, attention swung again to the almost forgotten matter of building the road.

Early in January 1865 Crocker's agents rescoured Sacramento, Stockton, and San Francisco for laborers, and the foothills north of Clipper Gap, quiet for months, again resounded to the axes of those clearing the way ahead, to the rumble of black-powder blasts, and the shouts of teamsters driving processions of dump-carts between cut and fill. In two months Crocker, again the sole contractor, had rails laid to Illinoistown, eleven miles beyond and five hundred feet above Clipper Gap. By late spring the Central Pacific was operating fifty-six miles of railroad. Passengers were carried at a flat rate of ten cents a mile; freight was fifteen cents per ton per mile. In June gross earnings from operations for the first time topped a thousand dollars a day.

Not money but labor was henceforth to be Crocker's problem. Of the thousands sent into the hills during 1863–4, an average of only two in five reported to the foreman on the job, and of these all but a few quit when they had earned enough to pay stage fare to Virginia City. Everyone who applied was put to work. Old age and extreme youth were alike welcomed. In 1865 Robert Gif-

THE COLTON AND CROCKER RESIDENCES, NOB HILL, SAN FRANCISCO, 1875

The Crocker house, on the left, is still under construction. Crocker's "spite fence," enclosing the Yung cottage, may be seen above the roof of the Colton house.

RESIDENCE OF E. B. CROCKER AT SACRAMENTO
*Now the Crocker Art Gallery. The wing to the left is a
later addition.*

HALLWAY OF THE E. B. CROCKER RESIDENCE,
SACRAMENTO

ford, aged twelve, walked the four miles from his home in Dutch Flat to Gold Run, ambitious to help build this railroad to the Atlantic Ocean. A heavy, florid man looked down on him from the great height of a horse's back and told him to report to one of the gang foremen and to say that Mr. Crocker had sent him. Young Gifford remained on the payroll three months. His job was to lead a team of horses that pulled a dump-cart, and his wages were seventy-five cents a day and board. But children, too, were scarce in the foothills and for months the labor shortage remained acute. In the company's new San Francisco office Stanford and Judge E. B. Crocker (brother of Charles and head of the Central Pacific's legal department) put their heads together and petitioned the War Department to send out five thousand Rebel prisoners to be put to work under the guard of a few companies of Union soldiers. But the war ended and the scheme had to be dropped.

A plan of importing, under contract, thousands of peons from Sonora and other Mexican states never got beyond the discussion stage; the constitutional inertia of the breed was too well known to California employers.

Another dubious possibility remained — the lowly Chinese. There were already thousands of them on the Coast, reworking the abandoned placers in the gold country, operating laundries and cheap restaurants, peddling baskets of vegetables through the residential streets of California towns, or crowded into the wretched warrens of a score of " Chinatowns." The suggestion that the Chinese be given a trial was first made by Stanford and

E. B. Crocker. Strobridge, stubborn and conservative, dismissed the idea as preposterous. In his opinion, and in that of nearly everyone on the Coast, the outcast Celestial's field was raising carrots and cabbages, washing shirts, or doing scullery work in the houses of prosperous citizens. The weight of the average adult Chinese was probably less than a hundred and ten pounds; to attempt to build a railroad over the Sierra with these rice-eating weaklings was rank nonsense.

Crocker, for once, failed to share Strobridge's opinion. His own servant, Ah Ling, had proved himself a marvel of endurance; moreover, in his storekeeping days in the placer towns Crocker had observed that the Chinese were at their gravel pits long before the white men were out of bed. He confronted the skeptical Strobridge with an unanswerable argument; hadn't the ancestors of these weaklings built the Great Wall of China? And didn't that construction job compare favorably even with this railroad to Nevada Territory? A threatened strike of his white crews proved the deciding point. Strobridge dubiously agreed to try the experiment, and fifty Chinese were herded on freight cars in the Sacramento yards and hauled to the end of the track. They disembarked, glanced without curiosity at the surrounding forest, then tranquilly established camp, cooked a meal of rice and dried cuttlefish, and went to sleep. By sunrise they were at work with picks, shovels, and wheelbarrows. At the end of their first twelve hours of prodding industry Crocker and his engineers viewed the result with gratified astonishment. Those who through the day had been momentarily expecting the weaklings to fall in their tracks from exhaustion permanently revised their opinion of the Chinaman's endurance.

Another gang of fifty was hired at once, then a third. Finally all doubt vanished and the Chinatowns of the state were searched for every able-bodied male who could be tempted by the bait of steady work and forty dollars a month. Within six months two thousand blue-clad Orientals were swarming over the line while cuts were sunk and fills leveled off at a pace beyond the hopes of the partners. Of course, the white laborers of the Coast resented the affront. The railroad, already unpopular on numerous counts, earned the antagonism of another powerful group. To counteract this injury, railroad spokesmen were presently referring to the Chinese as " the Asiatic contingent of the Grand Army of Civilization," and Stanford was incorporating in company reports long defenses for using them: " Without them it would be impossible to complete the line in time . . . they soon become as efficient as white laborers. . . . More prudent and economical, they are content with less wages." To charges that the Chinese were held in a state of virtual serfdom by the labor contractors with whom the company dealt, Stanford stated: " No system similar to slavery . . . prevails. . . . Their wages . . . paid in coin at the end of each month, are divided among them by their agents . . . in proportion to the labor done by each. . . . These agents are generally American or Chinese merchants, who furnish them with supplies of food, the value of which they deduct monthly. . . ."

By the end of 1865 the company was committed to the use of Chinese for most of their labor, and Stanford was hopeful that the force might be increased to fifteen thousand during the coming year. Of course no such supply was available in California, and a San Francisco firm, Sisson, Wallace & Company (of which another of the Crocker brothers, Clark W., was a partner) , contracted to bring in from China as many as might be needed. Accordingly boats from Canton were presently tying up at San Francisco piers, their rails swarming with yellow faces, while labor leaders predicted economic ruin for the Coast and threatened a variety of reprisals. At the camps in the hills, however, the anticipated opposition failed to materialize. The advent of the Chinese relieved the white men of pick and shovel work; many became gang foremen, others were promoted to be teamsters, powdermen, or stone-workers. Moreover, the Chinese lived in their own camps, cooked their own meals, and knew their place. Thus the superiority of the Caucasian was undiminished, his dignity enhanced. Harmony reigned in the Sierra canyons and real progress began to be made.

6

By midsummer of 1865, trains were running, three a day each way, to Illinoistown (soon renamed Colfax in honor of a visit from Grant's Vice-President) , while men and equipment were concentrated on the line ahead. The job was entering its difficult phase. In April 2,000 men and 300 wagons and carts had constituted Crocker's force. Six months later it had been increased to 6,000 men, mostly Chinese, and 600 teams. With plenty of money to spend and plenty of men, rapid headway was being made at last. That summer the Sacramento *Union* reviewed the road's current activities and pronounced it " the largest construction enterprise in the world, not excepting the Suez Canal." Crocker, more confident than ever that he had been cut out for a leader, announced to the world: " The work goes bravely on."

There were many who wondered that so large a man could be so tireless. In later years dozens retained the memory of his large figure slouched on the back of a steaming horse, weaving continuously back and forth over the line, roaring orders, finding fault; in his own words, " stopping along wherever there was anything going amiss and raising old nick with the boys." He later told of lying all night in his car at the railhead, unable to sleep for planning ways to speed up the job. " Everyone was afraid of me," he recalled with pride. " I was just looking for someone to find fault with all the time." The fault-finding became habitual; even on his rare returns to his fireside at Sacramento his wife found it impossible to please him.

Only once a month was his appearance among the construction crews greeted with pleasure. His big sorrel mare then labored under an additional burden, two leather saddle-bags, bulging with coins. The big boss — " Cholly Clocker " to the Orientals — rode into the midst of a group, produced a paper, and called off the names of the men. As each stepped forward he dipped into the saddle-bags — gold on one side, silver on the other — and dropped the coins into the lifted palm. It was a chore he insisted on doing himself. Riding up the noisy canyon with a hundred and fifty pounds of gold and silver in his saddle-bags appealed to his sense of the dramatic, and its distribution periodically confirmed a pleasant sense of power. Later he was to remark in sincere admiration: " My faculty of leadership developed more and more as I grew older."

But fifty miles of line had yet to be built before the summit was reached, and some of the problems were hardly suspected. Beyond Secrettown the climb to the snow-covered crest began in earnest; the grade stakes veered upward along the slanting side of the American River canyon, and the stream dropped far below. Mean-time surveying parties ran scores of experimental lines ahead, and here and there made minor changes in Judah's survey, avoiding occasional deep fills, substituting a wooden trestle for a cut through granite, trying — without success — to effect changes in the route that would ma-terially lessen construction costs or reduce grades and curvature.

Throughout the summer of 1866, " Crocker's pets," six thousand strong, swarmed over the upper canyon, pecking methodically at the broken rock of the cuts, troop-ing in long lines beneath their basket hats to pour wheelbarrow-loads of debris down the canyonside, thread-ing precarious paths with seventy-pound kegs of black powder suspended from both ends of bamboo poles, refreshing themselves at intervals with sips of tea kept near at hand in whisky kegs emptied and abandoned by their white confreres. The Chinese were presently found to be adept at the back-breaking work of drilling and placing blasts, by then a major part of the work, for the upper ridges were scraped clear of soil by the winter deposits of ice. The reverberations of the heavy blasts echoed at decreasing intervals through the canyons, and the consumption of black powder rose to five hundred kegs a day.

Track-layers followed close behind the graders, and locomotives pushed strings of flatcars loaded with construction iron, lumber, explosives, food, drink, and more men to the railhead. Cape Horn, a sheer granite buttress, proved the most formidable obstacle of the year; its lower sides dropped away in a thousand-foot vertical cliff that offered no vestige of a foothold. The indomitable Chinese were lowered from above on ropes, and there, suspended between sky and earth, chipped away with hammer and chisel to form the first precarious ledge, which was then laboriously deepened to a shelf wide enough to permit the passage of the cars. Three years later when overland trains crept cautiously along this ledge, passengers gazed straight down from their windows into thin air.

Cape Horn was successfully passed in May 1866. Dutch Flat — where Judah, five years earlier, had organized the road — was reached in July. Later that summer Crocker, Stanford, and Hopkins, hoping to convince still-skeptical Coast financiers that they were building no mere feeder for their trans-Sierran wagon road, celebrated the opening of the track to Alta. Ten carloads of citizens from Sacramento and the bay arrived over the new rails, gathered about tables set in the open air, and with appetites sharpened by the altitude ate a luncheon " worthy of Delmonico's " and made their choice of three beverages: lemonade for the ladies, ice-water for the hypothetical teetotalers, and a concoction named Pacific Railroad punch for all the rest. Thus fortified, the visitors listened to nine speeches, joined in three cheers for Huntington in New York, for Judge E. B. Crocker in Nevada, and for the editor of the Sacramento *Union,* whose whereabouts was not revealed.

The progress continued. In November the company's timetables in California newspapers were again revised, as Cisco, ninety-four miles from Sacramento and nearly six thousand feet high, became the new terminus. Two trains were operated each way; the running time was five and a half hours, an average of about sixteen miles an hour, and the passenger fare was $9.40. Twenty-eight miles of track were built during 1866, at a cost of slightly less than eight million dollars.

Cisco was fourteen miles from the summit and eleven hundred feet below. To build this section Crocker and Strobridge and the company engineers had to overcome difficulties new to railroad builders anywhere. One problem was the extreme hardness of the granite of the upper ridges, through which the road must pass in almost continuous tunnels and deep cuts. Here heavy blasts spurted back through the drill holes, leaving rock undamaged.

The points of picks and chisels flattened against its flinty surface. Their usual equipment useless, the engineers adopted a late scientific discovery. Presently a Swedish chemist, one Swansen, was installed to manufacture on the spot a temperamental new substance called nitroglycerin. Its characteristics were imperfectly known and accidents were frequent; moreover, the cause of premature blasts could only be guessed at, for the explosions usually obliterated both evidence and witnesses. Strobridge himself was a casualty, losing an eye when he chanced to be in the vicinity of a blast.

Summit Tunnel, a quarter-mile bore through the granite backbone of the mountain, emphasized the inadequacy of the rock-drilling equipment then in use. Begun in midsummer of 1866 and pushed with all possible speed, it was a solid year in the building. Not only was the work tackled from both ends but a shaft was chipped out from above so that work could proceed outward from the middle. Thus on four fronts Chinese crowded shoulder to shoulder and, working in twelve-hour shifts, chipped and hacked at the steel-like rock faces — and advanced at an average rate of eight inches a day.

At San Francisco, Stanford and Hopkins and E. B. Crocker received reports of this snail-like progress and compared them with news of the Union Pacific, then just hitting its stride in the easy advance across the prairies of eastern Nebraska. They foresaw their rival making good its boast to build to the California state line, leaving the Western company only the costly and unproductive road across the mountains. Crocker and Strobridge, grappling with as tough an assignment as engineers had ever faced, read impatient messages from headquarters and returned brusque answers inviting their critics to suggest means of doing better. The tempers of neither group were improved by the exchange; consequently when an inventor presently appeared at the San Francisco office with a new-fangled device he called a steam drilling machine, he was welcomed eagerly. Stanford, always fascinated by machinery, was particularly impressed. No possible flaws in a mechanized civilization were ever visible to his eyes, and this gadget instantly charmed him. Inventor and invention were dispatched to the summit with instructions to set to work at once, and the San Francisco group confidently awaited the result.

But Crocker's next letter from the mountains was openly contemptuous. Strobridge, stubborn and opinionated, had his own views on how to bore tunnels through granite, and these did not include steam-driven drills. Stanford and Judge Crocker dispatched exasperated letters insisting that the device at least be given a trial; Crocker's reply quoted Strobridge to the effect that to connect the drill would require stopping his hoisting engine, which would interfere with the removal of the loose rock from the center section of the tunnel. Stanford bought another hoisting engine and sent it up to the mountains; Strobridge, backed by Crocker, refused to install it. The matter, by that time something of an issue, hung fire for weeks. "There does not appear a will that they should succeed, and usually where there is no will there is no way," Stanford wrote sadly to Hopkins. Crocker's brother, E. B., accepted defeat less philosophically. " It puts me out of all patience to see how that drilling machine matter was mismanaged. . . . The truth is things have got to such a pass that there can't be a thing done unless it suits Stro. Whenever a man gets Charles' confidence, he swears by him and all he says or does is right."

The drilling machines were not used — and the Summit Tunnel continued to be pecked through by Crocker's stoical Chinese. The months lost enabled the Union Pacific to build hundreds of miles of the joint road they would not otherwise have accomplished, and the Western company spent a needless two million dollars hauling men and supplies about the uncompleted bore. Summit Tunnel was finally holed through in September 1867. It was the last major tunnel to be driven by hand. Within a year or two, power-driven drills were in use all over the world.

7

WHEN the first locomotive nosed its way through the east portal of the summit bore, signalizing the conquest of the Sierra's crest, it marked the end of the first phase of construction. Nearly five years had passed since the wet afternoon at Sacramento when ground was broken, and the line was still where its enemies had predicted it would end — " lost in the clouds of the Sierra." Another full year, 1867, was to pass before the tracks would reach the state line and flatten out on the floor of the Nevada plateau.

The prospect of building in the desert heat could hardly have been distasteful to Crocker and his thousands of workmen, for they had already had far more than their share of sub-zero weather. The winter of 1864–5 had been abnormally mild, but this was the period when financial matters and not construction had occupied the partners, and no benefit was gained by this bit of good luck. The next winter was a different story. Construction work by then was mostly above the six-thousand-foot mark — and the winter was as severe as any on record. Snow fell in quantity as early as October, and the next five months saw an almost continuous succession of storms. As ground froze and the tracks and construction line were blanketed under an icy mass fifteen feet thick, the work slowed down to a walk. Crocker, wrapped in furs like an Eskimo, patrolled the line continually; the work must go bravely on. It went on, even though nearly half his force of nine thousand were needed to keep the line clear of snow, and his reports showed so little progress that the partners in California were newly alarmed. In December, Stanford and Hopkins, up from balmy Sacramento to view the battle for themselves, stood shivering on a snowbank above Cisco while five locomotives strained futilely to drive a snowplow through thirty-foot drifts. They returned to the lowlands convinced that Crocker's reports of his troubles were not all imagined.

But the mileage race with the Union Pacific was on

THE HIGH SECRETTOWN TRESTLE IN THE SIERRA
NEVADA MOUNTAINS OF CALIFORNIA, 1877

This remarkable picture, taken when the trestle was being filled in with dirt by the Central Pacific, shows the meager tools with which the builders had to work. In those days there were none of the power implements that are so common to modern construction. Scrapers were not even used in the grading; dynamite had been invented, but was not in general use. Chinese coolies did the work with pick and shovel, one-horse dump carts, wheelbarrows, and black powder. At times it was necessary to lower the workmen over cliffs in baskets to ledges where they could level off a grade in the mountainside.

Courtesy of the California State Library

AN EARLY VIEW OF A SIERRA SNOWSHED

Courtesy of the California State Library

SUMMIT HOUSE AND SNOWSHED

Courtesy of Francis P. Farquhar

in earnest, and the Western forces could not afford to slow down. The snow-bound thousands continued the struggle straight through from November to May. Chinese in day and night shifts shoveled continuously to help keep the completed line open, but drifts formed faster than they and the steam plows could remove them. In the end the section above Cisco had to be abandoned.

Before winter was half over, work in the open had become impossible and thousands of half-frozen Chinese were shipped back to Sacramento or over the summit to the lower levels of the eastern slope. Only in the tunnels and deep cuts could construction go on, and even there the difficulties mounted. Food, powder, fuel, and all construction materials were laboriously packed in from Cisco. By January the task of keeping paths open between camps and the line was abandoned. Tunnels were dug beneath forty-foot drifts, and for months three thousand workmen lived curious mole-like lives, passing from work to living-quarters in dim passages far beneath the snow's surface. This eerie existence was complicated by constant danger, for as snows accumulated on the upper ridges, avalanches grew frequent, their approach heralded only by a brief thunderous roar. A second later a work crew, a bunkhouse, sometimes an entire camp, would go hurtling at a dizzy speed down miles of frozen canyons. Not until months later were the bodies recovered; sometimes groups were found with shovels or picks still clutched in their frozen hands.

Those sent ahead to clear the roadway down the east slope found conditions not much easier. In the heavily wooded Truckee River canyon, clearing the frozen ground for the graders proved a huge task. Sugar pines eight feet and more in diameter were felled, their trunks cut in sections and rolled out of the way, while heavy blasts were planted beneath their stumps, which were blown skyward in abrupt fountains of flying wood, frozen earth, and pungent black smoke. To supply this outpost army, thousands of tons of equipment, material, and provisions had to be hauled on sleds from Cisco over the summit to Donner Lake. Three locomotives, iron for forty miles of road, and forty cars were among the items freighted on sleds over the ridge, then loaded on wagons at Donner Lake and drawn down rutted, muddy roads to Truckee. The distance from Cisco to Truckee was only twenty-eight miles, but the expenditure in effort and dollars was enormous.

Months later, as spring thaws began to reduce the mountains of snow, Crocker and Strobridge moved their crews back to the summit and began chipping down through solid ice to the abandoned cuts and fills. The upper few miles of completed line on the west slope were presently cleared and Cisco again became a way station. The assault was resumed and intensified. Throughout 1867 twelve thousand workmen crowded along the forty-mile front from the summit to the eastern base of the mountains, hacking at the cuts and tunnels above Donner Lake, grading the roadbed down the steep slopes of Truckee Canyon. Tunnel No. 9 at Donner Lake and the adjacent deep cuts through solid granite proved tediously slow. Before that seven-mile gap could be closed and a connection made with the tracks ahead, winter again closed in and the experiences of a year before were repeated.

The construction record for 1867 — a scant forty miles, twenty-five of which were still unconnected with the main line — was not encouraging to the four partners, who were casting growingly anxious eyes at the Union Pacific. That year the rival road built six times as many miles as the Central; its officials planned to reach Ogden, five hundred miles beyond its railhead, by the end of 1868. Faced by the loss of hundreds of miles of easy construction across Nevada and Utah — where the government subsidy was easily twice the cost of building — the partners nonetheless could do little to remedy the situation. For the second winter proved as severe as the first, and the gap above Donner Lake remained unclosed. Moreover, the line over the summit became blanketed with such mountainous snowdrifts that the efforts of the company engineers failed to keep it open. Reluctantly the upper line was again abandoned; Cisco once more became the terminus, and the slow process of sledding over the summit had to be resumed.

News that this upper section had been closed for the second successive year confirmed still-active doubts of the company's critics on the Coast. Hostile newspapers, now including the once friendly *Union,* printed letters in which engineers proved conclusively that the line must remain closed for five months each year. One writer, borrowing a phrase from a book just coming into popularity, called the line the " Alice in Wonderland Trail." Another predicted that in the end the great transcontinental railroad would prove useful only to carry excursionists to the high Sierra on summer vacations. But these were critics who had earlier claimed that to build from Sacramento to Nevada over Judah's route would cost an average of half a million dollars per mile. The actual cost was high enough; nonetheless, two years of experience with the mountain winters had reconciled the associates to the expenditure of another unanticipated two million dollars. Because no other means of keeping the tracks open could be devised, construction of a long series of snowsheds was begun. During the next two years a dozen sawmills and two hundred carpenters were continually busy putting up the heavily timbered galleries that eventually covered thirty-seven of the upper forty miles of the road. A year or two later, when tourists began passing over the line, it was these sheds and not the vastly more difficult cuts and tunnels that aroused their admiration.

During the winter of 1867–8 work was pushed on the unclosed gap above Donner Lake, while rails were laid down the eastern slope and graders pushed into the sage-covered desert beyond. But until the gap could be closed all hope of successfully competing for mileage with the Union Pacific was futile. The correspondence of the group shows with what impatience they awaited the delayed spring of 1868. At the first hint of warmer weather, thousands of coolies were moved back to the summit to reopen the line above Cisco and to clear the ground for the uncompleted section. The bosses, from Crocker down, drove them unmercifully, but removing the thick crust of ice proved a colossal task. It engaged the picks and wheelbarrows of six thousand Chinese for weeks before the frozen roadbed was exposed and track-laying could begin. June of 1868 was well advanced before the rails joined and the tracks at last were made continuous from Sacramento to the state line. Immediately freight trains packed with supplies and materials started rolling down the eastern mountainside and out upon the Nevada desert.

8

To bring the road from Sacramento to the state line money had been spent with a lavish hand. Crocker's friend Strobridge later estimated that had speed been a less essential factor the cost could have been reduced seventy per cent. He had in mind, of course, the tremendous waste involved in winter construction on the blizzard-swept mountaintop, and the great expense of building in advance of the continuous line that was completed. With the upper thirty miles frozen solid from November to March, every cubic foot of earth had to be chipped or blasted loose, the workmen often occupying dim trenches between perpendicular ice cliffs thirty feet high. Moreover, when spring thaws reduced the frozen earth to mud, the newly laid tracks sank and buckled and three quarters of the work had to be done over.

Twenty years later the company's auditors fixed the cost of this California section at $23,000,000, but that was when the owners were trying to minimize their profits, and the figure was reached by listing at face value bonds that had sold at fifty cents on the dollar and less. In gold, the total was slightly above $14,000,000. Judah's estimate, in 1861, had been $12,500,000, a by no means reckless forecast. He had not foreseen the necessity for building thirty-seven miles of snowsheds, nor had he counted on a five-year war that skyrocketed costs of materials and labor and quadrupled freight and insurance rates.

In the early '60s manufacturing on the Coast had hardly begun. Everything needed in railroad building, excepting only lumber and masonry, had to be purchased, at inflated prices, in crowded Eastern markets. The controlling group had little reason to complain of the railroad acts of '62 and '64, but as the war advanced, one of the provisions grew irksome. It was specified that rails and spikes and rolling stock must be of American manufacture — and with every mill in the East jammed with wartime orders prices rose alarmingly. Standard twenty-pound iron rails that had sold at Pennsylvania mill towns at $55 per ton in 1861, reached a peak of $262 before the war ended. To Huntington's New York office came representatives of British ironfounders, and the thrifty New Englander endured the anguish of having to refuse contracts that would have placed rails on the Sacramento levee for a third less than he was paying at the American mills.

Not only must materials be bought in the ruinous Eastern market; they must be shipped across the Isthmus or round the Horn, and from 1862 to 1865 rates followed sharply ascending curves. Later, when their own monopolistic lines were adhering to the slogan " All the traffic will bear," the partners liked to remind shippers that they had not always been on this pleasant side of the fence. Not only freight rates but insurance advanced shockingly, for Rebel warships harried the sea-lanes off Virginia and farther south, eager to intercept cargoes of needed powder and iron. The danger was great enough to increase insurance rates fourfold.

As official buyer and forwarder for the company, Huntington had need of all his shrewdness, for he was dealing with millowners whose order-files bulged with lucrative army contracts. Only the fact that the Pacific Railroad was regarded as a quasi-public enterprise, the completion of which would help win the war, enabled him to place certain orders at all. More, until the material was at sea, he was never certain that the War Department would not take it over. A number of times Huntington's considerable powers of persuasion failed to prevent this catastrophe, and locomotives, rails, and cars ready to be shipped to the Coast, and urgently needed there, were diverted to the southern battle-lines.

These were some of the problems of supply the partners faced during the first four years. There were others. After persuading indifferent millowners to accept contracts, and after avoiding the danger of having the material commandeered by the War Department, there remained the problem of getting it to California. Available ships were few, and freight rates were whatever owners or agents chose to ask. In 1862 the horizon brightened momentarily when Huntington outwitted a shipping agent by chartering fifty ships at half the prevailing rate. But this was an incident. Freightage round the Horn averaged $17.50 a ton; via the Isthmus it was three times as much. In 1863 Crocker needed a new locomotive in a hurry. It was disassembled and loaded on a steamer at Philadelphia, transported to Panama, loaded on flatcars and sent over the twenty-mile Panama Raiload, reshipped on a Pacific steamer, deposited on a lighter in San Francisco Bay, hoisted to the deck of a riverboat for transportation to Sacramento, deposited on the levee, and trucked to the company's shops, where it was reassembled. The combined freight bill was $8,100, more than eighty per cent of its initial cost.

The collapse of the Rebellion failed to bring the anticipated drop in prices. In '66, when a contract was let for thirty-eight locomotives, the price averaged $11,000 each. The forty-foot passenger coaches of the period cost $3,500, flatcars $600, handcars $150. All other supplies were in proportion. Powder was $5 a keg; construction tools — shovels, scrapers, dump-carts, track-laying implements — remained far beyond what they had been in 1861. All prices were in gold; if payment was made in the inflated currency, bills mounted as much as sixty per cent. When the Sierra was surmounted and construction crews advanced into the unproductive Humboldt, new items of expense were added. Hay and oats for the hundreds of draft animals brought fantastic prices, and the cost of lumber rose in proportion to the distance from the Sierra forests to the advancing railhead. Ties were presently costing the partners as much as $8 each, delivered.

By then, however, cost was a lightly regarded detail.

88

The immense rolling plains of Nevada and Utah Territory lay before the Central's construction army; and less than a thousand miles beyond, crews of the rival company were pushing rapidly westward. The Union Pacific building crew under the management of General Grenville M. Dodge, with their ranks swelled by hundreds of newly disbanded soldiers, had for months been piling up mileage over the prairies of Nebraska and southern Wyoming — and all the while the Central forces, still struggling with the flinty Sierra tunnels, had been advancing literally by inches.

9

In April 1868 the Overland Telegraph carried a message from Vice-President Durant of the Union Pacific to Stanford at Sacramento. The Union Pacific's line had then reached Sherman's Summit, Wyoming, 8,200 feet above sea level. Stanford wired back: " We cheerfully yield you the palm of superior elevation; 7,242 feet has been quite sufficient to satisfy our highest ambition." By then the ambition of the Central Pacific group had been curtailed in another direction; they no longer planned to build as many miles of road as their rival. To extend their lines to Salt Lake and a little beyond, enough to give them control of the traffic with the Mormon capital, was all they hoped for. Even this goal was no longer certain. To realize it would require that they build faster than railroads had ever been built before.

But the stakes were high and, now that the mountains were behind, Crocker's native optimism reasserted itself. His huge building organization was functioning with admirable precision. "Give me the material I need," he announced, "and I can build a mile a day of completed railroad." His partners took him at his word and the material was forthcoming, though to supply it taxed the ingenuity of the entire organization. Huntington bought materials with an increasingly prodigal hand; at one time thirty ships were at sea carrying iron rails round the Horn. The winter of 1867–8 arrived while the snowsheds were still far from completed, and to keep the line open over the summit proved a tremendous task. Despite the efforts of six snowplows and 2,500 men, there was one discouraging two-week period when the road was closed and the outlook grew dark.

The railhead reached Reno, Wadsworth, and advanced eastward across the low sage-covered hills. Surveying crews worked far in advance, relocating the line over the rolling country, seeking a route with the fewest cuts and fills, the least amount of grading. Years later when the New York broker E. H. Harriman got control of the line, he spent millions realigning this Nevada section, eliminating scores of its snake-like curves and shortening it by dozens of miles. Mileage and speed, not economy of operation, had been the goal of Crocker and his associates; every mile built meant a profit of twice its cost.

Through the hot summer of 1868, six thousand men functioned with speed and ordered efficiency. Crocker's gangs of coolies, now expert with pick and wheelbarrow and horse-drawn scrapers, tirelessly threw up and leveled the nondescript roadbed, undeterred by the sizzling heat, the clouds of alkali-laden dust. Behind them other crews rushed culverts to completion, while still others embedded the widely spaced ties, working at top speed to keep ahead of gangs of Irish track-layers.

This perambulating army, living in long strings of boxcars that weekly moved to new sidings, made rapid advances across central Nevada's waterless plains, while Crocker boasted that he was directing the mightiest peacetime army ever enlisted in a work of civilization, and the partners on the Coast, no longer critical, sent him messages of congratulation and urged him to try a little harder. The winter of 1868-9, though it again brought trouble in the Sierra and washed out miles of earthen fills to the rear, was welcomed with joy by the sweltering crews along the construction line, and the pace continued. December 31 saw an advance for the year of 362 miles, only three short of Crocker's promise of a mile a day.

But the Union Pacific's crews, then numbering above five thousand, boasted that one Hibernian could outwork three Chinese, and the race went on. Control of the traffic with Brigham Young's prosperous colony became the prize for which both sides contended. During the fall and winter Stanford lived at Salt Lake and cultivated the goodwill of the Prophet by offering him lucrative contracts to grade long sections of Central Pacific roadbed. The two men (their physical resemblance was close enough to cause occasional mild embarrassment to the Central Pacific's monogamous president) became close friends, and there was some disapproval when word reached the Coast that the two addressed one another as Leland and Brigham.

As the year 1868 ended, the rival railheads were so near that the point of their joining became a matter of importance. Both had sent surveyors far beyond the other's rails: the Union Pacific almost to the California line, the Central hundreds of miles east of Ogden. Meantime building continued until the graded lines paralleled each other for miles. Chinese and Irish crews regarded one another curiously and with mutual distaste. By accident or design, boulders occasionally rolled down from the Central's line, higher on the hillside, while startled Irishmen dropped their picks and scurried out of their paths. The Union's powdermen sometimes laid blasts rather far to the right of their own line, and a thousand graders looked on in innocent wonderment as the earth parted and Chinese and scrapers, horses and wheelbarrows and picks fountained upward. The Orientals regathered their forces, buried the dead, and continued placidly about their business until another blast brought another temporary pause. But the sport ended when a section of the Union's line mysteriously shot skyward and it became the Irishmen's turn to take time out for grave-digging.

Meanwhile the point of joining was being fought out at Washington, with Huntington on hand as usual to protect the interests of the Western road. He had, however, a formidable rival in the Union Pacific spokesman,

General Dodge, for Grant then occupied the White House and Dodge was a close friend and fellow campaigner. After days of jockeying for advantage a compromise was reached, and on April 10, 1869 Congress designated Promontory Point, six miles west of Ogden, as the meeting-place.

Once this had been settled, the necessity for haste vanished. Tension relaxed all along the line; the Central's force was cut down, and officials of the rival roads found time to exchange visits. Toward the end of April, Dodge rode westward across the narrowing gap and spent two days in the camp of the Westerners. He found much to criticize in the methods of the Californians and a little to praise. The docile industry of Crocker's veteran coolies aroused his frank envy; his own gangs of ex-soldiers had for months been distinguishing themselves by qualities far removed from docility. He found time in a letter to his wife to weigh the advantages of hiring a Chinese servant — an idea probably suggested by observation of Crocker's matchless Ah Ling. Sitting down to dinner with a group of Central Pacific engineers, he made a further pleasant discovery: " The Californians," he wrote, " have plenty of strawberries." No such delicacies were provided by the Union Pacific's commissary, and the General planned a trip to California in July.

The visiting engineer was interested in other things besides strawberries and Chinese domestics. He was on hand the day Crocker's crews accomplished their widely heralded feat of laying ten miles of track in a day. Dodge was not particularly impressed. "They took a week pre-paring for it," he commented, "and embedded all their ties beforehand. . . ."

10

THE RAW April of 1869 ended and the seven-year job drew toward its close. The Central's rails reached Prom-ontory first, for an uncompleted rock fill held up track-layers of the rival road, and its rails did not reach the junction point until a day later. On May 2 General Dodge wrote his wife: "There will not be much of a time here — no demonstration; but in the east and further west I expect they will celebrate."

The prediction proved incorrect. Back at the Central's head office at Sacramento plans for a celebration had been under way for weeks. On May 7 the first of several special trains arrived at the railhead, its occupants ex-pecting to witness an immediate wedding of the rails. In-stead they found the little village drenched and forlorn in a driving rain, its sodden street an extensive mudhole, colored bunting hanging limp and dripping across the façades of its wooden shacks.

This was not the gala reception the Californians had pictured. A hundred feet from the Central's railhead the end of the Union's tracks could be seen through the rain. Of the eastern party and the trainloads of celebrants rumored to have left Omaha two days earlier nothing was visible. Stanford and his guests stared moodily at the landscape, then climbed gingerly down the damaged steps of his private car — it had been struck by a coasting pine log on its passage down the east side of the Sierra — to file messages of inquiry with telegraph operators of both lines, housed in adjacent damp tents.

But the storm was general throughout the Rockies, and the Union's headquarters at Ogden reported floods and washouts on its line east of the town. Nothing was said of a further complication; money was lacking to pay many of the Union's workmen, and Vice-President Durant had to cope with still another strike. Word reached Promontory that the Eastern party would not arrive until Monday. It was then Friday. Stanford's party faced without enthusiasm the prospect of three days' contemplation of the wet landscape.

Back on the Coast, plans had been made for elaborate celebrations on Saturday. Stanford wired news of the delay, but the West had always considered Saturday the proper day for celebrating, and the message was ignored. Thus while San Francisco, Sacramento, and a dozen lesser towns commemorated the event with bands and fireworks and illuminated parades, time dragged in the car of the Central Pacific's president. Some of the party relieved the boredom by a visit to the nearest Union Pacific construction camp. There Jack Casement loaded them into a battered coach and a long day was spent on a tour of flooded Weber Canyon. They returned to Stanford's car, tired and damp and hungry, late Saturday evening. The downpour continued. That night the car was drawn back thirty miles to a siding at Monument Point and the next morning its windows framed the same landscape from a new viewpoint, one that included the gray surface of Salt Lake. Throughout the morning the steward's shotgun was intermittently active on the lake shore, and at luncheon a mess of plover lent variety to the bill of fare.

Stanford's car had not been moved back from the end of the track solely to provide his guests with a view of Salt Lake. Two days of fraternizing among the officials had not meant that the rivalry was at an end. Both continued to jockey for advantages until the rails were joined. Rival officials recognized that the company building a siding at Promontory would have an advantage in the future control of the settlement. The Central Pacific's plans were laid in secret. A hundred miles back, a work-train had been made up, loaded with men and materials; only the storm delayed execution of the coup. Sunday night the rain ceased and the sky cleared. The Central construction train moved from the rear, timed to reach Promontory at daybreak. It arrived on schedule — and was greeted by derisive shouts from Casement's Irish track-layers. They had been working all night; the Union Pacific siding was completed.

It was the last skirmish before the lines were joined. Monday, May 10, was clear and cold. During the night Promontory's liquid street had turned to ice. The spot was five thousand feet high and the wind had a penetrating quality that kept unacclimated visitors shuttling between the town's five saloons and the glowing stoves of the cars.

THE DRIVING OF THE LAST SPIKE, MAY 10, 1869
*The man with the shovel in the center is J. H. Strobridge, C.P.
construction superintendent. Mrs. Strobridge is on his right; Mrs.
Mary L. Ryan on his left.*
Courtesy of the California State Library

STREET SCENE, PROMONTORY, UTAH, 1869
where the Central and Union Pacific lines were joined.
Courtesy of the California State Library

CONSTRUCTION IN THE SIERRA, ABOUT 1865
showing method of digging a cut.
Courtesy of the California State Library

**FIRST CONSTRUCTION TRAIN PASSING THE
PALISADES**

As the morning advanced, crews set to work closing the remaining yards of the gap. It had been planned that two special trains arrive at the same moment, from east and west, as an impressive prelude to the joining of the rails. Instead, battered construction trains rolled in from both directions, loaded with graders and track-layers and teamsters, all intent on seeing the show.

The entire population of the ephemeral town augmented the crowd, and throughout the morning other groups filtered in from near-by construction camps on foot or on the broad backs of draft horses. Stanford's party again made the thirty-mile trip from Monument and was pushed to the siding to make room for another flag-decorated special from the Coast. This bore other company officials, including lean, spare Mark Hopkins, his shoulders hunched against the wind. The two remaining partners were absent. Huntington was in New York, and Crocker, who always delighted in celebrations, had unaccountably remained behind at Sacramento.

Midmorning passed with no sign of the Union Pacific's special. The crowd faced the cold wind and gathered in shivering groups while work crews completed the final few feet of track, leaving one rail on the side nearest the lake to be placed later. Delay succeeded delay. Noon passed — it was after one o'clock, after two. Telegraph instruments on tables beside the track chattered impatient inquiries from east and west. What was wrong? The wind died down and it grew uncomfortably warm. The crowd, hungry and impatient, intruded on the cleared space and had to be periodically forced back. The stage had long been set and the audience was near the end of its patience. It was a lamentably late curtain.

At last the screech of a Union Pacific locomotive was heard and the crowd set up an ironical cheer. A group of Central Pacific officials, led by Stanford and Hopkins, descended from their car and tramped through the mud to greet the arriving dignitaries. Spectators surged forward, staring at Durant's shining Pullman, at the dapper vice-president's velvet coat, and cheered again as formal greetings were exchanged. The celebration took on an unplanned military aspect, for the train carried several companies of the 21st Infantry, and the regimental band, bound from Fort Douglas to San Francisco's Presidio. The soldiers were put to work forcing back the crowd and opening a lane for the cameramen, there to preserve the historic event.

Perhaps five hundred persons were present: Irish and Chinese laborers, teamsters, cooks, engineers, train crews, officials, guests, and parties of excursionists from California and Salt Lake City. The latter, to the disappointment of the Californians, did not include Brigham Young. The Prophet had sent his apologies and two aides: Bishop John Sharp and Colonel Savage, the latter carrying one of the heavy box cameras. A number of women were among the excursion parties, including the wives of two Central Pacific officials: Mrs. Strobridge and Mrs. Ryan. A group of Promontory's strumpets were also on hand, though their presence passed unrecorded in the official dispatches.

The belated wedding got under way. Ceremonial spikes, ties, and the final rail were carried forward by a picked squad of Chinese, their denim pantaloons and jackets newly scrubbed, their pigtails neatly braided and tied. While necks craned, a laurel tie was embedded, the rail put in place, the telegraph operators reporting each step over wires kept open throughout the nation. A Massachusetts pastor offered an invocation so comprehensive that at its end the telegrapher tapped out: " We have got done praying; the spike is about to be presented."

Not one, but several spikes were presented, each with a speech. One was of Comstock silver; another was an alloy of gold, silver, and iron, symbolical of Arizona Territory's varied mineral resources; gold and silver spikes from Idaho and Montana followed; then two of gold from California and a silver sledge-hammer for their driving. The spikes, except the final one of gold, were placed in holes provided for them, hammered home by inexpert taps of officials and distinguished guests. Nearly an hour was so consumed. At last the final spike was inserted, a telegraph line was attached to it and another to the hammer, so that the actual blows might be carried throughout the nation — to such devices were the ingenious driven in an age deprived of radio. The nation waited while Stanford raised his hammer for the historic stroke. The silver hammer missed the spike, but the telegrapher, prepared for the contingency, simulated the blow with his key. At once the magnetic ball dropped from its pole above the Capitol dome at Washington, San Francisco's dozens of fire bells began tolling, salvos of cannon boomed, and factory whistles screeched in scores of cities from coast to coast. In a country town north of San Francisco a boy under six was lifted on his father's shoulder and stared over heads at a sheet of paper newly pasted on a newspaper office door; he was told that all these men were cheering because soon everyone would be rich. In another town on the opposite rim of the continent neighbors spoke with sympathy of poor Mrs. Judah, who sat alone all that day in her brother's house, refusing to see her closest friends.

At Promontory, while the crowd shouted and locomotive whistles responded to taut cords, Amos Bouscher elbowed his way to the side of a San Francisco jeweler who was busily collecting five dollars from all who wished watch-charms made from the historic golden spike. Sixty years later Bouscher still retained his tattered receipt and a growing belief that the stranger must have been an impostor. Meantime, Vice-President Durant completed the driving of the spike. The 21st Infantry band played *America.* Photographers went through their routine as plate after plate was exposed. Two engines moved cautiously over the new-laid rail, touched cowcatchers, and their engineers were given the first drinks from the foaming neck of a champagne bottle. In San Francisco, F. Bret Harte, who realized that magazine verse should be timely, inquired in the pages of his *Overland Monthly:*

> What was it the engines said,
> Pilots touching — head to head. . . .

Officials and a few guests retired to Durant's shining car to frame a message to President Grant, while workmen, prudently detailed to the task in advance, drew out the silver and gold spikes, removed the laurel tie. Souvenir-hunters, undiscouraged, proceeded to cut chips from the substituted tie, even to hack bits off the iron rail. In the ensuing months both rail and tie had several times to be replaced.

By then the afternoon was nearly gone; officials hurried to a late luncheon on Stanford's car, and the *hoi polloi* sought the food and drink promised them by the two companies. They received both in abundance. By nine o'clock the celebration had reached a stage where a grand ball, a banquet, and a torchlight procession were in simultaneous progress. Two weeks later Central Pacific auditors O.K.'d bills totaling $2,200 " on account of celebration upon completion of the railroad." On the gray morning of the 11th the specials started on their return trips east and west; before nightfall transcontinental trains were moving cautiously over the new rails under the eyes of Promontory's diminished population.

11

THE COUNTRY-WIDE enthusiasm aroused by the completion of the road first informed many in California that Sacramento's former shopkeepers had become men of consequence. As a belated gesture of recognition, Sacramento citizens prepared to entertain the empire-builders at a testimonial banquet. Invitations were issued and accepted in elegantly phrased letters that were reproduced in Coast newspapers. In late September the four partners sat at one end of the high-ceilinged ballroom of the Golden West Hotel, faced half a hundred of their more prosperous fellow townsmen, and learned that their courage, industry, and vision had won the admiration of their home town. Stanford, official spokesman of the group, responded with an address, Crocker and Hopkins talked more briefly, Huntington not at all. But his new role of public benefactor proved not distasteful; he got to his feet long enough to announce that he would do anything for his good friends except make a speech.

The Sacramento banquet may have first informed the four that their careers had entered a new phase. During the construction period both they and the public had been too engrossed in the work itself to give much thought to how much or how little its completion might add to the renown of the controlling partners. The four had gone into the enterprise with no other experience than that of moderately successful merchants in a town of moderate size. In the beginning the railroad had made no large demands on their ability as organizers or financiers. Once launched, however, it had grown rapidly, its problems had taken on added complexities. So gradual had been the change that the partners themselves were hardly aware of it; Huntington once told that they sometimes paused to wonder at the power and responsibility that had been put into their hands. Crocker, who had begun his construction career with a force of two hundred men, was able less than two years later to announce that he was directing the largest single force of workmen ever assembled in the country's history. To Huntington the contrast must have been even more amazing. Until 1862 his business career had involved nothing more spectacular than attempts to gain temporary control of the local supply of potatoes or shovels or gunpowder; before the road was well started he was monthly awarding contracts that ran into the millions and chartering so many ships to carry the material west that he became the largest individual shipper in the world. Stanford, who felt that his career had reached its zenith with his election to the governorship, presently found himself at the head of a larger organization, one, moreover, in which he owned a quarter interest. Even placid Mark Hopkins, fresh from keeping the accounts of his and Huntington's hardware store, must have had periods of mild astonishment as he contemplated the size of the figures beneath his pen.

During the active seven years the partners bore their responsibilities because it was necessary that they do so. At the beginning their moderate personal fortunes were in the balance; moreover, it presently grew clear that the successful outcome of the enterprise would bring them fortunes beyond any ever before created on the Coast. The necessity for building up and protecting their property had kept them too busy to give much thought to what they would do with it after it was won.

Stanford's driving of the last spike marked the end of one stressful period and the beginning of another. The early weeks after the celebration, however, brought little change in the familiar routine. Construction crews were still active all along the line, repairing makeshifts adopted when haste had been the main consideration, putting the roadbed in condition to meet the requirements of the federal inspectors, assembling equipment, and perfecting schedules in preparation for the anticipated heavy traffic.

But by the beginning of 1870 the construction period was definitely over, and the partners faced an entirely different task. Building the road had proved an almost fabulously profitable undertaking; it was by no means certain that its operation would realize any profit at all. Only a few weeks after their line was completed, the Suez Canal was opened and Theodore Judah's roseate dream that the traffic between Asia and Europe would flow over the new railroad vanished. Moreover, by far the greater volume of freight between the two coasts continued to be shipped by water, and instead of the anticipated flood of passengers, the partners discovered that, once the initial rush was over, their one daily through train sometimes carried no passengers at all.

For seven years the four had been looking ahead to the end of construction as a time when they could enjoy their new fortunes. Instead of the anticipated period of ease, however, a variety of problems, entirely new, appeared and demanded solution. The tension did not relax, and the partners realized that the struggle to gain their fortunes was to be followed by another sort of struggle to maintain them.

Their letters reveal that it was a time of indecision. Should they embark on what Hopkins called " the certainty of continued years of anxious toil, and the uncertainty of how well and with what results we may work out the problem of final success " — or should they sell out, pocket their handsome profit, and pass on to others the complicated problems of operation?

That it was Crocker who first reached a decision and that he chose to sell out caused no surprise. Of the four, he was most definitely the man of action. The stress and noise and tumult of the construction camps had been exactly to his liking; he had thoroughly enjoyed every minute of the building period. To one who throve on physical activity, the prospect of an office desk and the routine of administration had no appeal. Moreover, he had developed strong opinions as to the injurious effects of too much mental exercise. There was the example of his elder brother, E. B. Crocker, the only one of the four brothers who had received a formal education. As attorney for the Central Pacific, E. B. had wrestled for six years with its complicated legal problems, and with what result? In 1868 he had paused one evening on the stairs of the Lick House, then had fallen at Stanford's feet, victim of a paralytic stroke. He had been an invalid ever since and was to die, still a young man, a few years later. Charles weighed the implications of this catastrophe. He then announced firmly that he would have no administrative job and invited his partners to buy him out.

Crocker's decision brought Huntington hurrying out from New York. The matter was too important to be negotiated by others. Hopkins was shrewd, but he lacked force in argument, and Huntington had more than once written that " trading is not one of Stanford's strong points." If Crocker were to withdraw, Huntington wished to be there to dictate the terms. Negotiations continued through the fall of 1870; the agreement finally reached also included the sale of the minor interest of Crocker's invalid brother. By its terms the three remaining partners were to pay the two Crockers $1,800,000, in three yearly installments of $600,000. Huntington left for the East, thinking the matter settled. Charles Crocker, however, delayed signing from week to week. When he presently asked certain modifications in the terms of the agreement, Huntington lost patience. " We bought Mr. Crocker out fairly and without an if, and I propose to do just what I agreed with him and nothing more." Huntington himself was then in one of his periodical dark moods and he went on to make a counter-proposal. If Crocker refused to sell, he suggested that Crocker, Stanford, and Hopkins buy himself out, presumably on the same terms offered Crocker. He went on to point out that their railroad holdings were potentially of great value, but that to realize on them would require " years of laborious toil." He was quite willing that those who did the work should make the profit. For himself he would welcome an opportunity to withdraw; if he had to stay he intended to reap the benefit of his work.

The logic of Huntington's stand was evidently made clear to the retiring partner, for late in 1871 Crocker signed the agreement and received the initial payment. Shortly after, Coast papers announced his departure with his family for an extended tour of Europe. Although Crocker was no longer a partner, he still retained very large holdings of Central Pacific stock, received as dividends from the construction companies that had built the road. The remaining partners, struggling with their new problems, thought of Crocker's carefree existence and concluded that he had not made a bad bargain. In one of his lucid letters to Huntington, Mark Hopkins wrote: " This gives them [Charles and E. B.] a productive fortune of a vast sum, and a reasonable expectation from C.P. stock of many millions more, so yoked with our interest in like property that we must realize to them their expectations, or do worse for ourselves."

Huntington's dark mood continued and through the fall of 1871 he made persistent though secret attempts to sell out and follow Crocker into retirement. The negotiations were conducted by a brilliant local attorney, Alfred Cohen, who had newly joined the company's legal staff. The plan was to form a syndicate of San Francisco bankers to raise the purchase price, said to have been fixed by the partners at $20,000,000. Cohen had numerous talks with D. O. Mills, president of the Bank of California, and sent progressively more encouraging letters to Huntington in the East. Both Stanford and Hopkins joined in the negotiations, although it was evident that Stanford had no real wish to sell. After an interview with Mills, Stanford wrote Huntington that the banker had not seemed " much interested." Huntington was not misled; his next letter to Hopkins contained this passage: " I do not suppose Stanford wanted to have us sell, and therefore I would not suppose that he would talk to Mills in a way that would induce him to buy, and then as he did not make his best effort he very likely would not make the trade. . . ."

The matter dragged on, the uncertainty of its outcome adding to Huntington's restlessness. He concluded that the reason Stanford wanted to remain was that he had a son (Leland Jr. was born in 1868) who would eventually carry on in his place. Huntington considered his own childless state and sent another pessimistic note to Hopkins: " The more I think of it the more valuable my interest on the Pacific Coast looks to me, and if I had some boys growing up to attend to this interest I hardly think I would sell . . . but as it is I know no reason why I should wear myself out for the sake of getting more money." This last admission would have astonished most of Huntington's friends. Later there was more in the same vein: " If I had someone growing up to take my place, I would hardly name a price that I would take, but as I have not, what the Devil is the use of my wearing myself out? " The sale remained a possibility for some weeks longer, then Cohen telegraphed that Mills had definitely turned it down. Huntington's gloom deepened. " I think we must make some change," he wrote Hopkins, " for I am losing my grip."

But no further opportunity for a change presented itself and the panic of 1873 wiped out all possibility of finding a purchaser. In face of this new threat Huntington promptly forgot both his fatigue and his self-pity. During the tumultuous third week of September, Huntington, in the midst of the bedlam, watched the financial structure of the nation disintegrate. On the evening of the 18th he found time to dash off a brief note to Hopkins: " This has been the wildest day on the 'change that I ever saw. The house of Jay Cooke & Co. gave notice to the stock board at 11 A.M. today that they had suspended & since then the newsboys in the streets have been crying their extras of this failure and that. God only knows where we will land. Help me all you can."

A few hours later Huntington learned that Fisk & Hatch, the brokerage firm that had been handling the sale of the railroad's securities, was in danger. The Central Pacific owed this house more than a million and a half. In the event of its failure the extent of the railroad's indebtedness would be made public, with disastrous results on its credit. On the night of the 18th the brokers called on Huntington for half a million dollars, which they hoped would see them through. Huntington sent urgent wires to Hopkins and Stanford, but the time proved too short to raise so much in San Francisco and before noon of the 19th Fisk & Hatch followed the example of dozens of other houses and closed their doors.

Huntington waited idly in the center of the tumult, recognizing like hundreds of others that nothing could be done. Occasionally he sent brief messages to the partners in San Francisco. On the 19th he warned them to prepare for the worst. At all costs they must sustain the Central Pacific — " everything depends on that." He added: " There is a terrible excitement on the street today but like everything else it will pass away." The first few days of disaster and meaningless activity were followed by a helpless calm in which no one knew what to do next. The editor of the Sacramento *Record* wired for a statement; Huntington sent back a reassuring message and apprehensively awaited further developments. For once his messages to the Coast were vague and uncertain. " I have little to report," he wrote on the 27th. "Everything is at a standstill. I stay in my office not knowing just what to do. There is no use in going out to borrow any money for however small the sum I should not be able to get it. Everyone is getting in all the money they can and locking it up. In fact, there never was such a time and I do believe and I hope to God there never will be again."

At that particularly inauspicious moment Crocker arrived in New York and produced the second of his $600,-000 notes. Since his return from Europe weeks earlier he had been presenting it daily to Stanford and Hopkins in San Francisco. He had received a great deal of information on economic conditions and on the shocking decline in the value of railroad securities, but not a dollar had he been able to collect. As always, the ultimate decision was left to Huntington, and Crocker had accordingly headed for New York. He walked into Huntington's office on September 26, an even week after the failure of Fisk & Hatch. That afternoon Huntington reported to Hopkins: " Mr. Crocker has just left the office. We had a long talk. He said he wanted his money. I told him we were to have a fearful fight with the government and that we could not pay him until the fight was over. He said it was our fight and not his, &c. I said he must help make the fight. He said if he helped make the fight he wanted his part of the profits, &c. He then said that he would come back now and take his position just as though he had not been out and give S. and H. & H. $100,000 each, and this I have telegraphed you . . . I well know that this is not what we want but is it not best as matters are? "

The partners agreed. Less than a month later California newspapers announced that Charles Crocker was again a director of the Central Pacific, and its second vice-president. The Coast editors were pleased: it was again possible to give the group its familiar name. Somehow, the Big Three had never had the right sound.

12

BY gaining control, in 1871, of the California Pacific, operating between Sacramento and the bay, the partners had succeeded in extending the transcontinental line to its logical terminus, San Francisco. Thereupon, preparations were made to move the main offices, and Stanford and Hopkins began building their impressive houses on Nob Hill. Not to be outdone, Crocker, newly returned to the fold, also acquired a site on the hill, a block west of his partners and on ground a shade more elevated. His property was gradually extended until he possessed, except for one small lot, the entire block bounded by California, Taylor, Sacramento, and Jones streets. The exception noted was owned by one Yung, a local undertaker, who persistently refused to sell. Crocker's efforts to oust the stubborn householder and thus round out his holdings later became something of a public issue.

Meantime Crocker started his mansion, a complicated wooden structure in a style his architect, Arthur Brown, catalogued vaguely as " early Renaissance." Twenty years later Willis Polk, fresh from the École des Beaux-arts in Paris and beginning his career as local æsthete, pronounced it " a delirium of the wood carver." The chief feature, aside from its cost — said to have been a million and a quarter — was a 76-foot tower, up which the 230-pound host delighted to pilot his guests to admire the panoramic view to be had from its top.

As the house neared completion its owner made another trip to Europe, this time to purchase furniture. The journey proved unfortunate in one respect. Soon after his return Crocker became active in the prosecution of Alfred Cohen, the former railroad attorney, then charged with having misappropriated fifty thousand dollars of Central Pacific funds. Cohen looked on Crocker as the instigator of the suit, and in his final plea in his own defense the attorney brought his considerable powers of invective to bear on that unhappy individual.

To the delight of the crowded courtroom, Cohen likened the trial to a comedy and the opposing witnesses to its actors. His consideration of the " cast" presently brought him to Crocker. That gentleman, he stated, had aspired to be the hero " who longed to languish in the scene as leading lover but, being too fat of diaphragm for genteel comedy, and too fat of wit for low comedy, was compelled to be content with the place of general utility man, whom the counsel would only trust to carry off the dead, light the lamps, and sweep the stage."

This, however, was a mere preliminary; the angry attorney was just warming to his work. He continued:

" Mr. Crocker showed a great deal of feeling in this case, and wishes to have credit for inaugurating it, but then Mr. Crocker is a great man; I do not think the most carping critic will deny that. He is a great man from any point from which you look at him. If you survey him from his broad pedal extremities to the narrow apex of his cranium, or whether you look at him longitudinally, you see that he is great; and if you walk around him, by the time you return to the starting point you are assured of his greatness.

" He has given us the benefit of his presence most of the time that this case has been progressing, and being desirous of making the best possible impression on the court and bar, he has reclined back in one of these chairs and with his feet elevated to the rail surrounding the jury-box, has presented to our gaze that portion of his person for which he has the most admiration."

The defendant reminded the court and the tittering spectators that he was not accusing the railroad official of "conduct contrary to the most orthodox rules of refinement":

". . . for Mr. Crocker is a 'travelled gentleman'; he told you that he had been to Europe, and he has been, he says, 'around the world.' He did not tell us whether he is the person commemorated by Mr. Jules Verne, who made the trip in eighty days, but I incline to the belief, from a knowledge of Mr. Crocker's attributes and from his appearance, that it was done hurriedly."

There was much more in this vein of not too gentle irony. Cohen ended by imagining the former drygoods merchant's soliloquy before he set out on his furniture-buying trip to Europe:

"I will drop the obsequious smile with which I used to roll up calico and tape for my customers, and in its place there shall come the arrogant, supercilious grin of oleaginous self-satisfaction. I will build myself a mansion, which I will set upon a hill. I will upholster and furnish it so that visitors shall be filled with doubt whether it is designed for a haberdasher's shop or a stage scene for a modern furniture drama. I will purchase Gobelin tapestries, and employ someone to tell me whether they should be hung upon the walls as paintings or spread upon the floor as mats. I will buy pictures from the galleries of the Medicis and employ Mr. Medici himself to make the selections. I will show the world how an intelligent patron of the arts and literature can be manufactured by the process of wealth out of a peddler of needles and pins. I will visit Europe until I can ornament my ungrammatical English with a fringe of mispronounced French. I will wear a diamond as big as the headlight of one of my locomotives; and my adipose tissue shall increase with my pecuniary gains until my stomach is as large as my arrogance, and I shall strut along the corridors of the Palace Hotel a living, breathing, waddling monument of the triumph of vulgarity, viciousness and dishonesty."

The charge against Cohen was dismissed and the regrettable personalities of the trial were in time forgotten. Moreover, the partners recognized that a man with so marked a gift for abuse had far better devote his talents to the company's interests than to those of its enemies. Cohen therefore quickly re-allied himself with his ex-enemies and devoted the next twenty years to a valiant championship of their interests.

Crocker occupied his new house late in 1876. A few months later the silver anniversary of his wedding was celebrated with a reception of such magnificence that local society editors remained lyrical for weeks. Descriptions of the attractions of the mansion appeared with regularity in the local Sunday supplements. Details of its 172-foot façade, of its 12,500 square feet of floor space, of its fully equipped little theater, in which amateur theatricals were regularly given, of the library and billiard room, became staple reading to thousands of wondering Californians. Crocker's paintings were particularly admired by the art-conscious community. On an easel in the drawing-room stood the prize of the collection: " The only Meissonier on the Pacific Coast, if we except his portrait of Governor Stanford. Mr. Crocker's Meissonier is called ' The Smoker.' . . ." Its owner had paid twelve thousand dollars for it, and the expression on the smoker's face was universally praised. Many visitors, however, preferred another work by an artist whose name has not been preserved, a canvas of generous size entitled " The Butcher Shop." It was a spirited composition depicting an old woman chasing a dog, which was making off with a piece of beef.

With his observation tower, his pictures, his travels, and his growing deals in San Francisco real estate, the next dozen years passed pleasantly for Charles Crocker. As his children grew up, his eldest son, Charles Frederick, entered the company and took over many of his none too arduous railroad duties. At the outset of his business career, the aging Charles gave his son some sound advice: " If it becomes necessary to jump off the dock in the service of the company, instead of saying ' Go, boys,' you must pull off your coat and say ' Come, boys.' " The young man was not called on to face this test, but he proved both shrewd and energetic; it was not long before he had made himself more influential in the company's affairs than his father had been for years. Charles Frederick's rise was sufficiently rapid to engage Huntington's attention and to persuade him to send his own nephew, Henry E., out to the Coast to represent his interests. Not unnaturally, the two young men were presently at odds, and a battle for supremacy between the factions they represented seemed inevitable. Only young Crocker's early death prevented such a clash and removed the last serious obstacle to Huntington's plan of assuming complete control.

The elder Crocker meantime continued to buy San Francisco real estate, visited the construction camps of such new lines as the Southern Pacific was building, and with his friend Dave Colton toured the West looking for " investments." Following Stanford's example — the latter had begun the creation of " the world's largest vineyard " at Vina — he took over great blocks of railroad subsidy lands in the San Joaquin Valley, formed the Crocker & Huffman Land Company at Modesto, and built an extensive irrigation system there. Discovery of a low grade of coal at Ione, in the Sierra foothills, attracted his attention and he became one of the leaders in an attempt to supply the state with one of the few important mineral products of which nature had deprived her. He purchased another large area of land in Nevada and set up one of his sons in the cattle business; for another, who wished to go into finance, he acquired a controlling interest in the Woolworth Bank.

For unknown reasons he failed to participate in the most spectacular venture of that entire period, the great diamond discovery of the '70s, although Dave Colton was a leading figure in it. The fact that he missed being taken in by that notable fraud — which fooled the shrewdest financiers of the city — confirmed his conviction of the infallibility of his judgment. " I have often said," he remarked in later years, " that in no enterprise that I have taken up, where I superintended it myself, was I ever unsuccessful."

Nonetheless, all was not smooth sailing. Crocker's egotism grew with his years and weight, and business associates found him increasingly gruff in manner, dogmatic in upholding his views, and intolerant of opposition. In the early '80s, having to appear on some matter of railroad business before the Los Angeles city council, he was kept waiting beyond what he considered a reasonable time. Enraged at the indignity, he stalked from the building, announcing that he " would make grass grow in the Los Angeles streets." Quite undisturbed, citizens of the arid town stated that they would welcome the miracle; after years of effort they had been unable to make grass grow even in their lawns.

In San Francisco, meantime, Crocker's feud with Yung waxed warmer, for the undertaker continued to refuse successively higher offers for his land. In exasperation Crocker took a drastic step. Dray-loads of lumber one day appeared on the hill and a gang of carpenters set to work surrounding the Yung dwelling with a wall forty feet high. The matter, of course, attracted city-wide attention and throngs daily climbed Nob Hill to stare at the " spite fence." In its weekly colored cartoon the local *Wasp* offered a helpful suggestion: the drawing showed Yung's cottage lifted high in the air on scaffolding and the undertaker again enjoying an unobstructed view.

The matter took a more serious turn. Dennis Kearney, the picturesque ex-teamster, had recently got control of the powerful Workingmen's party and the tone of his speeches in the sand-lots near the city hall was arousing concern. In the eyes of Kearney and his disciples, Crocker's quarrel with the undertaker was clearly a contest between capital and labor. The spite fence became a local symbol of the arrogance of wealth, and Kearney made effective use of it. In his speeches he promised his followers that he would personally tear it down and chastise its builder with the boards. The crowd's disapproval spread from Crocker to the whole group of Nob Hill nabobs, for were they not all employers of " cheap Chinese labor "? One night Kearney shouted to his fellow sand-lotters: " The monopolists who make money by employing cheap labor had better watch out. They have

CONSTRUCTION TRAIN AND CAMP IN NEVADA, 1868

Courtesy of the California State Library

CISCO IN WINTER

Courtesy of Francis P. Farquhar

A CENTRAL PACIFIC SNOWPLOW

at Cisco during the Construction Period.

Courtesy of the California State Library

built themselves fine residences on Nob Hill and erected flagstaffs upon their roofs. Let them take care that they have not erected their own gallows."

One summer evening in 1877 a caretaker looked out from the Hopkins residence while a crowd of three hundred climbed the hill and held a " political meeting " in the street, surrounded by the mansions of the capitalists. Kearney's characteristic speech demanded that the Stanford and Hopkins houses be taken over by " the people " and converted into asylums. He added that the crowd had assembled there to organize a Workingmen's party club for that ward. Addressing Stanford's darkened house, he shouted an invitation for its owner to come forward, promising that if Stanford would acknowledge that he was a thief he would forthwith be elected president of the Fourth Ward Club.

The group disbanded without violence, but a few weeks later mobs got out of hand and roved over the city wrecking Chinese laundries, beating their operators, and applying the torch to the wreckage. The exploit nearly brought on a wholesale conflagration, for the city was still composed largely of closely built wooden structures. Citizens belatedly awoke to their danger, revived the vigilance committees of the '50s, and succeeded in intimidating the sand-lotters. Kearney was arrested and thrown into jail, charged with inciting riots. He was eventually released, but during his long imprisonment and trial his following dropped away.

Crocker's spite fence thus ceased to be a political issue. Some time later the undertaker agreed to sell; both fence and cottage were thereupon pulled down, and Crocker realized his ambition to own the entire block.

13

His sixty-fifth birthday came and went, and doctors began to advise him on a variety of new topics. He was too active and far too heavy for his years. He should stay away from excitement, not hunt it out. His San Francisco real estate, his coal mines, his irrigation development in the San Joaquin, the current Southern Pacific expansion, all these were jobs for a younger man; his days of "storming up and down the line" were past. Crocker listened carefully to this sound advice and obeyed it to the letter — for a few days.

But he had always been too energetic to accept the role of invalid. The scrollwork mansion on the hill speedily became a prison and of course a man used to doing things could not forever sit talking to cronies in the bar of the Palace. Inevitably his restlessness returned and in a day or two he was off again; perhaps to the Merced development, where he one day drove a four-horse team through the tunnel of the world's largest irrigation canal and drew up at the far end to inform newspapermen that this project would eventually be recognized as a more important achievement than the railroad.

In the middle '80s, company officials contemplated their empty trains running over the tracks beyond San Jose and contrived to make a social asset of travel to the south. Southern Pacific capital produced a sprawling resort hotel among the oaks beside Monterey Bay and word was passed about that a week-end — or a summer — at Del Monte would be useful to anyone who wished favors of the company. Railroad officials made frequent visits with their families or groups of guests; society editors of friendly newspapers established regular correspondents at the resort and printed daily columns on the activities of guests. To be a frequent visitor to Del Monte became an easy but expensive way of attaining social importance. Ambitious dowagers from up and down the Coast rose to the bait and well-filled Pullmans were soon rolling in over the Monterey branch to fill the vacant rooms.

Del Monte became Crocker's special pet; there he spent the major part of his time during the hundred days while the big wooden structure was rushed to completion. He is remembered during that period wandering through the unfinished public rooms, sitting for hours in his carriage beneath a neighboring oak, looking on while the mass of towers and balconies and wide porches of " the largest resort hotel in the world " took shape. Upon its completion the place became his favorite residence. Probably this was because he had watched the driving of " every nail." He liked the structure, too, because it had a commercial purpose; it was intended to pay for itself and to make a profit, both of which it did handsomely. No such interest attached to his houses in San Francisco and Sacramento, which were the opposite of profitable investments. As for his New York house on West Fifty-eighth Street (which he had bought and furnished in 1886 at a cost of a quarter of a million), this attracted him so little that he spent only a few restless months there before presenting it to his daughter Hattie upon her marriage a year later.

The old man's distaste for New York was not lessened by his having been thrown from his carriage there and so badly shaken that he was in bed for weeks. Dispatches to San Francisco exaggerated his injuries; local editors recalled his age and weight — still above 225 pounds — and made ready to print his obituary. But Crocker was presently back on the Coast again, only slightly less active than before. Some weeks later fire destroyed one of his numerous San Francisco business houses, and he had the satisfaction of seeing a pet theory vindicated. For years he had " carried his own insurance," putting a percentage of the yearly earnings from his real estate into a special fund. Luckily, his one serious fire did not occur until the " fire fund " was large enough to rebuild the structure. This insurance matter was widely commented on in California and elsewhere; the old man's last months were brightened by another public vindication of his business shrewdness. Meantime his interest was centered on the Merced project, in which he had invested heavily. As it later proved, this development was less successful than the insurance fund, but to the end he remained confident that it would double his fortune.

Naturally a man involved in so many large enterprises refused to look on himself as an invalid, and the starvation diet prescribed by his physicians was often disregarded. The summer of 1888 found him again incapacitated. He paid another visit to Del Monte, confident that a few weeks at the new hotel would restore him to health. But diet this time proved ineffective and he grew worse instead of better. On August 14 word that he was in a diabetic coma reached San Francisco. A special train hurried his eldest son and a group of doctors to the hotel. It arrived too late by minutes for its passengers to see the patient alive.

He was one of the first guests to die at Del Monte. That night the special train carried the body back to San Francisco. A bow of crape appeared on the doors of the house on California Street; within, mirrors were covered and pictures turned to the wall. Two days later, accounts of his burial at Laurel Hill recorded that the Crocker casket was a replica of one in which John A. Logan had recently been buried, and the public reflected that a fellow citizen who sixty years earlier had sold newspapers on the streets of Troy had achieved a burial not less elaborate than that of a Civil War general.

HOPKINS

1

UNCLE MARK HOPKINS hunched his thin shoulders forward when he walked, and he had an odd, unhurried stride (which carried him over the ground with deceptive speed) , and when he spoke he stroked his beard hesitantly with a long, skinny hand. An observant friend once remarked that the latter characteristic made him seem older than he was.

He seemed older for other reasons. On the wet afternoon in 1862 when ground was broken for the new railroad, the future Big Four were all comparatively young men. Stanford, already Governor, was thirty-eight, Crocker was forty, Huntington a year older. Hopkins, always looked on as the graybeard of the group, was born, at Henderson, New York, on September 1, 1813, and so was a few months short of his forty-ninth birthday. But in the early '60s California was still preponderantly a young man's country, and anyone past his mid-forties was open to the suspicion of senility. The gold rush had been a movement of youth; Argonauts thirty-five and over were unusual enough to draw attention, and of course many thousands were still in their 'teens.

The survivors of this youthful horde, toughened by a

violent and contentious decade, were holding power in California when the Civil War began. Hopkins, past thirty-five when he left the East, was an old man from the moment he put foot ashore, constantly surrounded by those younger than himself. Easily and inevitably he accepted the title of Uncle Mark and adopted the mannerisms and the viewpoint of an oldster. From the first his partners looked on him as a kindly but slightly decrepit ancient, full of the wisdom of age, but hedged in by its conservatism.

He differed from his partners in still other ways. Three of the four were large men physically; Crocker normally weighed over 240 pounds, Huntington and Stanford not much less than 220. Uncle Mark was tall and bent and " thin as a fence post." His skinny knees and elbows were awkward and loosely hinged; it was as though he had never outgrown the gangling age. He had small gray eyes, a long thin nose set in a long thin face and surmounting a long thin beard, and he spoke (with a pronounced lisp) in a notably soft voice. He neither smoked nor drank, and he was sparing enough in the use of profanity to impress the eccentricity on the minds of acquaintances. Acquaintances were impressed too by his sparrow-like appetite. It is recorded that, at table with his partners, Uncle Mark would musingly consume half a cup of tea while the others applied themselves to a succession of steaming dishes. He ate almost no meat; even in a pre-vitamin age green vegetables were his staple, and the cost and difficulties of procuring a regular supply darkened his early years in California.

Perhaps because of his meatless diet, he disliked hard physical work and managed to avoid it all his life. From the age of twelve and under, his future partners had done the back-breaking labor required of farmboys of the period, but Hopkins was always an "inside man." At fifteen he was a clerk in a New York village store, and he remained a storekeeper, in New York and California, until he died. The firm of Huntington & Hopkins, founded in 1856, survived him more than twenty years.

Throughout his career he had the good fortune, or the good judgment, to ally himself with men of initiative. He was an accurate judge of his own strength and limitations, and one of the qualities he early recognized was that, while he could not create a business, he could make one go. Hence, his business life became a series of partnerships; beginning when he was twenty with Hopkins & Hughes, country storekeepers at Lockport, New York, and progressing through Williams & Hopkins, dealers in farm implements, and James Rowland & Co., commission merchants of New York City, to his association with Huntington at Sacramento and the final quadrangular partnership in the railroad venture.

"Hopkins' defect as a businessman," wrote one critic, "was that he was too cautious, but he was wise enough to overcome that weakness by allying himself with speculators." Alone, he would not have failed to gain a comfortable livelihood, for he was shrewd and industrious and, above all, thrifty. But he was too prudent ever to gamble for large stakes. He was one of that cautious type of men who are never penniless and almost never wealthy.

That he became possessed of more than twenty millions was "against his better judgment." The role of capitalist seemed to make him faintly uncomfortable, and he sometimes acted "as if he wanted to apologize for his millions." The attitude was novel enough to set him apart from other rich men.

Reporters who described him as a man of simple tastes used no facile newspaper phrase, for it was literally true. He disliked complexities, involvements, elaboration wherever encountered, whether in a business letter, a meal, a system of bookkeeping, or a manner of life. He was good-natured and pliant in nearly all his dealings, but when he chose to take a stand he could be "hell on wheels." The phrase is Charles Crocker's, who once recalled plaintively that: "When Hopkins wanted to be, he was the stubbornest man alive." As the affairs of the partners expanded, Uncle Mark's program of well-ordered simplicity was naturally harder to maintain and his minor revolts in support of his convictions grew more frequent. Stanford and Crocker usually opposed him, Huntington less often. Huntington had learned the futility of trying to argue him out of an opinion; moreover, he had come to recognize that when Uncle Mark took issue with others, investigation usually disclosed that the better arguments were on his side.

Of course his passion for simplicity regulated his private life, and for years his mounting wealth brought no change in his habits or surroundings. For a decade after his partners had adopted a more ornate manner of life his frugal and methodical routine continued. Because he failed to toss his abundant dollars about he was presently accused of penny-squeezing. The charge was not altogether just; Hopkins had no particular love of money. Most of the traits put down as miserly were merely symptoms of a persisting, inbred hatred of waste. Clerks were scornful when Uncle Mark paused on his way through the railroad's offices and rescued bits of still-serviceable blotting paper from the waste-baskets. When he chanced to go out on the line (Crocker said he made such visits not oftener than once a year), onlookers saw his lean figure bending constantly as he picked up a rusty bolt or spike, a stray bit of iron. Scrap-iron had a market value. Moreover, thrift in high places might conceivably set a good example for the underlings.

No less than waste, he abhorred paying more than a fair price for what he needed to buy. In early Sacramento the price of fresh vegetables often reached outrageous heights. Uncle Mark solved the difficulty by buying a few acres of riverside land below the town, putting a former truck gardener in charge, and growing his own. The soil proved unexpectedly rich and the little farm was soon producing far more than his table required. Of course the surplus was not wasted; Uncle Mark sold it to his neighbors — at full market prices. He had not intended to make a profit from his carrots and beets and cabbages, but when the chance for a profit came, he grasped it with pleasure. Preventing waste, reaping an unexpected profit, driving a good bargain, all regardless of the amounts involved — these were his favorite recreations, the only sport he enjoyed. But the public failed to see why a man reputed to be worth twenty million dollars should get his pleasure in this way. Such virtues were tolerable only in the poor.

Among those who shared this general opinion was his cousin, the former Mary Sherwood, whom Uncle Mark married in 1854.

2

THE GENERAL offices of the Central Pacific were moved from Sacramento to San Francisco in 1873, and Hopkins, Stanford, and Crocker duly followed. The two last named at once made plans for new residences in keeping with their increased wealth; while these were building, they leased the most pretentious houses available in the city.

Hopkins's change of residence was more casually accomplished. It is said that he finished work one evening at Sacramento, took a night boat down the river, went direct from the wharf to his new office, and there spent his usual busy day. After one of his canary-like meals in a restaurant he strolled out Sutter Street, regarding the to-let signs in the windows. Near Leavenworth Street a small cottage took his eye. He hunted up the owner, assured himself that the roof shed water and that the place could be heated without too much trouble or expense, and thereupon paid a month's rent — thirty-five dollars — and returned to the railroad's office for another hour or two of work.

He remained in the Sutter Street cottage more than five years. In fine weather he walked to and from the railroad offices at Fourth and Townsend streets; when it rained he rode the Sutter Street horsecars, which passed his door. The arrangement suited him perfectly. His work was hard and exacting, for he controlled the financial details of a large and expanding corporation; frequently he carried a bundle of papers home and the coal-oil lamp in his Sutter Street window remained visible until past midnight. He kept no carriage, entertained few guests, took no vacations. For recreation he tried stubbornly to raise vegetables in his sandy back yard, no doubt reflecting wistfully on the co-operative soil of his Sacramento truck-farm.

He would hardly have departed from this placid routine but for the growing insistence of his wife. Twenty years had passed since Mary Frances Sherwood, a lively, romantic girl, had married her quiet Cousin Mark, who had come home for a visit after five moderately prosperous years in the gold fields. He was then forty-one, almost twice the age of his pretty bride, and he could not have been a particularly romantic figure. But he was from California and, in 1854, to marry and go to live in that still glamorous land was romance enough for any adventurous girl east of the Alleghenies. Mary Hopkins seemingly found the early days of her married life full of variety and interest, for the two started west at once and the sea trip and the life of strange, hustling Sacramento must have been a succession of surprises.

But the novelty of the raw frontier town wore off and

MARK HOPKINS

from E. B. Redding's A Sketch of the Life of Mark Hopkins

THE MARK HOPKINS RESIDENCE, CALIFORNIA AND MASON STREETS, SAN FRANCISCO. THE STANFORD HOUSE IS AT THE LEFT

Courtesy of the California State Library

life fell into commonplace patterns. Uncle Mark, hesitant, methodical, cautious, hardly filled all the requirements of an ideal husband in the eyes of a romantic young woman half his age. The cousins remained childless. As the years passed, Hopkins devoted longer hours to work (first in the K Street hardware store, later in the growing railroad venture), and his wife moved in a progressively narrower circle. When they settled in San Francisco, the vivacious girl Uncle Mark had married nineteen years before had become a retiring, rather subdued matron, rarely seen in public.

Meantime the wealth and growing power of the partners had made them conspicuous figures on the Coast, and society editors sometimes wrote a column of brightly innocuous gossip about their wives. They seldom found much to say of Mary Hopkins. The management of her perfectly functioning household was her chief pleasure. She preferred the quiet joys of domesticity to the more worldly distractions of society. For the rest, she was cultured, handsome, and gracious, and reading was perhaps her favorite recreation. Friends " whispered " that she was a close student of the classics (an addiction to literature was then frequently mentioned in whispers), and she had besides a wide acquaintance with the better grade of English novels.

That Mary Hopkins was not completely reconciled to the genteel boredom of her existence was long unknown to the world. Uncle Mark, however, shared the secret. For she made it clear that to her mind living in a rented cottage and growing vegetables in its back yard were not the ideal existence for a multimillionaire. She saw no reasons why they should not maintain an establishment comparable to those of the Stanfords and Crockers, neither of whom raised their own turnips. And of the three local partners, why was he alone required to be at the office every day of the year? Both Stanford and Crocker found time to make trips to New York with their families, and every now and then they went to Europe.

Uncle Mark had no convincing answers to these questions. He had been living the life of a hermit because his tastes chanced to run toward simplicity and against ostentation. But he was also good-natured and inherently agreeable. When questions on which he held convictions were involved he was quite willing to make a stand, but for the rest he preferred to be accommodating. If his wife felt they should branch out a bit, he would be good-humored about it. He would put up with a certain amount of nonsense. And so, after twenty years of eclipse, the active, fun-loving girl of the '50s began surprisingly to reassert herself. Her emergence began the day Uncle Mark agreed to give up the Sutter Street cottage and to make inquiries as to the price of building lots in North Beach, then highly regarded as a residential district.

But, as always, Hopkins proceeded cautiously. While he was still investigating North Beach real estate, he stepped into Stanford's office one day and discovered that the latter (who had escaped the vice of frugality) had just paid sixty thousand dollars for a block of land on the steep upper ridge of Nob Hill. From habit, Uncle Mark concealed his astonishment and listened while Stanford described the attractions of his purchase. Stanford talked and Hopkins stroked his beard and weighed the possibilities. He decided to look into the Nob Hill matter; before his investigations were completed he had lost interest in North Beach.

The hill was then a treeless waste, bleak and windswept, but its high eastern shoulder dominated the growing town. The business section was already encroaching on its lower slopes, and Hopkins grew convinced that it must presently become the most valuable residential district of the city. He foresaw the possibility that, like his Sacramento truck-farm, a Nob Hill lot might eventually return a profit. When Stanford offered to share his purchase with him, Uncle Mark unhesitatingly paid him thirty thousand dollars and received a deed to the western half of the block.

In the early '70s, it required both vision and faith to foresee the future of the hill. Only a few small houses had yet been built on its crest, and for an excellent reason. San Francisco's uncompromising streets veered up its steepest sides at grades so abrupt that two horses had difficulty pulling a carriage up the sandy inclines. That streetcars would ever scale the height had until very recently been regarded as fantastic, and rumors that Stanford and Hopkins planned to build mansions there aroused reasonable doubts of their sanity. But a local manufacturer of wire rope named Hallidie had for several years been tinkering with a device intended to grip and release a moving cable buried in a trench beneath one of the slanting streets. By 1874 the invention had been proved practical to a degree and the partners' sixty thousand dollars' worth of " vertical real estate " promptly became a conservative investment.

It was not long before Stanford, always fascinated by mechanical gadgets, was promoting and chiefly financing the California Street Cable Railway, and by 1876 tourists were looking on in amazement as toy-like cars with no horses attached glided up the three steepest blocks from Kearny to Powell Street. The local *Alta's* comment that Hallidie's " grip " had perfectly conquered the problem of negotiating San Francisco's hills proved correct; after more than sixty years, the California Street cars are operated by precisely the same means, and with equipment not many years newer. Cable lines were presently crossing Nob Hill north and south and east and west. Comstock millionaires joined those of the railroad, and the late '70s saw a dozen mansions taking shape on the hill.

But this was still in the future when Hopkins and Stanford faced the problem of anchoring their houses to the slanting hilltop. The partners turned over the task to the Central Pacific's engineering staff, and gangs of graders with scrapers and dump-carts established themselves on the hill. For the next few months citizens looked on while the organization that had built over the Sierra demonstrated its skill at the city's doorstep. When the show was over, the block bounded by California, Pine, Powell, and Mason streets was girded by a slate-colored wall of masonry that on the Pine Street side reached the height of a three-story building. The rock was granite from the railroad's quarries at Rocklin; it was hewn and laid by the railroad's stone-masons, and the finished walls were identical with those of bridge-approaches and cut-facings visible every-where along the company's lines. Today, long after the wooden mansions it enclosed have disappeared, this great wall remains, a minor civic landmark. Passing citizens re-gard it speculatively, puzzled to account for its familiar texture and pattern; few recognize it as twin brother to the characteristic Southern Pacific rockwork.

For most of its length the wall is as devoid of ornament as the facing of a branch-line culvert. At the southwest corner, however, the uniformity is broken and it becomes surprisingly the wall of a medieval castle, complete with battlements and towers, narrow windows and thick arched doorways. " The effect," wrote a local authority in the '80s, " is as unexpected as it is charming. . . . It rivals the best efforts of Viollet-le-Duc and . . . brings a bit of ancient Carcassonne to the shores of the Pacific."

3

RESPONSIBILITY for this medieval touch lay with Mary Hopkins. Not for nothing has she, in her twenty years of seclusion, gained a reputation as a student of literature. Bulwer-Lytton, Ouida, Mrs. Southworth, and others of the romantic school of the period were purveying the literature of escape long before the phrase came into use. Mary Hopkins, thumbing their pages during her barren years, shared the trials and stresses of countless chaste and ultimately triumphant courtships, eagerly absorbing the background against which England's idealized virgins skirted the whirlpool to gain the safety of the altar.

When she closed her novels and returned to reality, the transition must have been more painful to her than to the average. She was no farmer's wife, no household drudge, to whom the parks and galleries of romantic fiction were as remote as fairy gold. By a turn of fortune's wheel as surprising as any she had encountered in fiction, her elderly, bearded husband had the means of providing her with a setting not less spacious than that of her favorite heroine. The society editors were right; Mrs. Hopkins was a serious and industrious reader of novels.

Thus, when Hopkins good-humoredly agreed to a more complicated manner of life, his wife was not at loss as to how to proceed, for her models were clearly in mind. Having bought the Nob Hill lot and authorized the building of a house too large for his needs or tastes, Uncle Mark turned over further details to his wife and re-centered his attention on the more predictable business of financing railroads. It was the wife who dealt with Wright and Saunders, the architects commissioned to prepare the plans. Mary Hopkins thereupon began what was to prove the major enthusiasm of her life: the building of a series of pretentious residences.

Under her instructions the plans were gradually changed until what Uncle Mark had hoped would be a comparatively modest dwelling — a somewhat larger version of the Sutter Street cottage — became the singular mass of towers and gables and steeples that for the next thirty years lent a slightly dizzying note to the hill's already fantastic silhouette. Successive alterations not only changed the structure's original outlines, but extended its walls horizontally and vertically. When the wooden framework at length began to rise, the city was astonished to discover that quiet Uncle Mark was building a castle beside which Stanford's by no means tiny mansion paled into insignificance.

During the construction period, descriptions of the future wonders of the place periodically filled the Sunday sections of local papers. Long before it was ready for occupancy citizens were familiar with its more remarkable features; a drawing-room modeled on one of the chambers in the Palace of the Doges; a dining-room large enough to seat sixty, paneled to the ceiling in carved English oak; the master bedroom finished in ebony and inlaid with ivory and " semi-precious stones "; a library " so beautiful that only poetry should be read there."

The house was a long time building. Meanwhile Uncle Mark and his revivified wife continued to occupy the cottage at the foot of the hill. Reporters drawn there to question him about his new palace found him in shirtsleeves, hopefully nursing the vegetable beds in his back yard. They broke into appreciative grins when the old man leaned on his hoe, gazed up at the unfinished cluster of towers and turrets, and inquired if his visitors thought the " Hotel de Hopkins " would ever pay dividends.

The remark confirmed suspicions that Uncle Mark looked forward with less than complete pleasure to the day when he would have to move to the hilltop and shoulder the task of living up to such magnificence. Fortunately for his peace of mind, no question was then raised as to the artistic excellence of his new house. A dozen years were to pass before young Willis Polk, already referred to, began poking mild fun at the palaces of the railroad kings. "They cost a great deal of money," he wrote in the *Examiner*, "and whatever harsh criticism may fall upon them, they cannot be robbed of that prestige." Citizens were entertained when he directed ironical attention to the "little embroidered ruching modestly flouncing the third story windows" of Stanford's mansion, and in the house next door admired the "lions supporting the crest of the House of Hopkins." San Franciscans found such comment amusing and began to suspect that it might also be sound criticism. But young Polk made the mistake of pronouncing David Colton's Nob Hill house, a severe Georgian structure without a single tower or bay window or jigsaw decoration, "the most beautiful home in San Francisco." Thereupon confidence in his judgment slipped away and the public began to reflect on the folly of sending a young man to Paris in the hope of educating him.

Few questioned the taste or beauty of the Hotel de Hopkins while it was building, and Uncle Mark's concern for its mounting cost was uncomplicated by a suspicion that his thousands were being squandered to create an eyesore. And he need not have worried about accustoming himself to the regime on the hill, for he died before the castle was finished.

Characteristically, he managed to achieve a forthright

and uncomplicated exit. The state of his health had always been one of the unimportant details about which he had refused to concern himself. Since the day of the railroad's beginning he had remained close to his desk, leaving vacations and European water-cures to his younger partners and persistently refusing to coddle himself. But he was never strong physically and during the wet winter of 1877–8 his gangling legs and arms tied up in rheumatic knots. For weeks he shuffled about with a cane in each hand before he allowed himself to be sent up to Sacramento for an unaccustomed rest. He returned sooner than anyone expected, and Colton reported to Huntington: " Mr. Hopkins has just come into the office, and I am happy to say is very much better. . . ."

But the improvement proved temporary and early in March 1878 Hopkins hobbled aboard a company train bound on an inspection tour over the new Sunset Route. He had a theory that the hot Arizona sun would bake the stiffness out of his joints and enable him to hurry back to his accounts. Secure in that belief, he stretched himself one evening on a couch in the car on a Yuma siding and dropped off to sleep. Presently one of the company's construction engineers, Arthur Brown, heard the old man sigh in his sleep, recalled that it was past his punctual bedtime, and stepped across to arouse him. But for once Uncle Mark was not concerned with being punctual.

He was a few months short of sixty-five. His body was brought to San Francisco and the pastor of his old Sacramento church hurried down to conduct a funeral far more elaborate than Uncle Mark would have desired. The ac-

counts of his death in California newspapers retain to
this day the ring of sincerity. Hopkins was unquestionably the best liked of the Big Four. By 1878 the railroad
was already unpopular with nine of every ten citizens,
but even those most resentful of its tactics hesitated to
blame the senior partner. He had defects and eccentricities; he was an unextravagant rich man and therefore a
miser. But he was modest and kindly and sometimes
quietly humorous, with none of the vanity and little of
the ruthlessness of his partners. Men he had known in
earlier days found him still friendly and approachable,
and this was not invariably so with the others. " I've often
crossed the street to shake hands with Mark Hopkins, and
I've done the same to avoid meeting the others," said one.

His body was later moved to Sacramento and installed
in a mausoleum his widow had built for him at a cost, it
was said, of $150,000. Its walls were great blocks of rose-
colored marble, so highly polished that they flashed and
glistened like mirrors in the hot valley sun. There were
massive bronze doors flanked by urns, and within was a
frieze of acanthus leaves. The body was sealed in its
niche and Mary Hopkins returned to her unfinished
mansion on Nob Hill. She had installed her husband at
last in a setting proper to his station.

4

THE TELEGRAM from Yuma announcing Hopkins's death
had the indirect result of projecting the public spotlight

upon his widow and of keeping it there for years. For she had come into unrestricted possession of one of the largest fortunes in the country, and millions who had hardly known she existed suddenly wanted to learn all about her. Pictures of the plump, square-faced, rather stern woman (Caption: " America's Richest Widow ") appeared in newspapers all over the land. Her activities became matters of public interest, and society editors no longer dismissed her as a retiring housewife with an obscure liking for novels. Instead, she was pictured as a figure as unreal and romantic as any ever imagined by her admired Mrs. Southworth. Readers of Sunday supplements were presently enthralled by drawings of the lonely widow, " mistress of fifty millions," gazing down on San Francisco from the windows of her Nob Hill castle, while bordering columns of text speculated on what Prince Charming would come riding to her rescue.

By such journalistic alchemy, Mary Hopkins was dislodged from a lifetime of obscurity and made into a newspaper immortal of the first magnitude. Of course the process was not to her liking. She was then close to fifty, reserved by nature, and this invasion of her privacy appalled and frightened her. While local papers continued their discussion of when she would remarry and speculated on the identity of the successful suitor, she took progressively less pains to conceal a growing dislike for the town. The announcement in one journal of her engagement to a retired naval officer (one of the group known to be eager to relieve her of the tedium of widowhood) proved the final straw. The heiress made emphatic and angry denial and left at once for the Atlantic seaboard.

But curiosity in California remained keen and accounts of her movements continued to appear in San Francisco newspapers. The widow settled at Great Barrington, Massachusetts — where her and Uncle Mark's common forebears had lived — and embarked on what the local *Examiner* called " a building spree." McKim, Mead & White were commissioned to design a huge stone château, modeled on Chambord; it eventually cost above two millions. But headstrong tendencies, later to grow more pronounced, were already in evidence. Before building began, she dismissed the original architects; a Boston designer followed, and lasted a month; and the work was completed under the management of a young protégé, Edward T. Searles.

The San Francisco castle had meantime stood unfinished and before long she returned and saw it to completion. The " building spree " was then in full swing, for she also acquired in rapid succession a New York house, at 60 Fifth Avenue, a summer cottage at Block Island, and yet another at Methuen, Massachusetts. During the first half-dozen years of her widowhood she was constantly building or furnishing one or another of these; often several at a time.

Other qualities, unsuspected before her emancipation, began to grow evident. With no preparation, she had been thrust into prominence, the power of virtually unlimited wealth had been put into her hands — yet many wondered when her subsequent behavior proved not altogether rational. The flattery and attentions given her as a result of her newspaper fame and stories of her huge fortune speedily transformed the once subdued matron. She developed dictatorial traits and an imperious manner; employees learned that to question her orders in the smallest detail meant instant dismissal, and business and social relations were often explosively terminated. Naturally, she was not on a cordial footing with the press. San Francisco's society-page gossips had early prejudiced her against journalism. Because she refused to grant interviews, the newspapers exaggerated her eccentricities, and recorded her comings and goings, her social activities, and her extravagances in terms of mild burlesque.

By degrees she became known as a hard and frivolous woman, egotistical and self-willed. Her often expressed dislike for California (which, local papers pointed out, had contributed the wealth she was industriously squandering elsewhere) was cordially reciprocated, and her occasional visits with groups of Eastern friends to Nob Hill aroused no local enthusiasm. A few realized that the widow had missed popularity not by design but because she lacked the experience and skill to cope with a difficult situation. At first lonely and confused, she presently grew bitter, convinced that she was being persecuted. She suspected and quarreled with old friends, developed a contempt for the opinions of others, and eventually contracted an extraordinary marriage.

During the twelve years that elapsed between Mark Hopkins's death in 1879 and that of his widow in 1891, the latter's business affairs on the Coast were in the capable hands of her adopted son, Tim. Of business she knew rather less than the average wife of the period, but her quarter interest in the railroad was important to the surviving partners, and she had no lack of advisers. Fortunately, she allowed her properties to remain undisturbed; to attempt to liquidate them would have had a disastrous effect on the railroad securities, the market for which the partners had been building up for years. But the income from her holdings proved equal to her by no means inconsiderable expenditures, and Hopkins's death necessitated only minor changes in the financial structure of the partnership.

Timothy Hopkins was well under thirty when Uncle Mark died. He was a son of Patrick Nolan, a New Englander who had arrived in San Francisco in 1862 and worked there as a dockhand while he accumulated funds to send for his wife and three children. On the day his family sailed for the West, Nolan fell into the bay and was drowned. One of his children died on the voyage; his widow arrived destitute, and found work in the Hopkins household in Sacramento. Young Tim often visited her there. Uncle Mark and his wife, childless, were attracted by the boy and he came to live with them. Later Mrs. Nolan married the farmer who operated Hopkins's truck-farm; other children were born, and the family moved to St. Louis. Timothy remained behind at Sacramento.

The boy grew up in Hopkins's Spartan household, attended Sacramento and San Francisco schools, and then went to work in the railroad's general offices at Fourth and Townsend streets. When Hopkins died, Timothy was assistant treasurer, one of the bright young men of the company's executive staff. To him his aging chief had delegated much of the routine work of his department. When the time came, Timothy was competent to step into the dead man's shoes, and he was duly appointed treasurer.

He became of course the widow's main reliance, overseeing the settlement of the estate and the management of the property Hopkins had acquired in addition to his railroad holdings. So close were their relations that the widow then took a step which had been contemplated while Uncle Mark was alive: Timothy was legally adopted. Later the bond was further strengthened by the wedding in New York's Windsor Hotel of the widow's newly adopted son and her niece, Clara Crittenden.

5

MRS. HOPKINS moved east and thereafter she returned to the Coast only for occasional brief stays. On one such visit, in March 1882, a young man from New York, an employee of Herter & Company, decorators, called at the Nob Hill house and presented a letter of introduction. Furniture was his major enthusiasm; he had heard of the wonders of the new house and was politely eager to inspect it. Their common enthusiasm for houses and furnishings was the basis of a close friendship that sprang up between the widow and twenty-eight-year-old Edward T. Searles. During the spring weeks an interested city regarded the stranger speculatively as, seated between the widow and her daughter-in-law in the Hopkins carriage, he accompanied them on daily drives through Golden Gate Park.

From the first, Tim Hopkins failed to share his wife's and foster-mother's admiration for the decorator. As the older woman's infatuation grew more evident, so likewise did Timothy's alarm. When Searles at length left again for the East, Mrs. Hopkins and a group of friends accompanied him to the Oakland Pier; then, as his train was on the point of leaving, the enamored widow threw her arms about him, gave him a resounding good-by kiss, and informed the startled spectators that they were soon to marry. Notwithstanding her foster-son's objections, Mrs. Hopkins soon followed Searles east, where their engagement was announced. From the Coast, Timothy continued to bombard her with arguments against the match — with the usual effect. These not only strengthened her determination to marry Searles; they aroused her resentment at what she considered meddling in her personal affairs. At length she wrote a curt note forbidding young Hopkins to mention the subject again; Timothy replied with still more arguments and the widow made good her threat by breaking off communications entirely. There was one partial reconciliation. On her last visit to the Coast before her marriage, the widow allowed herself to be seen at church one Sunday with Timothy and his wife. But she returned east, married Searles, and thereafter communications between her and Timothy were confined to matters of business. At one time she contemplated severing even that connection, and an agent was sent out from New York charged with selecting someone to succeed Timothy as manager of her California properties. But inquiry disclosed no one whom the agent could recommend for the job; he returned and reported that she was already represented by the most competent man available.

Hopkins accordingly remained as business manager, but his friendship with Mrs. Searles was never renewed. The feud and the reason for it were well known in San Francisco, and when, on July 26, 1891, she died, it was expected that Timothy would inherit only a minor share of the estate. But neither the public nor young Hopkins was prepared for what her will disclosed. The indomitable lady had contrived to enliven her exit with a final thumb-to-nose salute to her critics. To her precise, chair-loving husband she left unconditionally her entire estate. There were no bequests to relatives or to charity. Friends and family servants were alike unmentioned, and Timothy was specifically disinherited.

Her millions and her belated romance had already made her known to the nation, and her unorthodox will became news of the first importance. In New York, reporters gathered at the town house on lower Fifth Avenue and from disgruntled servants learned interesting details of the life and habits of the bereft husband. It became clear that while Searles may not have been a hero to his valet, he was at least a mystery. He was revealed as a man of great but curiously restricted enthusiasms. Unlike his recent spouse, whose passion for novels had persisted to the end, Searles was no lover of literature; none of the retainers could recall ever having seen him read a book or even a newspaper. He had, however, two passions: one was a persisting dislike of his wife's adopted son, the other an absorbing passion for furniture. It was related that his chief pleasure was to wander from room to room about his various residences, standing motionless and absorbed before a blank wall, contemplating the draperies of a window, examining the drawers and back of cabinets, the under side of chairs.

Servants reported that he would often spend an entire day in a room moving furniture about, hanging and rehanging pictures, rearranging bric-a-brac. Sometimes it was late at night before he had found an arrangement to his liking. The next morning he would return and resume his contemplation; usually he ended by restoring everything to its original position. If servants failed to replace every chair or table ornament in its accustomed spot, Searles would notice the fact instantly. He had, said they, a sharp eye for such details.

When San Franciscans read of Mrs. Searles's will, one question became uppermost: would Timothy contest it? Attempts to break wills were a favorite form of litigation among newspaper readers on the Coast, and this one promised to be more interesting than the average. But Hopkins was in Japan, and the citizens had to await his return. Soon, however, they had their answer. Within a week after his return to San Francisco, the suit was filed. Hopkins asked for a share of his foster-mother's estate, basing his plea on the grounds that the will had been

THE GROUND-BREAKING EXERCISES AT SACRAMENTO, JANUARY 8, 1863

From a mural in the New Southern Pacific Station, Sacramento. Stanford with shovel; Crocker speaking; Huntington and Hopkins standing below Crocker; Judah standing to the right of the speakers' platform, with hands behind him.

Courtesy of the California State Library

TIMOTHY HOPKINS
from an engraving made in 1886.

secured by undue influence and fraud, and that Mrs. Searles had been of unsound mind when it was executed.

The trial opened at Salem, Massachusetts, in September 1891. Called to the witness chair, Searles faced a tittering courtroom and revealed details of an extraordinary courtship. He testified that the widow had proposed marriage to him in New York in 1883, though at first he had refused to " entertain the proposition." His hesitation, he added, had lasted three years. Meantime he had accompanied her and a party of friends to Florida in 1886, and from 1885 to 1887 had superintended the completion and furnishing of the Great Barrington château. Under the prodding of Hopkins's attorneys, the witness stated that he had known his bride was twenty-two years his senior and that she was a woman of large means. The questions grew more searching. He denied that he had married her for her money; denied also that it had been a " love match." Finally he admitted unhappily that the motivating influences had been " both love and money." The court rapped for order and the cross-examination swung to a related subject. What had the witness gained in a material way from his marriage? As his wife's sole heir, he had received the Hopkins share of the railroad properties, the San Francisco mansion, improved and unimproved property at Sacramento and elsewhere in California, the Great Barrington and New York houses, an undetermined amount of cash and miscellaneous property. He fixed his current annual income at between $500,000 and $600,000. His attorneys refused to allow him to state what his income had been before his marriage. Court was adjourned and Hopkins's counsel announced that examination of the witness would continue the next day.

But the following morning spectators who jammed the Salem courtroom were disappointed to learn that an out-of-court settlement had been reached. By the compromise Timothy Hopkins received a sum which the Boston *Globe* stated was " between eight and ten millions." In San Francisco the *Call* commented: " Evidently Mr. Searles didn't want another day on the witness stand."

6

THE OUTCOME of Timothy's suit had an important bearing on the battle for supremacy over the railroad, and for that reason the semicomedy at Salem had been closely followed in both San Francisco and New York. The settlement left Searles in control of much the greater part of the Hopkins railroad securities. Searles's business agents, Thomas H. Hubbard and T. E. Stillman, therefore, held the balance of power between the Stanford and Huntington factions. Had events at Salem put Timothy in possession of the majority of the Hopkins stock, it is possible that Huntington might have been forced from the Southern Pacific presidency, and control of the road have returned to California. Huntington had realized the danger and, because of it, he had treated Searles with a benevolent friendliness that may well have astonished the latter. He had even allowed himself to be interviewed on events at Salem and to comment approvingly on the way Searles had conducted himself on the stand. The result was that the bulk of the Hopkins stock continued to be voted solidly as Huntington directed, despite increasingly hostile objections from the Stanford and Crocker factions on the Coast.

Rivalry between Huntington and the heirs of his partners persisted through the '90s. Stanford's estate was then in the hands of his widow and the university; the Crocker interests were represented chiefly by Charles F. Crocker, eldest son of the original Charles. Timothy Hopkins still remained a railroad official and controlled a minor share of Uncle Mark's original quarter interest. With all these Huntington was frequently at odds, and from time to time echoes of their differences found their way into the Coast newspapers. The quarrels were mainly caused by the fact that Huntington's autocratic tendencies, never a minor characteristic, grew with his years, and so likewise did his frankness. " When I was younger I sometimes had to tolerate fools," he snapped in one of his later interviews. ". . . That's one place where I draw the line now." A writer in the *Examiner* explained that there was nothing complicated about Huntington's definition of a fool: it was anyone who disagreed with him or opposed him. Huntington, he added, warred with his partners' heirs because he resented the fact that they had come into railroad money. " If he had had his way, his partners' millions would have reverted to the Southern Pacific's treasury."

Not being able to accomplish that, Huntington took little pains to conceal his low opinion of the ability or industry of the second generation. Accordingly, he began harping again on what for years had been a favorite grievance: the failure of others to work as hard as he did. In the middle '90s, he sent his nephew, Henry E. Huntington, to San Francisco to take charge of the railroad-owned streetcar system. The move was resented by the local executives because no one on the Coast had been consulted. Charles F. Crocker, then vice-president of the Southern Pacific, disliked the manner of Henry E. Huntington's coming; moreover, he disliked the gentleman himself. Their quarrel reached the public and on the elder Huntington's next visit reporters were waiting with questions. Had he sent his nephew out without consulting his associates on the Coast? Huntington retorted that on his last trip he had made two attempts to talk with young Crocker on the subject. " I sent word to his office one day at half past two and the next afternoon at two o'clock. Both times I was told that he had gone for the day." He added that investigation would disclose that his nephew kept longer office hours.

Huntington's suspicion of the descendants of his partners included Timothy Hopkins, but it is doubtful if the latter gave offense by failing to attend to business. The share of the railroad securities forced from Searles assured his continuance as a railroad official. He remained an active and useful citizen of California until his death in 1936. As for Searles, when he left the Salem courtroom in 1891, he retired gratefully from the public spotlight, content to remain in the background the rest of his life. He spent much time in travel, indulged his taste for furniture and its arrangement to his heart's content and presently passed unobtrusively out of the picture — one of the most curious figures in the entire gallery of those thrown into prominence by Central Pacific profits.

Although Uncle Mark was the first of the partners to die, his millions continued to occupy public attention for many years after interest in the estates of the other three had waned. Notwithstanding the fact that the probate court at San Francisco had ordered the distribution of his property in 1883, word got abroad that much of the estate was still intact. There were but two important heirs: the widow — who received by far the greater part — and Uncle Mark's picturesque brother, Moses, who had served as administrator. Thereafter for many years the matter remained quiescent; then, in the early 1900s, petitions began to be filed in California courts stating that assets of the estate had been fraudulently concealed and asking their distribution to a variety of claimants. The fortune — its value was placed as high as forty million dollars — was stated to be lying in the vaults of San Francisco and Sacramento banks. The rumor spread, and soon from all parts of the country persons who felt they had a claim to a share of it began to make themselves heard. Petitions of nearly a thousand lost heirs were filed in the federal courts. The lower courts in 1927 dismissed the pleas and two years later the Supreme Court ended the hopes of the expectant thousand by denying an appeal. But even that did not end the matter. New crops of heirs with new petitions continued to turn up in such number that in 1931 a San Francisco judge denounced the scheme as a country-wide swindle by which a group of attorneys were " beating innocent and usually ignorant people out of their savings by making them think they are heirs to Mark Hopkins."

What prudent, practical Uncle Mark would have thought of this horde of real or imagined descendants and their hope of sharing the mythical fortune must be left to conjecture. His meager dust had lain beneath the acanthus frieze at Sacramento for half a century. Meantime there had been changes. The Nob Hill house had become the first home of the San Francisco Art School; through the '90s and later its gilded chambers held sketching classes — intent circles of Beardsleyesque young men and intent girls struggling to surmount the merely photographic — while the great public, educated by *Trilby,* regarded its baroque exterior with wistful disapproval and Sunday papers used muggy views of the structure (made by the new halftone process) to illustrate perennial discussions of the nude in art.

Later still the post-war building boom produced a twenty-story hotel on the site, where Hollywood notables came to six-room hide-outs for rest and contemplation and " to get away from it all." College and high-school students swarm in the dining-room and bar on Saturday nights and the saxophone-player of the reigning orchestra intermittently croons into a microphone, beginning at nine. It is the Mark Hopkins, most frivolous of the local hotels; " the Mark " to the younger crowd. At dinner-dances lights are dimmed in the main dining-room and through its arched windows the ghostly roofs of the city grow visible. The dancers move in viscous rhythm, the music blares and throbs, youths in pairs slither in from the bar, merge in the gloom, and the mass of undulating bodies swallows them up. " The Mark." Perhaps it is well that Uncle Mark is safe in the little marble house his wife built for him at Sacramento. One cannot be sure that he had a sense of irony.

STANFORD

1

FOR thirty years Leland Stanford was one of the Pacific Coast's conspicuous figures, and in that time he had more than his share of praise and abuse. " Had he come at an earlier era," wrote one admirer, " he would have been a Christ or a Confucius." Others compared him, without irony, to Cæsar, Alexander the Great, Napoleon, and John Stuart Mill, to the disadvantage of all four. A California editor stated that more properly than Lorenzo he might be called " the Magnificent," and one of Hubert H. Bancroft's anonymous scribes thus began a biographical sketch: " If he [the biographer] starts with the simple assertion that he [Stanford] is the greatest man in the world today, it may sound like senseless adulation, yet it is no more than the truth. . . ."

On the other hand, his partner Huntington once described him tersely as " a damned old fool," and Alfred Cohen on a brief vacation from the Central Pacific's legal staff credited him with " the ambition of an emperor and the spite of a peanut vender." Ambrose Bierce delighted to print his name £eland $tanford, and Arthur McEwen suggested in 1894 that the arch above the entrance to his new university should bear the legend: " With Apologies to God." At Stanford University's dedication eight thousand citizens stood respectfully in the hot sun while praises were sung of " the noblest gift in the history of mankind." But many suppressed grins when they were asked to join in the closing hymn: " We Give Thee But Thine Own."

He was a large, heavy man, deliberate in thought and motion. All his life he was a notably slow talker. His hesitant speech grew more pronounced with his years, and most of the later interviews make reference to meditative silences, to the lengthy period that elapsed between the putting of a question and the moment when its answer began to issue from the Stanford lips. His extreme deliberation of thought was regarded by many as evidence of uncommon sincerity, of a desire to weigh the merits of a question, to consider its implications, and to frame his answer only after the matter had received detailed and sagacious analysis. But his grave pauses impressed strangers more profoundly than those who knew him well. The latter recognized that the length of the pause bore no relation to the complexity of the question. " How do you feel this morning, Governor? " required as long a period of brooding concentration as a query involving the safety of the Republic.

Stanford's low-geared thinking, the painful slowness with which he translated his thoughts into words, was the opposite of a handicap. It did much to make him a success in politics. Extemporaneous speaking was of course beyond him; campaign speeches and every sort of public address had to be written in advance. Brief remarks were memorized and recited; those of any length

were read, not from notes, but from complete manu-
scripts. This method gave him a twofold advantage over
more agile adversaries. For one thing, during his entire
political life he never made a statement that had not been
considered in advance, whereas most of his opponents
could be depended on to extemporize themselves into
trouble at least once during a campaign. But the chief
value of his handicap lay in another direction. It was the
spectacle of this big, earnest man on the platform, stolidly
reading his speech line for line, page by page, that won
the votes of his listeners. Here obviously was no speech-
maker intent on swaying the electors by the sinister force
of eloquence. The speaker was uninspired and he must
therefore be sincere; he was dull and hence very probably
profound; and of course only thoroughly honest politicians make thoroughly bad speeches.

Not long after the completion of his redwood mansion
on the San Francisco hilltop, an official of a British shipping company called on Stanford at the railroad's offices,
made a favorable impression, and was invited to dinner.
The Englishman had arrived by boat from the Orient;
it was his first visit to America, and Stanford's was the
first American residence he was privileged to enter. The
event seemed to him important enough to warrant more
than passing mention in his diary. " The house I later
heard spoken of as the finest in the western part of America, and in San Francisco I saw no others that rivalled it
in size. . . ." Silently and, his guest thought, somewhat
grimly, Stanford led him on an inclusive tour of the structure, topping off with a circuit of the steep grounds and

a visit to the stables, on the corner diagonally across California Street. Horses and shining carriages were duly admired, then the pair recrossed the street and sat down to dinner. Mrs. Stanford was indisposed and the two dined alone. After a long and, except for the guest's remarks, an almost completely silent meal, Stanford led the way across the hall to the library, on the walls of which hung paintings of the Governor and his wife.

" For the next half hour," the visitor wrote, " we talked. That is, I talked and Mr. Stanford sat silent. I do not say that he listened, for that I had no means of knowing. He merely sat, regarding me not impolitely but with a face from which all expression had been erased. He may have heard every word I uttered or he may have heard nothing. I began by feeling that I must be boring him, then by wondering if I had perhaps given him cause for grave offense. Next, it occurred to me that he might be sleepy; finally I became certain that he was ill." When the visitor at length got up and fled, Stanford accompanied him to the door, shook his hand affably, and remarked how much he had enjoyed their " chat," all with such evident sincerity that the caller was forced to believe him. The Englishman returned to his hotel and lay long abed reflecting on the eccentricities of American millionaires.

Stanford was not always loath to talk. He granted interviews far more willingly than most prominent men, and he actively enjoyed the noise and crowds and hubbub of political campaigns. He was seldom able to resist the temptation to run for office. Before he had been in California two years he was serving as justice of the peace at

Michigan Bluff, a cluster of canvas shacks in the Sierra foothills, and he had hardly settled in Sacramento before his name was on the ballot as a candidate for alderman. He received 87 of 991 votes. Undeterred, he ran for state treasurer the same year and was again badly defeated. A little later he helped organize the new Republican party in California, and was elected Governor in 1862. He served a two-year term, retired from politics for twenty years, then decided to go to the Senate.

A week after the California legislature of 1885 had elected him, a reporter for the *Examiner* met James G. Fair, Senator from Nevada, in the lobby of the Palace Hotel and asked a question about which half the state was curious:

" Senator, how much do you suppose Stanford's seat cost him? "

The mining man shifted his toothpick and made some rough calculations. " Well, judging from what I had to pay up at Carson, my guess is not a cent less than a hundred thousand."

Other guesses were higher. More or less directly this was the cause of his final break with Huntington, a piece of bad luck that cost him many times a hundred thousand. But Stanford was a hard man to discourage. Five years later, during the last of his conversations with the young man he had imported from Indiana to be president of his university, he remarked: " I learn every year more and more to love the landscape, and this the poorest man in California can enjoy as well as the richest."

His religion has been partially defined as Unitarian

Methodism, and David Starr Jordan once wrote of " a rarely beautiful smile which illumined his otherwise impassive face." He was currently believed to have paid the editor of a San Francisco weekly ten thousand dollars a year to write admiringly of his activities. In his old age dependants listened brightly while in hesitating tones he coined numberless wise maxims. The following has survived: " If it rained twenty-dollar gold pieces until noon every day, at night there would be some men begging for their suppers."

2

ONE of eight children, Stanford was born on March 9, 1824 in Watervliet Township, New York, not far from Albany. A family tradition states that soon after his birth, the Marquis de Lafayette, traveling the post-road between Albany and Troy, spent a night at the Bull's Head Tavern and condescended to hold the proprietor's infant son on his patrician knee. The elder Stanford was one of the numerous group of farmer-inkeepers who in stagecoach days lined well-traveled roads and pieced out their income from agriculture by supplying meals and lodgings, or casual glasses of ale, to travelers. Josiah Stanford moved several times during Leland's childhood, seeking a better location for his inn and a larger share of the stage travel that was rapidly diminishing as railroads were built. He was presently operating the Elm Grove Hotel, on the turnpike between Albany and Schenectady, where he also owned some three hundred acres of wooded land. As his picturesquely named sons (one was Jerome Bonaparte, another De Witt Clinton) grew old enough to swing an ax, they were set to chopping firewood for the Albany market. There is record of a contract with one of the new railroads for twenty-six hundred cords; helping to fill this kept Leland busy throughout his sixteenth and seventeenth years.

During that time he first met the daughter of Dyer Lathrop, an Albany storekeeper. At once he formed the habit of making elaborate detours about the Lathrop house on Washington Avenue so that the girl might not encounter him in his rustic clothes, perched on top of a load of firewood.

Perhaps with some of the profits from the wood contract, the elder Stanford decided to give one of his sons professional training. Leland was chosen and he set off in 1841 for a school near Utica. Later he transferred to Cazenovia Seminary, near Syracuse, a Methodist school conducted on the Spartan principles common to such academies. There he was in intermittent attendance until 1845. Although he was never graduated, and apparently never distinguished himself in the classroom, he came to be regarded as one of Cazenovia Seminary's distinguished sons. Stanford in after years made substantial gifts to the school. One of these was a painting (a life-size portrait of himself) intended to be hung on a wall of the chapel.

The Cazenovia period was followed by three years in

LELAND STANFORD
from a photograph made in Paris about 1885.
Courtesy of Edwin Grabhorn

MRS. LELAND STANFORD
from a photograph made in Paris about 1885.
Courtesy of Edwin Grabhorn

the office of an Albany law firm. This time he was at less pains to avoid the storekeeper's daughter, and by the time he was admitted to the bar in 1848 he and Jane Lathrop were engaged. Following what was then a well-established custom for newly accredited professional men, he elected to settle in one of the new towns on the Western frontier. His choice fell on Port Washington, a village on the lake-front some miles north of Milwaukee, of which great things were expected. Stanford married and took his bride out to Wisconsin. There he formed a partnership with another fledgling attorney, settled himself in a rented house, bought a " business lot," and prepared to grow up with the country. Three years later it had become obvious that Port Washington was not to be another Chicago. Stanford's early enthusiasm evaporated and when a fire destroyed his office, his library, and the businesses of most of his debtors, he left the declining town without regret and returned to Albany.

The year was 1852. While he had been trying to begin a professional career on the shore of Lake Michigan, five of his brothers had been drawn farther west by the general exodus to California. Reports filtered back to the family at Oak Grove telling of moderate success and of progressively brighter prospects. Leland was in a mood to be persuaded. Within a few weeks after his return to Albany he was again headed west, this time by steamer to California. His wife remained behind with her parents.

Stanford was twenty-eight when he arrived in San Francisco, considerably more mature than the average Californian. The crest of the gold rush was of course well past, and with it had gone the myth that nuggets were to be picked up like pebbles in the streams. But this Argonaut of '52 had no intention of mining; he had come west to join his brothers in a less romantic but more stable calling: the grocery business. The elder Stanford, Josiah, had opened a store at Mormon Island in 1850; later he had established a central store at Sacramento, and as the others arrived he had put them in charge of branches set up in various foothill camps.

Leland took his place in this primitive chain-store system. With his brothers' help he acquired an interest in a one-room store at Cold Springs, a camp between Hangtown and Coloma, then mostly inhabited by Chinese. But the placers there were nearly worked out, business was poor, and Stanford and his partner moved to another mushroom camp: Michigan Bluff. This settlement, as it chanced, was still on the up-grade; population tripled during the year after Stanford arrived; and for three years the store grew and its owners prospered.

The Sacramento store, managed by Josiah and another brother, Philip, had meantime flourished to a like extent. By the middle '50s Stanford Brothers was a wholesale house of standing, dealing in groceries, liquors, tobacco, flour, and produce and the usual miscellany of miners' supplies and equipment. When Josiah and Philip acquired interests in San Francisco and moved " down to the bay," a deal was made whereby Leland took over the sole management of the Sacramento store, then housed in a new fireproof building at Front and L streets.

Through the store, it was inevitable that Stanford

should be brought in contact with what was still almost the sole industry of the region, gold mining. One such connection proved particularly remunerative. Among the customers of Stanford Brothers were a pair of store-keepers, Hanford and Downs, in the town of Volcano, fifty-five miles southeast of Sacramento. They had acquired an interest in a quartz mine at near-by Sutter's Creek and, like thousands of others, had proceeded to bankrupt themselves trying to develop it. Stanford was among their creditors, and the two merchants settled their bill by turning over to him 76 of their 93 shares in the Lincoln mine. Very soon thereafter the mine began to produce heavily and continued for years. In 1872 Stanford and the other owners sold out for $400,000. Counting his dividends over a period of years, he is said to have realized over half a million by the transaction.

During this early period Stanford had no intention of living permanently on the Coast. He shared the common ambition to accumulate a fortune as quickly as possible, then to settle down as a substantial citizen of his home town in the East. This plan he was able to put into effect in 1855. He returned to Albany with three major objectives: to go into the wholesale grocery business there; to rejoin his wife; and, characteristically, to buy a certain imposing Albany residence he had admired in his youth.

But here again his experience paralleled that of other returned Californians. After the accelerated tempo of the Coast, life in older communities seemed impossibly sedate and humdrum. The novelty of the return, of greeting old friends, and of patronizing the stay-at-homes wore off after a week or two. Thereupon the adventurer usually developed an unaccountable restlessness and fell to studying the schedules of the Panama steamers.

Stanford's desire to return to California was seconded, unexpectedly, by his wife. He soon learned the reason. Albany was not a large town in the '50s and the Lathrop family was well known. During Stanford's absence in the West his wife had continued to live at her father's house. As time passed and the missing husband failed to reappear, friends and neighbors came to regard her curiously, with glances of obscure sympathy. Convinced that she was looked on as a deserted wife, Jane Stanford developed a dislike for her native town that she retained with admirable consistency as long as she lived. As a place of permanent residence California, to her mind, was none too remote from Albany. Her wishes fell in with Stanford's own, and the two were presently on a steamer headed for the west coast. Stanford once remarked that Albany's gossips were indirectly responsible for making him Governor of California.

3

THEN and later Stanford had a sustained and ponderous geniality, considerable personal vanity, and a naïve love of display. Of the Central Pacific's Big Four, Huntington, of course, was easily the dominating figure. But Huntington, until late in life, avoided whatever would make him personally conspicuous, choosing to sit in the wings while others carried out his wishes before the footlights. Crocker, energetic and blustering and physically domineering, was essentially a subordinate, a man to take orders and carry them out, and Hopkins never rose, nor ever desired to rise, above his position as the keeper of the company's accounts.

There remained Stanford, who had all Huntington's craving for leadership and much of his ruthlessness, but who lacked the other's adroit cunning and his talent for moving in a direct line to a desired end. In the battle that presently arose for leadership Stanford, heavy-handed and slow and often stupid, was easily outmaneuvered, and from the beginning to the end of their association his was the secondary place. Denied actual leadership, he seized nominal leadership as the most attractive substitute, a decision made easier by Huntington's liking for obscurity.

There can be no doubt that Stanford's failure to dominate the affairs of the Central Pacific profoundly influenced the course of his career. Having failed of the real leadership his nature desired and which he thought he deserved, the final thirty years of his life became a struggle for self-justification, an unremitting effort to convince himself that nominal leadership was actual leadership, that the man whose heart's desire was to lead was actually leading. He succeeded far better than most men so situated ever succeed. Although he was defeated in the end and died knowing he was defeated, there were long periods when his seeming success was indistinguishable from reality.

His enforced secondary place in the railroad's affairs had a familiar result. To counteract the consciousness of defeat he set about surrounding himself with the visible evidences of success. As the formidable profits from the railroad enterprises became available, by far the greater part of his share went to create the background against which he played his late-Victorian version of political leader and financial king.

It was a magnificent production, put on with a total disregard for expense. The Stanfords moved from Sacramento to San Francisco in 1874, and the following year occupied the most desirable suite in the newly finished Palace Hotel, then rented a house on Pine Street, from the windows of which they could oversee the building of the latest of their series of elaborate houses. For that year Stanford startled San Franciscans by encircling two acres of sand on the crest of Nob Hill with a thirty-foot wall and constructing a mansion that dominated the city like the castle of a medieval hill town.

Descriptions of the attractions of the place filled the California journals for months after its completion. From its marble steps fronting on California Street, visitors stepped into a circular entrance hall, the stone floor of which was inlaid with the signs of the zodiac in black marble, and which was filled with a curious amber light from a glass dome in the roof seventy feet above. A wide hall bisected the ground floor, terminating in a conservatory at the far end. From the hall, sliding doors opened into various high-ceiled chambers: a reception room finished in the style of the East Indies; a library which the

Governor — this was his favorite title; he retained it long after he left office — used as his home office and in which he received callers; a communicating door led to a billiard room. Beyond, on the sunny Powell-Pine corner, the windows of which, hung with purple and gold velvet, overlooked the entire business section of the city, was what was known as the downstairs sitting-room. There the family and guests gathered evenings, listened to hymns and occasional waltzes, admired the birds brought in from the aviary, and radiated the elegance of Victorian domesticity.

To this prim chamber one winter evening in the late '70s came a certain Miss Frayne, a young woman journalist who was preparing for a California weekly a group of articles on " Our Millionaires at Home." She found the Stanfords simple and kindly and, except for the upholstered luxury of the setting, leading lives not different than that of humbler Christian families. Neither Stanford nor his wife cared for social life in its more frivolous aspects. The Governor liked nothing better than quiet evenings at home. His chief hobby was his business; next to that, the breeding and training of horses. The latter also had a serious purpose: that of improving the strain and developing thoroughbreds in California.

Mary Frayne made careful note of the fact that Stanford had no interest in racetracks and gambling. He had never bet a dollar on a horse race and he never intended to. He no longer cared much for travel, but he considered it an elevating experience for those able to afford the luxury. A trip to the Old World, undertaken in the right spirit, was educational; America had nothing to compare with

Europe's art galleries. It was the duty of rich men to have good copies made of famous paintings and to allow humbler citizens to see and study them and so develop a taste for art. Mrs. Stanford was normally content to let her husband speak for both of them. Her family's comfort and the management of the household were her chief concerns, but she also devoted some time to church activities and to charity. Stanford usually turned over to her all letters containing requests for money. These were investigated and worthy cases often received help. Some of the requests, however, were found to come from unworthy or unscrupulous sources. Mrs. Stanford was not opposed to women entering the business world, provided surroundings were wholesome and the work was not beyond their strength. There was a place for women in journalism and in the arts, and of course in nursing and teaching school. As to the propriety of female doctors — then a much debated subject — she felt definitely that this was a profession better left to men.

A storm had come up and flashes of lightning grew visible through the sitting-room windows. Mrs. Stanford was concerned for her caller and wished to have the coachman bring round a carriage to take her home. Did she live far and were her shoes stout? Dry feet were the secret of good health. But the storm fortunately abated and Mary Frayne withdrew. She hurried down the wet marble steps to California Street, admiring the unaffected simplicity of wealth, a thorough young convert to benevolent capitalism.

But unaffected simplicity was not always a characteristic of the Stanfords. Soon after the completion of the
railroad, his wife presented its president with a private
car, the " Stanford," in which they annually spent many
weeks. Word went through the railroad organization that
when the Governor traveled he liked to receive the attentions due him as president of the company. Consequently
news of his approach was telegraphed ahead so that groups
of employees could be in evidence at crossroads stations
to salute the passing of his car. At division points the
Stanford's sitting-room became the setting for brief levees
as officials in their best uniforms filed past to pay their
respects and to inquire after the president's welfare. Section crews stood at attention while the special roared past
in a swirl of hot dust, engines of freight trains waiting on
sidings sounded long salutes, and the crews of roundhouses
and repair shops were marshaled at points sure to be
visible from Stanford's window.

What Huntington, whose passage over the line bore
less resemblance to a Roman triumph, thought of these
attentions was not made known. Nor did all signs of deference cease when Stanford's car passed on to the tracks of
rival railroads; these did business with the Central Pacific,
and its president was received as an honored guest. Even
in England, Stanford's arrival was such as to convince
other passengers that here was no ordinary traveler. The
steamer was met in the Mersey by a tug; Stanford and his
party were hurried ashore, ushered into a private car,
and dispatched to London well in advance of the regular

boat trains. There his usual suite at the Hotel Bristol was ready, presided over by the same servants who had attended his wants on earlier visits.

4

THROUGHOUT the '70s and '80s much newsprint was consumed to describe Stanford's spacious California background. First at Sacramento, then on San Francisco's Nob Hill, and later at Palo Alto, the Stanford establishments aroused interest that persisted from year to year. The depth and texture of the Stanford carpets, the quality of Stanford lace curtains, the unimagined intricacy of Stanford gas-lit chandeliers and cornices and iron fences were known and discussed in the remotest corners of the state.

During the final two decades of his life he moved restlessly from extravagance to extravagance, hardly beginning one before he was reaching toward another that promised even greater opportunity for spectacular spending. In the middle '70s his San Francisco house claimed his attention. Because the ascent to Nob Hill was too abrupt for convenient scaling by horse and carriage, he built the California Street Railroad and, to the measured click of the underground cable, carloads of natives and tourists passed in daylong procession before the stone gateposts and marble steps.

But the next year, as already recounted, Mark Hopkins

abruptly abandoned a lifetime of frugality and began his mansion next door; the extension of the granite wall soared higher than Stanford's and was topped at the corners with medieval turrets. A year later Charles Crocker went higher still and the railroad profits added another complex silhouette to the Nob Hill skyline. A group of miners from the Nevada bonanzas acquired adjacent sites on the windy upper slopes, and the screech of jigsaws and the hammers of a hundred carpenters announced an eruption of wooden mansions on the hill.

Its noble isolation gone, Stanford lost his first interest in the Nob Hill house, and his thoughts focused on a larger enterprise. The Palo Alto farm, a nine-thousand-acre block of foothills and oak-studded meadow, provided a suitable background for indulging the then genteel taste for blooded horses. There he proceeded to ride his new hobby as it had never been ridden elsewhere. An army of workmen made camp among the oaks, and descriptions of the wonders of Palo Alto began to appear regularly in the press. The residence — Stanford's fourth in a decade — had " all the luxuries of a beautiful manor "; the two racetracks and the sixty-acre trotting park were " rolled and sprinkled daily "; its lines of stables, attended by the farm's hundred and fifty employees, were brightly painted studies in perspective.

The roll-call of Stanford's horses, published and republished, added pleasant new luster to his name: " 10 full-aged stallions, 50 young stallions, 250 brood mares, 250 colts and fillies less than three years old." California's most celebrated crop became the carrots from the sixty-acre patch planted yearly for the Stanford colts. Supremacy on the racetracks of the world became his goal, and boards of strategy met regularly in the clapboard mansion to plan and perfect the campaign. Across the meadow, hour after hour, six days a week, Stanford's horses circled the flawless track; there ninety colts were kept in training and each was exercised twenty minutes daily. In addition, near-by stables housed "twenty selected colts in careful training for the Eastern race courses two seasons in the future," and beyond were the quarters of the notable stallions Shannon and Flood, and of thirty brood mares sired by celebrated studs of England and America.

One of the Stanford horses was to reappear briefly in the nation's newspapers sixty years later. This was Gloster, purchased in the East in 1873, and the first trotter to cover a mile in under 2:20. Gloster was trained on the Palo Alto tracks and sent east for the racing season of 1874. Before the journey was well begun, the horse was killed in a train wreck. Much later, Franklin D. Roosevelt, then President-elect, varied a dull press conference at Albany by retelling the story of Gloster's achievements; his father had sold the horse to Stanford.

The names and reputations of other horses in the Palo Alto stables revive memories of the forgotten reverence then paid to turf and paddock: Piedmont, which Stanford imported at a cost of thirty thousand dollars, Clay, Frolic, Electioneer, Fiddler, fastest stallion ever bred in England, Musk, Fetterlock, Ison, Macgregor, Hermit, Lowlander, Salvador, Peregine. . . . The Palo Alto farm became the center of horse-breeding in the West, and memories of the period focus on the stocky, aging figure of the Governor in his shining sulky, making his rounds over the dustless roads of the farm, inspecting recent purchases, hastening the completion of still more stables, sitting for hours beside the track while his trainers put likely prospects through their paces.

But the time came when even his racing hobby failed to monopolize all Stanford's attention. His interest turned to farming, and it became his determination, in the new enthusiasm as in the old, to make himself unquestionably first. At a cost of an even million dollars he acquired a 55,000 acre block of land in the northern end of the Sacramento Valley. There another baronial estate was presently in the making — and again California journalists marshaled their superlatives to describe it. Grapevines to the number of 2,800,000 were planted in a single 3,500-acre block, " incomparably the largest vineyard in the world." Wineries were built, extensive and complicated irrigation systems were installed; the town of Vina came into being.

It was the plan eventually to extend the vineyard to such epic size that a man might start walking at daybreak at the beginning of one of the rows and be overtaken by night before he reached its end. Stanford was to supply the Western world with wines of choicer quality than the best Europe could provide, and the descendants of the group of French vintners imported to bring about this marvel today lend an unexpected Gallic atmosphere to several valley communities north of Sacramento. These, and the ruined wineries, and a few thousand acres of stumps of dead grapevines, are the only present remainders of this grandiose scheme. For soil and climate refused to co-operate and the wines of France were not supplanted.

During the years Stanford was conducting his Vina experiment he had no doubt of ultimate success. His chief concern was not that of finding a market for his products but of convincing the public that the enterprise had a higher purpose than that of producing intoxicating beverages. His intention was to make the ranch's chief product, Vina brandy, of such quality that it would be used exclusively for medicinal purposes. To this end, the expatriate Frenchmen toiled in August temperatures such as they had never known in their native foothills, trying to practice an ancient craft in an alien environment. Later, oak casks were shipped to San Francisco and stowed as ballast in the holds of the grain-carrying clipper ships. There they remained five years, the brandy aging to the accompaniment of a gentle agitation provided by the seven seas.

The scientific and æsthetic implications of the Vina experiment were, however, lost on the public. To thousands of citizens a distiller was a distiller, however he might disguise his nefarious trade. For by the '80s the battle on the demon rum had already reached a stage where the outcome might have been forecast. The disapproval of alcohol's enemies was seldom merely theoretical. In 1892 Llewellyn Bixby, landowner and pioneer citizen of southern California, looked about for a suitable school at which his daughter might complete her education. Stanford University was then newly opened and the California journals had emphasized that its faculty was as brilliant as any in America. But the fact was indisputable that its founder not only bred racehorses but also distilled intoxicants, and Sarah Bixby was sent east to Wellesley.

5

THE VINA farm had hardly passed its experimental stages when Stanford's main interest again shifted, this time to the most spectacular enterprise of all.

For nearly twenty years after their marriage the Stanfords had remained childless. Leland Jr. was born at Sacramento in May 1868 and for the next fifteen years the child's welfare was a determining factor in every decision his parents made. The family moved to San Francisco in 1874 partly so that he might not grow up in the provincial atmosphere of a valley town; the Nob Hill house was planned on an elaborate scale because his father and mother expected that some day he would dispense hospitality there as one of the Coast's leaders of industry and finance. Even the purchase of the Vina ranch was influenced by the thought that its 55,000 acres would give the active boy room for exercise and be beneficial to his health.

He grew to be a normal youth, quiet by nature and of a studious turn of mind. In due time, of course, he was expected to succeed his father in the management of the Stanford properties, and his training was planned with that in mind.

That his responsibilities would be heavy Stanford himself well knew, for he had not found his millions an un-
mixed blessing. " It is pleasant to be rich," he told a
Washington reporter at one of his hesitant interviews.
" But the advantages of wealth are greatly exaggerated . . . I do not clearly see that a man who can buy
anything that he fancies is any better off than the man
who can buy what he actually wants. He can easily gratify
his whimsies, to be sure; but there are some positive dis-
advantages." One disadvantage was the constant demand
of those who, for reasons good or bad, or for no reasons
at all, wanted some of the Stanford cash. " My wife and I
are worried almost to death by beggars, between whom
it is very difficult to discriminate. Most of them are regular ' rounders,' who solicit, implore, entreat, and command
that there shall be given them at once certain stipulated
sums of money. Of course there is no pleasure in being
thus tormented. . . . A man's annoyances increase with
his wealth."

This was a condition from which Leland in later life
could not well be protected. There were other matters,
however, from which he might be shielded by his parents'
foresight. Of the elder Stanford the interview quoted
above stated: " In the first place, the life he was compelled
to lead in order to accumulate wealth probably prevented
that cultivation of taste for art, music, and letters which
is essential to the highest enjoyment. . . ." There had
been regrettable deficiencies in Stanford's education. Despite the presence of his portrait in the chapel at Cazenovia
Seminary, his grammar was never faultless, and such

blemishes as " rout " (for " route "), " tussell," " Baron Rothschchild," and " Black Mail " sprinkled such of his letters as did not pass through the hands of a secretary. Moreover, he knew no foreign languages, and he discovered belatedly that his taste in art was not to be relied on.

Young Leland was to be spared all this; he was to be trained from childhood to be more than a " mere businessman." Accordingly, at an age when he had scarcely graduated from the nursery, he was studying music, taking dancing lessons, conjugating French verbs, and, in the art gallery of the Nob Hill house, examining under the guidance of his tutor such Stanford canvases as Leloir's " A Christian Martyr Led to the Arena." In 1876, when he was eight, his parents took him to Philadelphia so that his mind might be broadened by a study of the arts and crafts assembled in the galleries of the Centennial Exposition. While Stanford and his wife bought furniture and bric-a-brac for the California Street house, Leland's interest focused on wood-carving. He carried a set of tools back to San Francisco. Some months later his parents, delighted at this early flowering of artistic talent, exhibited a group of his carvings at the annual Mechanics' Fair.

At eleven, Leland was deemed old enough to benefit by foreign travel. From 1879 to 1881 the boy and his parents moved here and there over England and the Continent. Stanford and his wife took the cure at various spas, gratified their whims for jewels and paintings, had their portraits done by currently fashionable artists, and followed the pattern of conduct expected of rich and conservative Americans on the Continent. Leland meantime continued his studies, squired his mother when the Governor was absent on business trips to America, visited galleries, improved his accent under " the best teachers money could hire," and began the formation of his celebrated " museum."

The boy's passion for collecting antique coins and medals, fragments of pottery and sculpture, was coupled with an eagerness to study the periods that had produced them, and some natural taste in their selection. Had he lived, it is not unlikely that the bulk of the Stanford fortune might eventually have been invested in an intelligently selected collection of antique art; in its field it might have been comparable to another institution created by Central Pacific profits, the Huntington Library. Before Leland was fifteen, his collection filled three rooms on the top floor of the California Street house; this, with the additions made during his last trip to Europe and the Near East, eventually found its way into the Stanford University museum, where it may be seen today — the naïve and promising beginnings of what might have been a life enthusiasm.

Leland was already preparing for college when he returned to San Francisco in 1882. That fall he presided for the first time as host at the Nob Hill house, entertaining groups of boys and girls from San Francisco's eligible families in the big downstairs ballroom. The parties were in the nature of a farewell; the family soon returned to New York, where Leland studied for the entrance examinations to Harvard. His parents, meantime, unwilling to be separated from him by the width of the continent during the coming four years, had leased a house on Fifth Avenue and prepared to make that their headquarters. It was never occupied. Stanford's health gave concern and doctors advised a water-cure in Bavaria. Early in 1883 the three crossed the Atlantic again, spent the summer in Germany and France, and in November started for Athens. There, during December and January, Leland made notable additions to his collection and cemented his devotion to the antique. But the weather continued bad and the boy became ill. The three sailed for Naples in February, continued on to Rome. Then, as Leland grew sick in earnest, they hurried to Florence, in the hope that the climate would be beneficial.

There his persistent fever was diagnosed as typhoid. Physicians from Paris and Rome were summoned to his room in the Hotel Bristol. For some days, while blinds were drawn over the windows facing the Arno and the street outside was covered with straw to deaden sounds of traffic, the issue remained in doubt. But the methods of treatment — including a periodical wrapping of the patient in sheets dipped in ice-water — proved ineffectual, and on March 13, 1884 the youth died. He was not yet sixteen.

In later years Mrs. Stanford several times revisited Florence. Not until nearly two decades later did she bring herself to drive down the Via Ponte Carraia and to glance briefly at the windows behind which the losing battle had been fought. In 1907 a group of Stanford students caused a memorial plaque to be set into the wall of the hotel, where it has since been read by thousands of uncomprehending natives and tourists.

6

In Paris, five weeks after Leland's death, his father and mother rewrote their wills to provide for the endowment of a memorial to their son.

What form the memorial was to take was not at once determined. For a time the Stanfords considered founding a " museum of artistic and natural curiosities," thereby completing what the boy had tentatively begun. How the decision to found a university was reached is not definitely known; several individuals later claimed the honor of having first suggested it. One theory, frequently advanced, held that the determining impulse was not of human but of divine origin. The revelation was said to have been made soon after the Stanfords' return to America in the spring of 1884; the intermediary was Maud Lord Drake, a notable figure in the wave of spiritualism then sweeping the country. The Stanfords, accompanying General and Mrs. Grant to one of the medium's séances at Washington, had been impressed by the supernatural powers of the priestess. Other visits had followed, and the two were soon among her disciples. Stanford's intention to found a memorial college in California was made public at that time, and at once the belief became widespread that the project was the result of instructions received during one of Mrs. Drake's séances.

The spiritualists were solidly behind the theory and did much to spread it abroad. They succeeded in stirring up a lively controversy and in keeping it alive for half a dozen years. Unfortunately for the thousands who were convinced of the supernatural origin of the new university, however, Mrs. Drake was presently detected in the practice of fraud at one of her table-tipping séances, and the divine hypothesis began to collapse. It received its final blow when Mrs. Stanford in 1892 publicly repudiated the theory of supernatural guidance — a statement thankfully received by members of the Stanford faculty, already lecturing in the new halls.

During the early stages of the project the Stanfords had intended establishing, not a university, but a technical school — a decision probably influenced by Stanford's admiration for mechanical ingenuity in any form. This enthusiasm was well known to his friends and was often commented on. Examples of it are numerous. It is known that he once spent half a day in rapt contemplation of a medieval catapult in a Paris museum. His visits to Europe's historic castles were often inconveniently prolonged while he inspected the mechanism of drawbridges and studied the methods by which moats were filled and drained. His insistence, in the late '6os, that Engineer Strobridge employ newfangled gadgets called compressed air drills to pierce the Central Pacific's Summit Tunnel precipitated a quarrel that almost split the partnership. Much later, when a San Francisco photographer named

Muybridge proposed photographing one of Stanford's racehorses with a battery of cameras lined up beside the track, Stanford willingly financed the experiment. He also financed the publication of Muybridge's book, *The Horse in Motion,* and his name thereby became permanently linked with the beginnings of the yet unborn motion-picture industry. Finally, in the art gallery of his California Street house Stanford's chief pleasure was to show guests, not his collection of canvases by the period's most admired artists, but his orchestrion. The latter was a complete orchestra, mechanically operated, housed in a handsome cabinet that reached the ceiling. After visitors had listened to the orchestrion, their host took pleasure in demonstrating yet another technological marvel: no less than a collection of mechanical birds. These, perched on the branches of potted trees in the art gallery, were operated by compressed air. When the Governor touched a concealed button they startlingly opened their tin beaks and sang.

While plans for the memorial were still in the embryo stage Stanford considered making his technical school a part of the already functioning state university at Berkeley. Accordingly, he had the Governor appoint him to the university's board of regents. But the state legislature unexpectedly refused to confirm the appointment, as was necessary. Stanford had already attended several meetings of the board, and the rebuff was a severe blow to his dignity. Of course it ended all possibility of joining forces with the Berkeley institution.

Details of the Leland Stanford Junior University were

announced in the summer of 1886. In most quarters the project was regarded as a monumental piece of folly. California journals greeted it reverentially, but those of the East were skeptical. Stanford's plan to take a tract of farmland in a sparsely settled state and by the expenditure of five million dollars to convert it into a world-renowned center of learning aroused little enthusiasm beyond the Rockies. The fact that the University of California after functioning for years had an enrollment of less than three hundred was taken as evidence that there was no need for another college less than forty miles distant. The prediction was made that for decades to come Stanford's professors would " lecture to empty benches in marble halls." One Eastern editorial writer stated that " there is about as much need for a new university in California as for an asylum of decayed sea captains in Switzerland." These confident forecasts were, of course, wrong. Less than a generation later, Stanford authorities were struggling to find a means of keeping the enrollment down to manageable size, and the Berkeley institution, swollen from 300 to 18,000 and reorganized on a quantity-production basis, was straining to absorb the ever increasing crowds that streamed through its gates.

But newspaper gibes about building marble palaces on his wheatfields and buying five million dollars' worth of intellectual center had no visible effect on Stanford. During the fall of 1886 his car shuttled over the network of Eastern railroads and in its rosewood-paneled drawing-room the founders perfected details of their memorial and interviewed the Eastern talent. At Baltimore the Johns

Hopkins University initiated them into the mysteries of research, and Massachusetts Institute of Technology and Cornell impressed Stanford anew with the value of the applied sciences — the latter so much so that its ex-president, Andrew D. White, was urged to come west and preside over the unfinished halls. At Cambridge they were momentarily taken aback when Charles Eliot Norton with habitual directness informed them that a university was an expensive hobby and that they must be prepared to spend every penny of the advertised five millions. " Mrs. Stanford looked grave," wrote Norton later. But the five millions were duly expended and eventually a great deal more.

One Saturday afternoon the Stanford car was shunted to a sidetrack and half the population of Bloomington, Indiana, hurried to the depot to stare at its curtained windows. At five the next morning the thirty-nine-year-old president of Indiana University, situated at Bloomington, returned from a speech-making trip. A breathless friend appeared out of the darkness and announced that the " Governor of California " was at the village hotel and wished to see him. The meeting took place; Stanford and his wife described the stone quadrangle taking shape on the Palo Alto meadow and announced that their joint estate, the bulk of which was eventually to go toward the university's endowment, was valued at thirty million dollars. Phrases of the interview have been preserved: in his hesitant speech the founder stated that it was to be a university of the highest order, where students were to be trained for usefulness in life. It was to be a center of in-

vention and research, coeducational and interdenomina-
tional, and there was to be no tuition. Moreover, it was
to be free from political control from any source, and in
particular from meddling at the hands of the California
legislature.

The emolument of its president was to be ten thousand
dollars a year. Stanford had often paid far more for a
likely racehorse, but the sum was a staggering one to the
young man to whom the job was offered. David Starr
Jordan hurried home for consultation with his wife, and
Mrs. Stanford and her secretary set off to attend the
Sunday morning services at a local church. The chronicles
of Bloomington record that she dropped five dollars in
gold on the collection plate and took occasion, when the
student preacher hurried up to inquire if a mistake had
been made, to tell him that his vengeful, Old Testament
God was unlike the gentle deity of her acquaintance. How
Stanford spent the morning is not recorded.

Meantime Dr. Jordan had decided " with some enthusiasm " that he would become the first president of the new
university. On a June morning a year later, with an infant
son on one arm and three pieces of baggage in the other,
he stepped from the train at Menlo Park. The democratic
arrival caused an acquaintance, waiting with Stanford in
the latter's carriage, to remark that he guessed the newcomer would " stay hitched." Jordan, as it proved, stayed
hitched for nearly four decades.

On a hot afternoon in October 1889 the university for-
mally opened its doors. From a platform at one end of the
quadrangle, Stanford, with Jordan holding an umbrella

187

over his head, slowly read an address to 415 prospective students (a youth from Oregon, one Herbert Hoover, among them) and to a dense crowd of visitors.

The Coast's newest educational plant began to function. It functioned with reasonable smoothness for twenty months. Then, on June 20, 1893, Stanford unexpectedly died, and hidden weaknesses came to light that threatened to bring its brief history to a close.

7

THE BEGINNING of the trouble extended far back to the early days of the Central Pacific. For always behind the university and the racehorses, vineyards and mansions of the spacious Stanford setting was the railroad, source of the dollars that made the rest possible. And behind the railroad, with competent fingers on all its regulating wires, was the cynical and frigid person of Collis Huntington. It was one of fate's ironies that Stanford's gilded career should have been shaped in every important phase by the hand of his enemy; the cold New Englander was ever the ghost at the Governor's banquet.

Stanford's later difficulties were, however, largely of his own making. His grandiose activities, no less than his vanity, had led him into extravagances that even his quarter share of the huge railroad profits could not bear. The intervention of his partners had several times been necessary to extricate him from financial tangles. A letter to

Huntington from the company's financial manager, David Colton, reveals that Stanford's ability as a money-spender was well developed as early as 1877. On January 4, 1878 Colton listed the amounts the four partners had drawn from the treasury for their personal use since August 1 of the preceding year. Huntington had withdrawn $57,000, Crocker $31,000, frugal Mark Hopkins but $800; Stanford, however, had taken out $276,000.

But the chief reason for the later difficulties was merely that Stanford became unnecessary in Huntington's scheme of things and with characteristic directness the latter proceeded to lighten ship by dropping him over the side. For Stanford's preoccupation with matters unrelated to the railroad Huntington had neither understanding nor patience. Reserved and unsocial by habit, he was aroused to uncomprehending contempt by his partner's liking for display and for the applause of the mob.

In the early days of the road, however, Huntington had been willing to forward his partner's ambition to shine in public, and from the first Stanford was the company's representative before the people. He became president when the project was still a paper railroad of dubious future, and he continued to hold the office for twenty-eight years. That he was more or less a figurehead was recognized by a few from the beginning, but for years it was a part of company policy to keep the fact from the public. When Stanford became a candidate for Governor in 1862 he received, of course, the support of all his partners. His election was a valuable asset to the new corporation, for to have its president in the Governor's chair gave the project a semi-official air. The benefits were enhanced by the fact that Stanford's term covered the years from 1862 to 1864, when the war fever enhanced loyalties and stilled opposition. Moreover, the prestige remained long after he had left office, for hardly had the armies been disbanded when the powerful Civil War tradition began to take shape and to be molded, in California as elsewhere, into an effective political weapon.

Through the '70s and early '80s the fact that California's War Governor was its president continued to be helpful to the Central Pacific. Later, when the country, after a thorough trial, lost faith in the integrity of Civil War reputations, Stanford's political reputation faded rapidly. Perhaps it was in the hope of regaining some of his lost prestige that he re-entered politics in 1885, and the railroad-controlled legislature sent him to the Senate.

Huntington, who had expected his friend Aaron Sargent to be made Senator and who had obtained Stanford's promise to support Sargent's candidacy, presently learned that Stanford was himself seeking the office. This became, and remained, the chief source of Huntington's enmity, but there were other factors.

By the middle '80s the time was drawing near when the government's thirty-year bonds, loaned the company to help build the road, were to mature. Huntington for years had been laying plans to force cancellation (or at worst a drastic scaling down) of the huge debt, on the grounds of the Central Pacific's extreme poverty.

Stanford's spectacular extravagances were, of course, frequently embarrassing to the " poverty lobby " Huntington was maintaining at Washington. On one occasion the question of debt cancellation was being argued before Congress, and Huntington's lobby was functioning furiously to convince the lawmakers that the railroad and all connected with it were in abject poverty. Stanford, never oversensitive to the warnings of expediency, chose that particular time to buy his wife a hundred-thousand-dollar diamond necklace — a transaction that was recorded, with appropriate editorial comment, by newspapers from coast to coast. The building and endowment of the university — Huntington habitually called it " Stanford's circus " — seemed to him another particularly ill-timed piece of folly, and Stanford's humane announcement that " the children of California will be my children " left him cold.

To finance the building of his university, Stanford spent all his available cash and in addition borrowed large sums on short-term notes, which he expected to meet with an anticipated division of railroad profits. But shortly before the payment was to be made, Huntington, who knew of his partner's predicament, informed him that no profits were to be distributed, blandly explaining that the money had been " loaned out." The only explanation Stanford ever received was that " it helped the standing of the railroad to have the money out at interest." But the transaction was far from helping Stanford's own standing.

Other factors complicated the situation. The business depression of the early '90s decreased the value and negotiability of Stanford's railroad securities; the world's greatest vineyard (the upkeep of which cost five hundred dollars a day) had proved a failure so far as profits were concerned, and the stock-farm and mansions and, above all, the university made increasingly heavy demands on his involved and shrunken fortune.

Stanford's last months were given over to uneasy efforts to find a way out of his difficulties. During that period Timothy Hopkins chanced to call at the Palo Alto house. Stanford announced that he had been revising his will and wished Hopkins to witness it. With Hopkins and Mrs. Stanford as audience, he proceeded to read the document. As he named a long list of cash bequests to relatives and friends, Mrs. Stanford looked increasingly grave. When he had finished, she ventured a mild protest:

" But, Leland, you know times have been bad. Don't you think you are being too liberal to some of these people? "

Her husband smiled a bit grimly. " They won't think I'm so liberal," he announced, " when they come to collect."

He succeeded in staving off a financial crash, but only because of the drastic intervention of fate, and the debacle followed soon after his death.

8

THE NEXT few years saw a curious drama played on the new campus at Palo Alto.

Out of the confusion emerged the strong-willed and competent figure of the widow, Jane Lathrop Stanford. While her husband lived, Mrs. Stanford had followed tradition by remaining discreetly in the background, contenting herself with overseeing the domestic machinery and with minor charitable and religious duties. Her husband's death, however, projected her into the midst of a complicated situation. The estate was immediately tied up by lawsuits, the most important of which was one filed by the federal government attaching the assets until the question of the railroad's $57,000,000 debt was settled. Meantime, expenses went on. The university, then in full operation, was requiring an unexpectedly large sum to finance, and the upkeep of various other Stanford properties raised the monthly expenses to impressive heights. The Palo Alto farm alone had 150 employees and its annual operating cost was close to $250,000.

Stanford's death threw his involved estate into the probate court. Outstanding debts, and gifts provided in the will, reached a total of $18,000,000. It was necessary that debts be satisfied before distribution of the remainder of the estate could begin. No capital and no adequate revenue were available, and the university entered a period of short rations. The force of Charles Eliot Norton's warning that a university is an expensive hobby was driven home. Expenses were slashed and a tuition charge levied on the students. Hundreds of racehorses were sold from the inactive stock-farm. The immense Vina ranch was summarily shut down, and its thousands of acres of young vines were left to parch beside dry irrigation ditches. In professors' contracts the stipulation as to salary was given a qualifying clause: " — or as much of this sum as may be available."

A sympathetic probate judge by stretching several points was able to provide relief by ruling that the president and instructors of the university might be classified as Mrs. Stanford's personal servants and their salaries included in her household allowance. The struggle went on. In the midst of the starvation period President Jordan received a dole of $1,200 from the court. He carried the canvas sack back to Palo Alto — the sum had been paid in twenty-dollar gold pieces — and set out to pay fifty dollars in back salary to each of twenty-four professors. But not one of the impoverished two dozen had change for twenty dollars and Jordan compromised by dispensing his windfall in alternate amounts of forty and sixty dollars.

The belief got abroad that the expense of the university (the salary roll was $15,000 a month) was jeopardizing the interests of the estate's creditors and there were demands that the college shut down until a settlement was reached. Huntington expressed his remedy concisely: "Close the circus." When this suggestion was disregarded, he had another card to play. The time when the railroad's debt to the government would reach maturity was almost at hand, and the question of to what extent the Big Four was liable must soon be decided. The Hopkins and Crocker estates had already been distributed; Stanford's was still intact. If the matter could be brought up at once, the Stanford estate — and not Huntington — would be forced to bear the expense of contesting it. The question was duly brought up. The government served an injunction preventing distribution until the Stanford share of the debt — a sum in excess of $14,000,000 — became due and was paid. An interested spectator, Huntington watched the legal battle take its leisurely way through the District Court, the Circuit Court of Appeals, and finally the Supreme Court. The decision was favorable to the Stanford estate. It was both favorable and inexpensive to Huntington.

But the litigation consumed many months and the Stanford interests continued to tighten belts. The widow took a leading part. Economy became a game into which she entered willingly, even with enthusiasm. All but two or three of her household servants were dismissed. She ordered work stopped on the park-like grounds surrounding the Palo Alto house, in the landscaping of which dozens of gardeners had been engaged for years. Her eagerness to shave expenses, to stretch every dollar to its limit, carried her to surprising lengths. Household accounts were closely scrutinized and all but absolutely essential items were lopped off. One day a San Francisco friend was astonished to see the old lady in her flowing black weeds laboriously climbing a hill to make an afternoon call. She hurried to the door and admitted the visitor, her face expressing her surprise. " My dear," said Mrs. Stanford, " you *know* I can't afford a carriage."

Soon after Stanford's death the widow decided to close their Washington residence, the Brady house at Seventeenth and I streets. Early in 1894 she set off for the capital to oversee the removal of the furniture. She left with $500, determined that this should cover the expenses of the trip. She made the journey in her private car, paying nothing for transportation, since every railroad in the country granted her passes as long as she lived. During her stay in Washington she lived in the car, thereby saving hotel bills. She returned triumphantly to Palo Alto with $340 still unexpended.

There were times when despite such feats of personal economy the question of whether the university could be kept open remained in the balance. One memory of the period revolves about Mrs. Stanford's week-end visits to Palo Alto from San Francisco. At a certain point on the railroad below Menlo Park the campus first became visible, and Mrs. Stanford each week gazed anxiously from the window for a glimpse of the tall smokestack of the university's heating plant. If smoke was issuing from its top she knew the coal was holding out, that classes were in session, and the university still functioning.

Those who followed the widow's career during that period inevitably compared her to Queen Victoria. The indomitable young Widow of Windsor, in her rustling black silk, forcing to completion every one of Albert's projects, had her counterpart almost half a century later in this aged and invincible daughter of an Albany merchant. The comparison extended well beyond the externals of physical likeness, for the two women were similar in temperament, and each within her own sphere chanced to be placed in a position to exercise unrestricted power.

It was natural that Jane Stanford should herself see a similarity between her plight and that of the bereaved Queen, and that her letters should rather closely follow Victoria's epistolary style. " Your poor Queen's mind is constantly overtaxed " is paralleled in scores of messages from Mrs. Stanford to her personal Lord M., Dr. Jordan. ". . . It exhausts my ingenuity and resources to such an extent that had I not the University so close to my heart I would relieve myself from the enormous burden and take rest and recreation for the next year." Victoria's martyrdom, the wistful pleasure of sacrifice, permeated the wooden mansion on Nob Hill as thickly as it had ever hung over the halls of Windsor. " Gladly would I live on bread and water to do this, my part." " Every dollar I can rightly call mine is sacredly laid on the altar of my love for the University, and this it shall ever be." And again: " I could lay down my life for the University. Not for any pride in its perpetuating the name of our dear son and ourselves, its founders, but for the sincere hope I cherish in its sending forth to the world grand men and women who will aid in developing the best there is to be found in human nature."

Her physical resemblance to Victoria became to her mind ample compensation for the fact that she was not beautiful. A short figure with an inclination to stoutness, a florid complexion, and large, slightly protruding eyes — like Victoria's — these are remembered characteristics. She consciously made the exalted old lady of Buckingham Palace her model both in statesmanship and deportment, following her lead even in the choice of her clothing and in her stiff, erect bearing.

In her last years Mrs. Stanford was not always content to admire her model from afar. She had caught glimpses of the Queen on earlier visits to England, but when the date of Victoria's Jubilee approached, she was determined to be present. She did not go merely as a sightseer, however, for the journey had a serious purpose: she had decided to sell her jewelry in order to buy books for the university library. So, early in 1897, the determined figure of the lesser martyr set off for the shrine of the greater, her bag of jewels tightly clutched in her hand. Not once did the old lady let them out of her sight; she considered both insurance premiums and safe-deposit fees excessive and so became her own watchman.

To those who remained behind in the West, her pilgrimage seemed a morality play come to life. The sentimental '90s followed the unfolding drama with damp enthusiasm, and the California widow descending on London in her suppliant's role, proffering her bag of gems to the guests at Victoria's glittering celebration, became a symbol of Western womanhood. The fact that her mission was unsuccessful, that none of the assembled notables would pay the prices she had set on her treasures, failed to spoil the picture. The interested watchers on the Coast could see no reason why even a pilgrimage should not be conducted on a business-like basis. The suppliant returned to Palo Alto with only a few minor pieces of her collection sold. She turned the remainder over to the university's board of trustees, to be disposed of when the market improved.

But the old lady did not allow this business disappointment to spoil her pleasure in the Jubilee. The latter's high point was, of course, June 22, the sixtieth anniversary of Victoria's ascent to the throne. Mrs. Stanford was up before daylight. By seven she was driving through the decorated streets, following the route the Queen herself would presently take. The drive ended at a house on Fleet Street, where a second-floor room had been leased for the day. Before its windows Victoria would pass on her way to St. Paul's. A long wait ensued, but for once the California widow was not impatient. This was Jane Stanford's opportunity to view her admired model at close range and she was determined that there be no errors. Nor were her expectations disappointed. The head of the parade appeared, passed down Fleet Street to Ludgate Circus, then up the hill to St. Paul's. By the time Victoria came into view, the first sections were just reaching the cathedral. Congestion ahead caused those farther back to slow down, then to stop. By great good luck, the royal carriage halted directly opposite the Fleet Street windows. Victoria lowered her parasol, looked about. Her eyes reached the Stanford window; for an electric moment they rested on the eager face of the California widow. Her Majesty bowed perceptibly and her gaze traveled on. Mrs. Stanford returned the salutation and in addition blew a kiss in the direction of the royal carriage, which had already started forward and in a moment was out of sight.

Mrs. Stanford tarried two weeks longer in London, but the high light of her visit remained that dramatic, face-to-face encounter. She was never able to accomplish that again, although she two years later spent some weeks in close proximity to the Queen. Victoria was at Windsor and Mrs. Stanford engaged rooms at the White Hart Inn, the windows of which looked directly out upon the main gate of the castle. Throughout her stay she kept careful watch on the carriages that passed in and out; unfortunately, the Queen was ill and never once left the grounds.

But her vigil was not entirely in vain, for during her stay Mrs. Stanford received an invitation to one of the garden parties at Windsor. There she was presented to Victoria's daughter-in-law and to others of royal blood. But the aged Queen was visible only as a tiny figure in a white cap seated in an upper window, high above the scene. Of course there was no possibility of a further exchange of salutations. Jane Stanford strained her eyes at her remote counterpart, then walked, an erect, plump, tightly corseted figure, across the crowded east terrace, past the flowerbeds and statuary and the blaring military bands, and at last reached the quiet of her hotel room.

9

SHE thoroughly enjoyed the role of Lady Bountiful and she continued to play it, not always with restraint, as long as she lived. It became her habit to descend on relatives, many of whom she had not seen, or apparently thought of, for years, and to rearrange their affairs after her own ideas, all with the utmost kindliness and vigor.

Mostly the beneficiaries were grateful. In 1869, on her first visit east over the newly completed Central Pacific, she and Leland Jr. visited at her mother's house in Albany. After California the house seemed cold, particularly for Leland, then an infant. The visitor enlivened her stay by having a new heating system installed, topping off this gift with a shining brass rail for the front steps.

Hunting up relatives and the graves of admired forebears became a hobby of her later years. Once, on a midwinter trip to Norwich, Connecticut, she combined both errands. Upon arriving in the city, she learned that her ancestor, the Reverend John Lathrop (over whose grave she had planned to erect a monument) had been buried elsewhere. However, she discovered two distant cousins living in the neighborhood and these received her bounty instead. Before her visit ended she had made plans to take the elderly sisters abroad with her the following summer. They would engage a house on the Thames — not too far from Windsor. Perhaps on afternoon rides they might encounter still another old lady, one who bore a rather startling resemblance to Mrs. Stanford herself. Other matters intervened, however, and the Norwich cousins spent the summer at home.

Another of her pilgrimages took her to an upstate New York town to visit an aunt of whom she had not heard in years. The ancient lady was found to be living on a farm. The house was so unlike the farmhouses the Stanfords maintained in California that Mrs. Stanford saw another opportunity for helpfulness. She hurried back to the town, engaged a suite for her Aunt Marinda at the hotel, arranged to have her meals served in her rooms and for the payment of her monthly bills through the local bank. The rest of the afternoon was spent buying furniture and clothing for the pensioner. The next day the latter was informed of her good luck — and flatly refused to move to town. The philanthropist sent her gifts out to the farm-house, settled a monthly pension on the rebel, and returned to New York.

Clergymen shared with relatives the pleasures of her bounty. Always deeply religious, Mrs. Stanford nonetheless was able to regard the clergy with a realistic and sometimes critical eye. At no time did her faith in Christianity include a belief in the infallibility of its interpreters. But on the other hand she was an ardent churchgoer, one who could be depended on to contribute liberally when offerings were asked, and her support of any cause close to an admired pastor's heart was seldom withheld.

When her husband acquired the Palo Alto farm, one of her first concerns was to investigate the spiritual facilities of the near-by village of Menlo Park. She found its one tiny church badly equipped and in miserable repair, the communicants few, and the pastor and his family living in cramped quarters. Immediately she undertook another of her reforms. Paint and carpet and a new organ lent the structure attractions that brought wandering members back to the fold. Meantime a modest but comfortable cottage was mysteriously being built on a neighboring lot, furniture was moved in, and in due time the good news leaked out: this was to be the new parsonage. But the pastor proved unequal to the occasion; he committed the *faux pas* of insisting that certain changes be made in the house before he would move in. About that time, Mrs. Stanford began to doubt the soundness of the man's theology. Presently it was disclosed that he had been in the habit of going to San Francisco two days a

LELAND STANFORD JR.
from In Memoriam: Leland Stanford.
Courtesy of Edwin Grabhorn

THE STANFORD AND HOPKINS RESIDENCES, NOB HILL, SAN FRANCISCO

taken from Powell and Pine streets.

Courtesy of Edwin Grabhorn

week, where he had addressed curbstone crowds in advocacy of a redistribution of the national wealth. This time even the pleas of his wife (who appreciated philanthropy and abhorred Socialism) did not prevail and the new parsonage soon had another tenant.

To Mrs. Stanford this was but one of a series of disappointments. Another revolved about Dr. John Newman, a Methodist divine with leanings toward spiritualism, who visited the Stanfords at San Francisco not long after Leland Jr.'s death. Announcement of the foundation of the university had only recently been made, and it was assumed by many that it would be a religious school. Wires were more or less adroitly pulled by members of several denominations in the hope of placing the institution under the wing of their particular sect. The Washington medium, Mrs. Drake, had not yet been exposed, and although Stanford's ardor for spiritualism had cooled, his wife's interest was still keen.

Dr. Newman and his wife became guests at the California Street house and tactfully sought to have the new college designated a Methodist institution, with perhaps the Doctor himself as its president. When Stanford failed to warm to the proposal, Dr. Newman (whose wife habitually referred to him as Saint John) resorted to séances in the hope of having his recommendations endorsed by higher authority. The matter was brought to a climax when Mrs. Newman burst into the family sitting-room one evening and announced that Saint John was in receipt of a message from Heaven directing not only that the Stanford fortune be devoted to religious ends but that it be administered under Methodist auspices. The Stanfords were evidently not convinced of the authenticity of the command, however, for Saint John and his wife soon returned east.

A third major disappointment in her spiritual advisers occurred to Mrs. Stanford many years later. This revolved about the selection of a pastor for the Memorial Chapel at Stanford. The building and decoration of that structure, which was to be a memorial both to her husband and to her son, had for years been one of the widow's chief concerns. During her travels it was her habit to keep a sharp eye on the details of ecclesiastical architecture and decoration. If a window or a carved doorway or a mosaic floor or an altar painting seemed to her attractive, she had a sketch prepared, which was duly forwarded to the architect with instructions that he incorporate it in his plan. Her enthusiasm for such matters was mainly responsible for the fact that the Memorial Chapel remained under construction for years after other university buildings were completed. In the intricacy of its design and decoration, the structure far outshone anything else on the campus, or, for that matter, in all California. A contemporary account did no violence to the truth when it stated that " no artifice known to the stone-cutter, no secret of the artist who shapes bits of colored stone into rich patterns, no device of the ecclesiastical painter, but has contributed its part to this grand building, the spiritual temple of the students and their mentors."

Of course, Mrs. Stanford did not lightly undertake the

task of choosing a shepherd for this handsomely housed flock. After examining the records and credentials of many prospects, she eventually gave tentative approval to a certain Dr. Heber Newton. The chapel was dedicated early in 1903; Dr. Newton was duly installed in a house provided for him on the campus. Mrs. Stanford, considering the matter satisfactorily disposed of, prepared to set off on a trip abroad. But it was not long before doubts again assailed her. Dr. Newton was a man of advanced years and, as it developed, uncertain health. Moreover, a variety of things had happened that caused him distress. A trunkful of favorite sermons had been lost en route from his last pastorate. The furniture of his campus house was not completely satisfactory, and he several times wished that something might be done about the hymns. In his New England church he had been allowed the luxury of a well-trained — and well-paid — choir. The singing in the Memorial Chapel, while it was spirited and enthusiastic, was by students, and strictly amateur.

Never noted for her patience with complaining clergymen, the widow one afternoon stopped her carriage before the Newton cottage, listened to the Doctor's plea that he be allowed to bring out at least the soprano from his Eastern choir, then lost her temper and informed him that his services were no longer wanted.

Dr. Newton's dismissal caused a stir on the campus and the beginnings of a revolt. Faculty members signed petitions requesting that he be reinstated, asking each other meantime if their jobs too might not depend upon the whims of this strong-minded old lady. But she remained unshaken and Dr. Jordan smoothed the waters with characteristic tact.

After the banished cleric had returned east it began to be said that it was not the loss of his sermons or the lack of a trained soprano that had disconcerted and unnerved him; it was the church itself. The theory was that the chapel's lavish decorations and Oriental coloring had formed a background altogether unsuited to the lean and sinewy brand of salvation he had spent a lifetime teaching.

10

STANFORD's period of short rations finally ended, and as the century closed, the widow began to relax her close supervision over its affairs. In 1897 she deeded the San Francisco house to the university's board of trustees and received in return the right to occupy it as long as she lived. Six years later she took the final step of transferring to the trustees the executive control she had exercised for a decade. The period that followed was probably as happy as any of her life. She was by then well known wherever she went, and much of her time was spent in travel. From 1894 onward the university had been sending annual crops of graduates out into the world. Often during her travels some alumnus would appear at her hotel to pay his respects, much to the old lady's delight. On her last extended tour, while her steamer was lying at

Perth, on the west coast of Australia, she learned that a young engineer and his wife, both Stanford graduates, were due to arrive from India. At once the steamer was thrown into turmoil. Arrangements were made to hail the incoming vessel and to inform the couple that Mrs. Stanford wished to see them at once. Meantime she insisted that her trunks, which had been stowed in the hold, be brought to her stateroom so that she might select a suitable gown. She prevailed on the captain to delay the hour of sailing. But the India steamer was unaccountably behind schedule, her own ship could wait no longer, and Herbert Hoover and his bride missed a last opportunity to exchange greetings with the old lady.

Other graduates proved less elusive, and as time passed, reunions with " her boys " grew frequent. The university became internationally known; in foreign lands she was quite frequently received with official honors as its founder. On all her later travels she carried a supply of books made up of photographs of the university buildings. These she autographed and presented to those from whom she received official favors. The books were bound in several different styles (some in cloth, some in leather, a few handsomely gold-tooled) and she was therefore able to choose a binding that closely approximated the rank or importance of the recipient.

She was a tireless traveler at home as well as abroad. Her private car was then nearly thirty years old and its rosewood and plush sitting-room impressed visitors as curiously like a museum. But Mrs. Stanford found it comfortable and in it she annually spent many weeks shuttling between the two oceans or on shorter jaunts up and down the Pacific Coast. Her car was passed free over every major railroad in the country. On the lines controlled by the Southern Pacific she continued to receive many of the courtesies that had been accorded her husband during his lifetime. Such attentions were of course known to Huntington and approved by him, a circumstance that may have puzzled Mrs. Stanford, for she had long looked on Huntington not only as her husband's chief enemy but as a leader of the group that had tried to destroy the university — a sort of Satan in a black skull-cap.

This view of him persisted until the turn of the century. Then, on one of her last visits to New York, the old lady's secretary unexpectedly confronted Huntington at his Mills Building office with the news that Mrs. Stanford wished an appointment. Huntington was obviously astonished. He suggested that he stop off at Mrs. Stanford's hotel on his way home that evening. Informed that Mrs. Stanford wished to call on him, he fixed the hour at eleven the next morning. The secretary, present at the meeting, saw that Huntington had had an armchair moved into his barren office for the visitor, watched the two shake hands, and observed that the old lady's face was colorless as she said: " Mr. Huntington, I have come to make my peace with you." The latter took both her hands, had her sit down, mopped his brow, and ejaculated: " Well, I declare! " Clearly, here was a situation with which he did not know how to cope. His visitor went on firmly. They were both old. Soon they would join their group — they were then its only survivors. The time was past when they should bear grievances or hold unkind thoughts. Huntington said: " Of course! Of course! " and the onlooker thought she saw tears come into the eyes of these old people (both long past seventy) as they shook hands again and Mrs. Stanford went downstairs to her carriage.

In her California Street house one January evening in 1905 Mrs. Stanford poured a glass of mineral water from a jar that stood on a table beside her bed. After she had consumed about half the liquid she discovered that it had an unfamiliar, bitter taste. She called a servant, had her taste the water, and grew alarmed when the latter confirmed her suspicion that it contained a foreign substance. The next morning the residue in the jar was sent to a chemist for analysis. His report was sensational: the water contained strychnine.

Never unsuspicious by nature, the delusion that she was being persecuted had grown on her with age. She was promptly convinced that an attempt had been made to murder her. News of the incident reached the newspapers, and soon the entire Coast was reading of the sensational " Stanford poison plot." Police and reporters thronged the California Street house while servants were questioned and the big building searched from cellar to roof for " clues."

Meantime Mrs. Stanford had grown really ill, either from fear or from the effects of the poison. She was sent away to recuperate, and on her return found excitement still high and the house in a state of virtual siege. Police guards were stationed about it; servants were forbidden to leave, and only qualified persons could gain admittance. It was another of the newspaper-police investigations dear to San Francisco since its beginnings. The badly frightened old lady stayed a few days in a downtown hotel, read newspaper accounts of efforts to apprehend the criminal, and in active fear for her life fled by the next boat to Honolulu.

The excitement simmered down. No evidence was found to support the poison-plot theory, and police adopted a more prosaic explanation: that the jar had formerly contained cleaning fluid and had not been properly rinsed out. Newspapers turned their attention to other sensations, and the public had nearly forgotten the episode when a cablegram from Honolulu announced Mrs. Stanford's death.

There was an immediate revival of the theory that she had been murdered. A statement by her attending physicians that death had been due to natural causes was received in San Francisco with open skepticism. Stanford University authorities appointed a group of specialists to re-examine the evidence; they reported unanimously that she had died, not of strychnine poisoning, but of old age.

She had survived the illustrious Victoria by less than four years, her husband by thirteen, her son by twenty-one. Her body was returned to California and buried in the family mausoleum on the Stanford campus. Today students hurry past the structure and glance with unconcern at the high bronze doors. They speak of the sleeping three within as the Holy Family; this is tradition, however, not irreverence.

HUNTINGTON

"YOUNG MAN, YOU CAN'T
FOLLOW ME THROUGH LIFE BY THE
QUARTERS I HAVE DROPPED."

1

" A HARD and cheery old man, with no more soul than a shark." Thus, at the end of the century, Arthur McEwen greeted Huntington's last visit to San Francisco. The phrasing of the salute is worth attention: Huntington often had the grudging respect of his enemies. An unknown epigrammatist called him " scrupulously dishonest " and added that the old man's distaste for claiming virtues he neither had nor respected made him the Coast's least convincing hypocrite. In its story of his death the San Francisco *Examiner* remarked that he had always been " ruthless as a crocodile " and went on to state that he had met death as he had met other and earlier reverses: head-on. " Had he been a soldier," wrote C. C. Goodwin, once editor of the Virginia City *Enterprise,* " he would not have depended upon tactics . . . he . . . would have struck directly at the enemy's center." Goodman likened his methods to those of Mark Hanna. The public recognized a heroic quality in the old man's ruthlessness, and journalists who set out to revile him commonly lost heart after the first few paragraphs. There was an abundance

211

of ammunition but few vulnerable spots at which to aim. Ridicule and abuse slid off his broad, bent back as lightly as chaff. From the '60s until 1900 San Francisco's newspaper writers were as uninhibited as any in the country. Yet when they set out to flay Huntington they commonly made a bad job of it. They went through the motions, but their hearts were not in the task.

The reason is obvious. Methods of attack that had proved effective against others of the city's millionaires — and so lent spice to the game — were useless against the grim New Englander. Ridicule of his social ambitions invariably angered naïve, good-natured John W. Mackay. Huntington had no social ambitions. Attack Stanford's personal popularity from any angle and at once the dailies and weeklies under his control were spurred to furious counter-attacks. Huntington was not only indifferent to popularity, it was actually distasteful to him. Thin-lipped, dandified William Sharon, in most ways as frigid as Huntington himself, could be reached by well-aimed thrusts at his political aspirations. Huntington's letters to his red-haired confidant, Dave Colton, advertised his unyielding contempt for public offices and for those who held them. He was accused of hoarding dollars while men of less wealth were winning renown as philanthropists. He cheerfully admitted the charge. Philanthropy was no more attractive to his eyes than such kindred imbecilities as social climbing and a desire to sit in the Senate. When he astonished the West by contributing twenty-five thousand dollars to help beautify the bleak sandhills of San Francisco's new city park, he specified that the money be spent for an artificial waterfall. If one paid out cash and got nothing in return, logic demanded that it be spent for a useless purpose.

In a period when open-handedness was a primary ob-ligation of every rich man, Huntington took pains to spread his reputation as a penny-squeezer. " I'll never be remembered for the money I've given away," he once told a visitor to his New York office, almost certainly with the knowledge that he was understating the case. Years later a young civil engineer in the employ of the Central Pacific wrote: " He liked to have us think he was close in money matters," then went on to record his astonishment when, after a noontime meeting in a restaurant, the miser casu-ally paid for luncheons for five. Huntington's remark to a clerk at the Palace Hotel after he had found and cor-rected a twenty-five-cent overcharge in his bill was re-peated for decades, frequently by Huntington himself: " Young man, you can't follow me through life by the quarters I have dropped."

He once went so far as to admit: " While money-mak-ing is a good indication in a man and is evidence that he is a good man, it is not the highest quality in the world." This place was reserved for a related activity — that of saving it. Advice to the young was in the '80s and '90s a necessary part of any interview with any rich man. Hun-tington's prescription followed a fixed formula: work hard and save money. He reduced success to the ultimate in simplicity; put money in the bank. The trick was not in making it but in holding on to it. One of his few public speeches was addressed, in 1891, to the youth of the village of Westchester, New York, and his two minutes of wholesome advice led inevitably to this climax: " Learn to live on a little less than you earn and thus always have a balance in the bank." Save! Don't leave a trail of quarters dropped. Nothing else was of particular importance.

In business he was cold, crafty, hard, and frequently dishonest. But there were rumors that he had a softer side. Some professed to see a trace of sentiment in the fact that he named his private cars Oneonta I and Oneonta II after the New York town where he had spent his young manhood. In his last years he sometimes grew almost poetic when he recalled certain of his early exploits in wresting dollars from the reluctant palms of his elders, and he once reproved his two-hundred-pound stepson for shooting a bird.

There is no record that he ever wanted to reform anything or, except when personal interest was involved, to change anything. He had none of the qualities of the militantly good citizen. Social and civic consciousness were meaningless phrases; a man's responsibility was to himself. He was neither a democrat nor a snob. The man who worked hard and saved his money had his respect, whatever his station. A Negro porter in his Broad Street office bought and paid for a house out of his microscopic wages, and Huntington's pleasure in the feat was spontaneous and real. In the middle '70s the ex-policeman and small-town politician Dave Colton embroidered letters to his chief with occasional references to " our class " and " us moneyed men." Huntington's replies contained no such nonsense. Whatever stood in his way he fought

COLLIS P. HUNTINGTON
Photograph by Taber, San Francisco, about 1880.

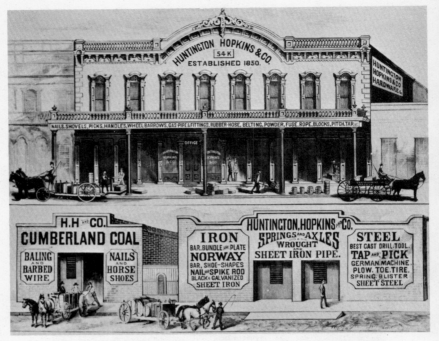

THE SACRAMENTO STORE OF HUNTINGTON,
HOPKINS & CO.

*formerly 54 K Street; now 220-228 K Street. The store extended through
to the next block; the lower part of the picture shows the L Street
frontage.*

Courtesy of the California State Library

stubbornly and with every evidence of pleasure; everything else was immaterial, a waste of time. This attitude, often mistaken for tolerance, was merely indifference. A plan to build a local railroad north of San Francisco was brought to his attention. " Let them do what they damn please," he wrote. " But see that they keep out of our way." This attitude was maintained with admirable consistency as long as he lived. Persons who kept out of his way might do what they damn pleased. But there was one exception. The man had dignity himself and the absurdities of other rich men brought forth brief and capable bursts of profanity. Office-holders, newspaper editors and publishers, men who wanted to reform something, these were expected to be mountebanks; one could tolerate that. But a man who had made — and kept — twenty million dollars should avoid behaving like a circus clown. He shouldn't " paint himself red and climb a pole."

To the end, Huntington refrained from pole-climbing, but as he advanced into the seventies he allowed himself certain frivolities. In 1899 when he arrived for what was to prove his last visit to the Coast, reporters met his private car at Oakland Mole and accompanied the old man across the bay. Back at their offices, one reported him " as bald as the American Eagle on our dollar, and as white as one just minted " — but still as keen as a man of fifty. He was likened to Atlas, " holding up, controlling and guarding the mighty enterprise that he and his partners had created, after all his first associates had died, and he himself was an old man. . . ." There was no lack of metaphors. He was a lordly oak, towering above the forest of ordinary men. " As the first forest melted away and a new one of different species succeeded, this oak still stood; warded off all storms that were hurled against it; turned aside the damp and the frost; waved its arms in the face of the hurricane; beat back decay; healed its own wounds, sheltered its own eagles. . . ."

Not only old age, but the loss of his hair caused him annoyance. Sensitiveness over the glistening expanse of his great domed scalp was responsible for his familiar black skullcap and for the fact, often mistaken for arrogance, that his hat usually remained on his head when good manners dictated that it should be removed. On the last visit to San Francisco he was persuaded to pose for a photograph by William Keith and again the hat was not removed.

That portrait deserves a passing word. Keith's fame as the " California Turner " was then at its height; to have one of his dim meadows in the parlor was as much a badge of social consequence as a summer at Del Monte. Purchasing a Keith landscape was no sordid business transaction; those who had experienced it recalled unsmilingly a young woman writer's remark that " to visit the Master's studio is to step into the anteroom of God." God's anteroom had black velvet curtains across one end, before which patrons sat while on the other side the Master superintended the placing and lighting of his painting. He then appeared, issued a quite unnecessary command for silence, and the curtains parted in the middle and moved slowly back. After this prologue to refuse to buy, or to haggle over the stiff prices, required more courage than most of his visitors could summon.

Keith's photograph of Huntington — perhaps it was preliminary to a portrait that was never painted — was several times published after its subject's death a few months later. It is that of a tired old man, stubbornly wearing his broad-brimmed hat, his trimmed mustache and short beard snow-white. The pose of his head and the expression of his eyes are characteristic; he is looking, attentive and watchful, straight ahead. His heavy shoulders are bent. Perhaps it was cold in the velvet-hung studio, for the old man had kept on not only his hat but his black overcoat, a panel of satin in its lapel catching a high light. A worn, austere figure, all black and white, against a somber background, with but one touch of frivolity: the wrinkled hand on the chair-arm has a narrow gold ring on its smallest finger.

But this Keith photograph belonged definitely to Huntington's later period, after old age had done its best to reduce him to the common level of decrepit rich men. Looking at it, much of the nonsense of his last years becomes credible; his garrulous interviews to the press, his collections of books and paintings and French furniture, his box at the Metropolitan. This tidy, benign old gentleman might have been a United States senator, or a retired grocer or clergyman living on a pension. The journalist who invented the "man of oak" simile had certainly never seen this portrait.

Another of the few photographs he permitted to reach

the public is more typical. Taken some years earlier, it has no suggestion of a bulldog with its teeth drawn. Huntington there is hunched over the littered desk of his New York office, a broad, heavy, static figure, the skull-cap close down to his ears. This was his normal environment, without velvet curtains: plain oak table, walls bare except for a framed photograph behind his chair, of the Newport News shipyards. The room was perhaps twelve feet square. It might have been the station-master's office in any village along the eleven thousand miles of railroad under his control.

The simplicity of his seventh-floor office in the Mills Building in New York reflected a lifelong dislike for elaborate settings in business — for what a later age termed " front." As far back as 1862 one of his early acts as a railroad man had been to reject a plan for an office structure for the yet unbuilt Central Pacific. He had glanced once at the drawing, then turned the sheet over, sketched a building that was described as " a slightly over-sized tool-house," and stubbornly refused to approve any other. A dozen years later, when work began on the new San Francisco headquarters at Fourth and Townsend streets, appointments of the private dining-room and of the executives' offices were described as " worthy of an exclusive club." Huntington reached the Coast in time to prevent such folly and on its completion the structure was found to have all the devitalizing luxuries of a warehouse.

While he lived, the railroads under his control had no part in the business of pampering the traveling public. Rolling stock and roadbed must be kept in operating condition and it was desirable that leaks in the roofs of freight-sheds be promptly repaired. But railroad stations were utilitarian structures; he saw no point in making them look like Gothic cathedrals or Roman baths, and until after his death no Central or Southern Pacific station bore any such resemblance. In hundreds of towns and cities of the West the original barren sheds persisted from decade to decade, their rotting boards re-covered at intervals with mustard-yellow paint of an unvarying shade, notable examples of unmitigated ugliness. " Mr. Huntington's views on architecture," wrote Willis Polk in the middle '90s, " would shame a Digger Indian."

Curiously, when in later years he came to select the settings for his leisure hours, his taste ran to the extreme of over-elaboration. Both his New York and San Francisco houses were crowded with French furniture and decorations of the most ornate and fragile design. A generation after his death a roomful of carved desks, marquetry cabinets and sideboards, satin-covered chairs and sofas and love-seats was exhibited in a San Francisco museum. Sunday afternoon visitors regarded the one-time owner's statue on an adjacent pedestal and wondered vocally that these fragile sticks had withstood the weight of his massive haunches.

2

THE RAILROAD partnership had not been in force three months before Huntington began to be referred to as the

brains of the group. With this opinion he was not inclined to quarrel, but what he most admired in himself
was his ability to make an investment earn a profit.
Money so earned was money created; the man who built
up a paying business enriched not only himself but the
world. In his old age he liked to compare his methods
with those of Jay Gould, picturing himself as the practical
railroad man and Gould as the speculator. He once told
his secretary, George Miles: " I wouldn't go into the stock
market against Gould, for he would whip me at that game.
That is his business. When it comes to building and
operating railroads in the most efficient and economical
way, I can beat him, for that is my business."

Yet beginning with Theodore Judah, dozens of his
critics have stated definitely that he was not a railroad
man, notwithstanding the fact that he died controlling
more miles of railroad than any man before him in history.
What was meant was that while railroads were good for
Huntington, Huntington was not good for railroads. He
entered the transportation business direct from a Sacramento hardware store, and the shopkeeper's viewpoint
shaped all his subsequent actions. To him a railroad was
merchandise in exactly the same sense as were a dozen
shovels or a keg of nails. In Sacramento he and Mark
Hopkins once managed to corner the supply of blasting-
powder and the coup netted them thousands of dollars.
Easy money! Huntington had not been in the railroad
business a week before he was planning similar exploits:
a corner on the freight and passenger business between

Sacramento and Nevada. Later the plan was enormously broadened. It became a scheme to control the traffic of the entire Pacific Coast. In his K Street store he had been in the habit of charging as much as he could get. What he asked for an article was determined not by what it had cost him but by how badly the customer wanted it. That was the way prices were fixed in California through the '50s; it was the way Huntington operated his railroad system as late as 1900. He was not disturbed when shouts of indignation greeted the Big Four's admission that they fixed tariffs on the basis of all the public could pay; his climb to business success had been accompanied by a series of similar shouts. He had come to regard them as a normal reaction on the part of the customer; they were a bad sign only if they were followed by a dropping off in the volume of trade. It was just a matter of striking a balance. If the buyer protested at the top of his lungs but still bought, then the merchant knew that he was making a reasonable — that is, the maximum — profit.

Born at Harwinton, Connecticut, on October 22, 1821, son of a tinker who was regarded as miserly even by his close-fisted neighbors (and who died leaving three thousand dollars in cash), Huntington needed few lessons in the arts of accumulation. In his father's household, thrift was no abstract virtue to be acquired through a reading of the pleasant axioms of Poor Richard; it was a cardinal law of existence. In rural Connecticut a century ago, cash was an extraordinarily esteemed article, to be gathered in and held at virtually any cost. At any time during Huntington's boyhood the appearance of a spendthrift in his Litchfield County countryside would have been a hardly less astonishing apparition than a live dinosaur.

In the '90s, when it had become the obligation of rich men to boast of a youth spent in poverty, the railroad magnate never had to draw on his imagination for harrowing details. Poverty, plus industry, plus thrift; this was his formula for success, and of the three, industry was not the least important. " From the time I was a child until the present I can hardly remember a time when I was not doing something." With this sentence Huntington began one of several biographical interviews, and he commonly returned to the subject every paragraph or two. What productive enterprises occupied his time until he was fourteen are not now known, but it is known that by then he had earned — and saved — over a hundred dollars. His fourteenth year (1835) was spent as " hired man " on a neighbor's farm; he received seven dollars a month and his clothes, and of course every penny was saved. With the eighty-four dollars, plus his earlier accumulations, the young Crœsus — still a month short of fifteen — left New England for wider opportunities in rural New York. " From that time on," he wrote, " I have been very busy."

At Oneonta he invested his capital in a country store, in partnership with an elder brother, Solon. But he spent little time behind the counter; he had already discovered that the world is full of men eager to do routine work for low wages.

During the next dozen years one catches glimpses of the brawny, square-jawed young man pursuing the goddess of excess profits down a variety of byways: peddling jewelry to farmers' wives in Ohio and Indiana, tramping through the pre-war South on the lucrative business of collecting unpaid balances of notes bought for a few cents on the dollar; selling butter in New York City, and turning his hand to whatever else promised a quick return.

The significance of events in California subsequent to January 24, 1848 was not overlooked by the young trader. There is no evidence, however, that Huntington ever seriously intended to become a miner. In later life he looked back to the half-day he had once spent shoveling gravel from a creek-bed as one of his major mistakes in judgment. When he sailed from New York in March '49 (aged twenty-seven), he was definitely no romanticist, light-headed from the contemplation of a prospective easy fortune. He saw the gold rush merely as a more than usually promising business opportunity, and he joined the westward scramble in his usual capacity of trader. With him on the *Crescent City* went a stock of merchandise, including a number of casks of whisky, which he planned to sell — at maximum profit, of course — to the *bona fide* Argonauts.

Few adventurers who set out for the gold fields were less affected than he by the prevailing attitude of improvidence and specious optimism. Huntington foresaw the impracticability of the " mining and trading companies " then being formed everywhere in the East, and he refused to join forces with any of them. After he reached Panama, he was able to put some of these disintegrating organizations to his own use. " They quarreled," he later remarked, " and came to me. They all seemed to come to me." The quarrels commonly meant a distribution of assets — and, as the latter were usually in the form of merchandise, Huntington was able to buy stocks of desirable goods at bargain prices. Before he was on the Isthmus a week he was carrying on the most active trading of his career. He bought whatever promised to meet his two simple requirements: a quick turnover and a large profit. During his three months' enforced stay on the Isthmus — a period less industrious Argonauts spent bemoaning the lack of boats to carry them north — Huntington took a flyer in the importing business. " While I was down there, I went down to Estebula and bought a little schooner called the *Emma* and filled her up with jerked beef, potatoes, rice, sugar and syrup in great bags and brought them up to Panama and sold them." Profits averaged well above a thousand dollars a month. His buying and selling required frequent trips through the fever-laden jungle between the two coasts. Huntington estimated that he made the crossing at least twenty times. " It was only twenty-four miles," he recalled. " I walked it."

3

HE was, then and later, strong as an ox, and healthy to the point of absurdity. When he was nearly seventy he remembered only one serious illness; in Sacramento in the early '50s he once fell victim to the current scourge, dysentery. Before the summer ended, his weight had fallen from over 200 to 125 pounds. Not until old age was upon him did he confess that he could no longer " eat everything," and at seventy-five he publicly deplored an inclination to lie abed mornings. Hard physical exercise was his key to health. At Oneonta he scorned to buy his winter fuel already chopped; sawing and splitting logs were the best form of calisthenics — " it exercises you all over." But there were no chopping-blocks at his house at Fifty-seventh Street and Fifth Avenue, or on his private cars, and in later years his muscles grew soft and his weight increased to above 250 pounds. The Oneonta woodcutting was habitually done before breakfast, and the sound of his ax ushering in the sunrise may have inspired the legend — kept alive by Huntington himself — that in his eight years there he had never been seen wasting his time in a saloon or hotel lobby, the town's only social centers.

Huntington's apprenticeship was completed long before he reached California; it was a finished trader who landed in San Francisco in the spring of 1850. On the trip he had managed to increase his capital from $1,200 to $5,000. In later life he liked to recall that on the day the ship docked he lent some fellow passengers enough to buy a hearty meal in celebration of their arrival; Huntington himself dined on crackers and cheese.

To follow his activities during his first five years in the West is to witness an expert demonstration of the art of accumulation under unusual and fluid conditions. His formula was simple: " I kept my warehouse full when prices were low, and when they went up I sold out." But supply and demand reached an equilibrium only rarely and by accident, and nothing resembling stable prices could be expected for more than a week at a time. Huntington shuffled between Sacramento and the bay — by boat, the distance here was too far to walk — keeping one eye on the supply of merchandise at both places and on the rate at which it was being consumed. The other eye was cocked at the Golden Gate, the only source of new shipments.

To keep closer tab on the incoming ships, he bought the most powerful field glasses he could find, and a dory which he kept moored to the wharf at Clark's Point.

During the ensuing months the masters of scores of sailing ships were first hailed in the harbor by this one-man reception committee. Huntington's frail craft came precariously alongside and its occupant shouted an inquiry as to what cargo was carried. If it chanced to be salable merchandise, Huntington scrambled aboard and concluded a deal on the spot, paying a deposit from the pouch of gold dust he always carried, strapped about his waist. Once he said that had his little craft overturned he would have sunk like a rock. Until 1862 he dealt in everything that was not perishable. Huntington liked to hold merchandise until he got his price, and the possibility of having to sell it cheap to avoid spoiling was not part of his scheme.

To control the supply of a needed product was the common aim of San Francisco's scores of speculators — an aim that was realized less frequently than biographies of the pioneers imply. Huntington achieved his ambition once, by cornering the shovel market and reaping a handsome profit — his first real killing. Later at Sacramento, as already mentioned, he and Hopkins had another partial success, this time with blasting-powder, and still later he managed to sell for a dollar a pound a consignment of iron bars he had picked up for twenty dollars a ton. But in general he had to be content with lesser exploits. When, as was constantly happening, too much of a product was dumped on San Francisco's waterfront, he was always willing to buy heavily, provided prices were low enough. Unlike the shoestring speculators, he had both capital and facilities to hold his merchandise for the probable advance. In Sacramento before long it required six large tents to hold his stock.

Huntington recognized the value of his reputation as one speculator who would buy whatever was offered, and he did what he could to promote it. " Everybody used to come to ' Old Huntington,' " he recalled. (He was then in his early thirties.) " I had a Panama hat that was very broad-brimmed, and used to come down to my shoulders . . . so I was well known."

Even that early he had original ideas as to how a business should be conducted, and his partnership with Hopkins, effected in 1853, allowed him to put some of them into effect. Hopkins occupied the same relative position as had Solon Huntington in the earlier Oneonta venture: he saw that things ran smoothly at headquarters, leaving Collis free to rove about on his bargain-hunting expeditions. Goods shrewdly bought on a depressed market jammed the big brick K Street store that presently succeeded the tents, and the firm was soon among the largest in the state.

Huntington took an almost paternal interest in the welfare of their score or more clerks, who lived in a combined dormitory and recreation room in the rear of the store. This was furnished, not with the packing boxes and empty kegs usual in early California interiors, but with tables, chairs, and bunks having the luxury of straw-stuffed mattresses. More, he committed the extravagance of buying at auction, for twenty-nine dollars, a box of books that unexpectedly showed up at a local sale, and established one of the first free circulating libraries in California.

To this room employees were required to return immediately after supper; at nine o'clock they were safely in bed with the candles extinguished. Thus the morals of the firm's personnel were protected: the town's bumper crop of gamblers and prostitutes received not one penny of their wages, and, to a man, they reported for work with clear heads, steady hands, and non-alcoholic breaths. With Huntington, this little pool of Y.M.C.A.-like rectitude in a roaring current of wickedness was a matter not of morals but of business. His young men were expected to save their wages, to remain sober and chaste, and to get eight hours' sleep a night. This was probably good for them; unquestionably it was good for their employers.

Huntington's stand for righteousness was not, of course, carried to unprofitable extremes. Neither he nor Hopkins nor their young men drank intoxicants — but the trade in whisky was a large and profitable side of the business. No employee was permitted, under pain of dis-

missal, to enter the gambling houses or the dens of prostitutes; but as customers the owners of both had their good
points. They bought liberally of the best, they paid
promptly and seldom quibbled about prices.

There were, however, a few triumphs of conscience over
profit. In later years Huntington delighted to recall such
incidents. One day a Mrs. Caswell, keeper of a bawdy
house at Third and K streets, sent her colored porter to
ask the cost of preserved peaches. Huntington chanced to
have the only supply in town and he named a high price
— ninety-six dollars — for the lot. The porter returned
and stated that the madam was agreeable and wished them
sent over. "You tell Mrs. Caswell," returned the merchant loftily, "that if she pays ninety-six dollars and takes
the peaches along I have no objection, but my boys cannot
go into her house."

A similar episode remained so clear in memory that
half a century later he was able to repeat his exact words.
One of his cut-rate purchases had been a thousand-barrel
lot of corn meal. This had proved so bulky that storage
facilities were taxed and the overflow had to be piled on
the sidewalk before the store. The price was ten dollars
a barrel. One day, however, when he saw another of the
town's madams approaching, he could not refrain from
hoisting the figure sharply.

"She came along with a silk dress trailing half way
across the street and asked for corn meal. She said:

"'What do you ask for a barrel?'

"Said I: 'Two ounces a barrel.' [$32.00]

"Said she: 'Do you think I am a damn fool?'

" ' No,' said I. ' I will be frank with you. I have not thought anything about you one way or the other.'

" She gathered her skirts up and went across the street."

4

IN the late '80s Hubert H. Bancroft, California's efficient businessman-historian, called on Huntington at the latter's suite at the Palace Hotel. Bancroft outlined a plan for compiling a history of the building of the Central and Southern Pacific, one that would tell the story of that feat in greater detail than had been possible in his seven-volume *History of California*.

Huntington listened without comment while the plan was outlined. He refused, however, to commit himself even when Bancroft made his usually effective vanity appeal: that Huntington himself would have the deciding voice in the creation of this portrait by which he would be known to posterity. But the interview was not a complete failure. Before the publisher walked back up Market Street to his headquarters in the next block Huntington had agreed to allow one of Bancroft's writers to accompany him back east.

At intervals during a four-day run from Oakland to New Orleans the old man submitted to questions by D. R. Sessions, Bancroft's scribe. Under his prodding he recalled incidents of his youth and of the early years at Sacramento, stated his opinion on a variety of subjects upon which rich men were usually interrogated, and delivered short, confused pronouncements on such questions as railroad subsidies, the future of the Negro, and his personal tastes in art and literature.

The result, 128 foolscap pages, literally transcribed, is an uncommonly interesting document. In it one is privileged to see Huntington as he chose to be seen. The self-posed portrait is that of a man by no means disappointed in himself. Looking back — he was then in his late sixties — he saw nothing in an active lifetime that he would have changed in the least degree. He was born of poor parents and had thereby learned the virtue of frugality. His schooling had been limited to four months a year and had ended entirely when he was thirteen; he was convinced that formal education was a waste of time. His temperament was not of a sort that inspired close friendships; this, too, became a virtue in his eyes. " I never had any chums . . . I ran in a crowd by myself." " I am not a sociable man . . . but I get as much out of life as any man in America. . . ."

Hunched forward in his chair and regarding through the windows of the Oneonta II the waterless wastes of southern Arizona, he accommodatingly searched for revealing anecdotes of his past. The incidents he recalled were commonly those in which he got the better of an opponent in a business deal or conquered adverse circumstances by shrewdness and hard work. Industry, frugality, the ability to drive a bargain, these were qualities to be admired wherever found, and Huntington most frequently found them in himself. Tenacity stood high in his list of the virtues; a man must stick to a thing and see it through. For the man who divided his interests and thus dissipated his energies he saw no hope. His favorite derogatory adjective was " restless "; to call a man that was to catalogue him as past redemption.

Although he continued to preach the Spartan axioms that had guided his youth, he had by then adopted most of the conventional follies of the rich men of his time: houses, travel, *objets d'art,* even, in a guarded and tentative way, philanthropy. From the early '80s onward, reports of his new enthusiasms drifted out now and then from the East, causing old-time California acquaintances to shake their heads in confusion. During his life on the Coast he had been heard to boast on two subjects only: his personal strength and endurance and his ability to protect himself in a business deal. Huntington in some of his new roles — as a connoisseur of paintings, for instance — seemed contrary to all sense. Self-hypnotism of that sort might be expected of other rich men, but they had looked to Huntington to remain rational despite his millions.

Those who gave the matter close attention, however, recognized definite Huntington characteristics even in this hobby. In 1888 he paid twenty-five thousand dollars for a painting of what he termed " a religious scene." This any of a hundred rich men might have done — but the reasons why he had purchased it were Huntington's own:

" There are seven figures in it — three cardinals of the different orders of their religion. There is an old missionary that has just returned; he is showing his scars, where his hands are cut all over; he is telling a story to these cardinals; they are dressed in luxury. One of them is playing with a dog; one is asleep; there is only one looking at him — looking at him with that kind of an expression saying what a fool you are that you should go out and suffer for the human race when we have such a good time at home. I lose the picture in the story when I look at it. I sometimes sit half an hour looking at that picture."

One imagines the old man, seated gingerly in one of his Louis XV chairs, fixing the canvas with a searching, grim stare. Long before the half-hour is up, the scene comes to life, peopled by figures no longer unfamiliar. For do not these luxury-loving cardinals resemble Huntington's own associates? There is that one in particular, the idle fellow who plays with the dog — or is it perhaps not a dog but a racehorse? " Stanford has his horses and his ranches, and Crocker likes to run off to Europe," he had once informed Hopkins in a letter complaining that his strength was not equal to the work piled on him. One begins to see why Huntington, regarding his twenty-five-thousand-dollar painting, " loses the picture in the story " — for the story is his own. Who is the weary wretch in the center who has spent himself doing what needed to be done while the idle cardinals gave themselves over to worldly pleasures — who but Huntington himself?

It was another manifestation of his habit of picturing himself as a martyr to his duties. Unquestionably there were times when he drew too heavily on his strength, and in the depressed periods that followed wondered if the game was worth the effort. " What the devil is the use of my wearing myself out? " he demanded of Hopkins in the early '70s. He was sure then that his health would break under the strain, and in almost daily letters he repeated and emphasized his desire to sell out. But he was only partly serious. In the midst of his dissatisfaction the panic of 1872 broke, seriously jeopardizing his fortune and of course multiplying his problems. He promptly forgot himself in the struggle, and his letters thereafter had no room for self-pity.

This crisis effected a permanent cure. Huntington not only outworked his partners; he also outlived them, and during the final decade of his long life he liked to boast that he could do more than men half his age. An English journalist who interviewed him in 1899 found him quite seriously planning enterprises that would take him twenty years to complete. On one of his half-yearly visits to California a friend remarked that he was looking well; Huntington replied with emphasis: " Five years ago I thought I might live until I was a hundred. I know now I'll reach a hundred and ten." The Huntingtons, he liked to point out, were a long-lived family; his father had remained hale and hearty until long past ninety. In New York toward the close of the century a notable banquet was given to Sir William Van Horne. A score of leading financiers were present, and Levi P. Morton, who had been Vice-President under Harrison, remarked to C. P. Stubbs, general passenger agent of the Southern Pacific: " This gathering comprises some of the most wonderful men in the United States, and that old man is the most wonderful man of the lot." The reference was to Huntington and the next day Stubbs repeated the compliment. Huntington's face showed no pleasure as he demanded: " Did he say *old* man? Did he say *old* man? Why didn't you kick him? "

5

HUNTINGTON married in September 1844, when he was in his twenty-third year. His bride, the former Elizabeth Stoddard, conformed admirably to Victorian standards of how a dutiful wife should conduct herself, and for the nearly forty years of her married life she accomplished a virtually perfect feat of self-effacement. While Huntington was shouldering his way up the financial scale from country storekeeper to leading figure in American transportation, the primary fact of her existence was known only because newspaper accounts of his movements sometimes ended with such sentences as this: " He is accompanied by his secretary, G. E. Miles, and his wife." So far was she removed from public knowledge that when one comes across a statement that she started on her first trip to California with but two hours' notice, the information seems a slightly scandalous violation of her privacy. For the rest, it is known that the couple remained childless, that in the small-town neighborliness of early Sacramento she was well liked by the wives of her husband's partners, and that she and her husband undertook to bring up Clara Prentice, daughter of her deceased sister.

The child was then but ten months old; she grew up in the household and in later years Huntington often remarked that he treated her exactly as though she were his own daughter. Her presence compensated in part for the fact that he had no children of his own, particularly no sons — a lack that was frequently on his mind. " I don't blame Stanford for not wanting to sell," he remarked in the early '70s, when the question of selling their railroad property was under constant discussion among the partners. " If I had a son growing up nothing could persuade me to get out." There were other references to the fact that he alone of the four partners had no male heir. Crocker had several sons and Stanford one; even Mark Hopkins, without children of his own, had taken young Timothy Nolan into his house and was bringing him up as his son. But Clara Prentice presently became known as Clara Huntington and letters passing between the partners began to refer to Huntington's new status as a man of family. " I am sorry to learn of Clara's illness," wrote Colton on May 2, 1878. " I hope she is quite well. . . ."

As she grew older, the girl adapted herself with no difficulty to the ornate life Huntington's millions made inevitable. The old man indulged her extravagances, even to the extent of expending, in the late '80s, a sum advertised to be two and a half million dollars to accomplish her well-publicized marriage to Prince Hatzfeldt of one of the minor German noble houses. This speedily came to be recognized as the worst investment Huntington ever had made, for the Prince's exploits remained staples of American scandal-sheets for a generation.

Long before Clara's marriage, however, Huntington's almost mythical first wife had died, and not many months later, in New York, on the morning of July 12, 1884, the widower took a second bride. He was then almost sixty-three. The second wife was Mrs. A. D. Worsham, born Arabella Duval Yarrington, a native of Alabama and then, by a current newspaper account, " quite a prominent woman in New York and the subject of considerable comment as being very ambitious." She had one child by her former marriage, Archie Worsham, who adopted his stepfather's name and, as Archer Huntington, became well known for his philanthropies and as a Hispano-American scholar. Huntington, himself a large man, admired size in others; he was once heard to boast that young Archie, at sixteen, weighed 220 pounds.

The new Mrs. Huntington did not share her predecessor's unshakable liking for personal obscurity. Under her influence Huntington dropped one by one his accustomed austere habits and began surrounding himself with a setting proper to his position as one of the dozen wealthiest men in America. His belated plunge into luxury proved not so bad as he had feared. He was presently, and with no visible signs of revolt, making a long succession of profitless investments: houses in New York and San Francisco, a summer camp in the Adirondacks, multiple roomfuls of French furniture, bronzes and tapestries, a box at the Metropolitan, hundreds of square yards of innocuous paintings by currently fashionable European artists. " I suppose I have half a million dollars' worth of pictures," he told an interviewer in 1889, and went on to add with pride that Henry Ward Beecher had once asked to see a newly hung canvas.

Beecher had performed his second marriage. Some weeks later, off on a lecture tour with his manager, J. B. Pond, the preacher amused himself by cleaning out the accumulated litter in his pockets. Pond looked on while Beecher brought forth a mass of papers, glanced through them briefly, tearing up such as he didn't want and tossing them out the car window. From the watch pocket of his trousers he pulled out a tightly folded envelope, stared at it blankly, then recalled that Huntington had passed it to him after the ceremony. The envelope was torn open and its contents drawn forth — four thousand-dollar bills. Later Pond was invited to admire what the fee had bought: a bright new rug for the churchman's living-room in Brooklyn. Huntington was proud of Beecher's friendship and remained loyal through the tremendous scandal in which the latter became involved. After Beecher's death Huntington befriended his widow, providing her periodically with railroad passes that she might visit her son, who lived on Puget Sound.

Although Huntington brought himself to spend prodigally, personal extravagance remained permanently beyond his powers. To the end, he boasted that he had never spent above two hundred dollars a year on personal adornment. Even after he had acquired the baroque setting of his later days, he continued not only to preach but to practice the virtues of frugality. With amusement he once confessed that his wife and daughter had constantly to remind him to ring for servants rather than to perform household duties for himself. In a day when a French chef was a necessity in every rich man's kitchen, he liked to tell dinner guests about his Chinese cook, who worked for small wages and wasted nothing.

He understood the problems of those in lowly stations and, if they met his rigid requirements, was quite willing to help them. Lacking even the beginnings of diplomacy, he sometimes publicly referred to laboring men as " inferiors "; but more clearly than most large employers of his time he recognized their rights, and there were few strikes on enterprises under his control. He had the respect of his servants, and sometimes their affection. When news of his death reached San Francisco, the only locally shed tears were almost certainly those of the Irish caretaker in his house on Nob Hill. Early one summer morning in the year 1900 Mary Foley dabbed her eyes with the lower hem of her apron and assured reporters that Mr. Huntington had been a fine and unassuming gentleman, and that he had never put on airs although she was prepared to state without reservation that he knew everything.

The personal affairs of John, the Negro porter in his Mills Building office, engaged his interest. Huntington encouraged him to buy a house, then withheld $40 of his $75 monthly salary to make sure that the monthly payments were met. This was a device he used, with varying success, with other employees who lacked the fortitude to save voluntarily. Slightly different was his treatment of " Uncle George " Bromley, a California ancient whom he had known since early Sacramento days. Word reached him that Bromley, long celebrated on the Coast for his humorous after-dinner speeches, was hard up. One day Bromley was summoned to the Southern Pacific's San Francisco office and informed that, on Huntington's instructions, he was being put on the payroll. He was not then told what duties were expected of him, nor did he ever learn. The salary was paid with regularity until Huntington's death, five years later, when it stopped. Thereupon the pensioner, quite understandably, felt himself abused at being tossed into the world again. A few years before Bromley began receiving his railroad pension, newspaper readers were charmed by the story of another Huntington benefaction. A dispatch from El Paso related how the magnate had left his private car and driven off for a two-hour visit at the cottage of an old friend, recently retired from a lifetime of bossing a Southern Pacific section gang.

Toward the end of 1898 Bailey Millard, Sunday editor of young W. R. Hearst's *Examiner,* heard an Oakland schoolteacher read a poem at a literary gathering. Millard, impressed, saw an opportunity to enlist the *Examiner's* methods in the novel cause of literature. No work of an unknown poet was ever launched with a greater splash. After days of preliminary advertising it was given to the public, accompanied by a column of editorial praise. Rival papers jeered, but "The Man with the Hoe," made the hoped-for sensation and Edwin Markham leaped into prominence as " The Poet of the People."

The poem became effective propaganda in the hands of the Socialists and so came to Huntington's attention.

Millet's painting, the poem's inspiration, was owned by the Crocker family. Indirectly, Central Pacific profits had supplied ammunition to the enemy, and this may have had something to do with Huntington's decision to wage counter-warfare. Another possible reason was the fact that the *Examiner* was then Huntington's most ruthless enemy on the Coast. Clearly, Huntington thought the poem dangerous; like many rich men he had taken serious alarm at the rising tide of Socialism. He considered the matter important enough to grant one of his infrequent interviews. " Is America going to turn to Socialism over one poem? " he asked a reporter for the *Sun*. " Markham's Hoe Man has a hoe. Let him rejoice. The only man to commiserate is the man who has no hoe; the man who cannot help to enrich the world."

Through the *Sun* an anonymous donor put up a prize of $750 for the best poem " answering " Markham's possibly dangerous work, and personally outlined the rules of the contest. Needy poets throughout the country rallied to the defense of the existing order. Five thousand " answers " resulted. The prize went to John Vance Cheney for his poem " Responsibility." Huntington died before he learned to what extent his $750 had confounded the Socialists.

6

EASILY overshadowing his fear of the Socialists, however, was his dislike of his slow-thinking partner. That Hun-

tington and Stanford were mutually antagonistic had
been known to a few almost from the beginning of their
association. As early as 1863, references were made to
their lack of harmony on questions of policy, and a few
years later a San Francisco paper pointed out that "a
money-maker and a money-spender cannot pull together
as a business team, however well that combination might
work in the matrimonial harness."

Temperamentally the two were as far apart as the poles,
and an open break was merely a matter of time and expediency. Personally Huntington would have welcomed
it years before it came. He had little talent for concealing
his dislikes, and Stanford's most conspicuous qualities
were precisely those he found hardest to endure. But
Huntington also realized that a public quarrel would be
bad business; that internal conflict would inevitably hurt
the prestige of the company. Through the '70s and '80s
he convinced himself that the Big Four must present a
united front to a world that grew increasingly antagonistic. So, for the sake of policy, Huntington stifled his
dislike for his stolid and vainglorious associate. It was
prudent to wait. He could settle the score later; there
was plenty of time. He waited, as a matter of fact, nearly
a quarter of a century before he considered it expedient
to bring the quarrel into the open.

Stanford's first election to the Senate in 1885 was the
spark that eventually set off the explosion. The circumstances can be briefly sketched. The term of one of California's senators was about to expire and the railroad
group, casting about for a man who would be useful in

Washington and who deserved this reward, decided on Aaron A. Sargent. From both standpoints there was nothing wrong with their choice. Sargent had been a staunch Central Pacific man since the inception of the road. During his first term as Congressman in the early '60s, he had helped Judah get the original Pacific Railroad bill through the House, and by all his subsequent acts in Washington he had proved himself a statesman after Huntington's heart. Sargent had served California, and the railroad, for some years in the House, following this with a term in the Senate. Then in 1874 he had retired to private life. Friendly with both Huntington and Stanford, he was one of the few men for whom the former had a genuine liking. His ambition to return to the Senate after ten years of retirement met with the approval and encouragement of both men.

Railroad support was promised Sargent at a meeting in Huntington's New York office in the spring of 1884. Word of the decision was duly communicated to California and formalities leading to his election proceeded with their customary smoothness and order. In November, local elections in California gave the Republicans a large majority in the state senate. There remained only the routine business of uniting on Sargent as the party's candidate and of casting a few ballots as a courtesy to rival candidates before voting Sargent into office. Sargent himself shared the opinion of political observers that he was as good as elected. The final step was for Stanford, as the Southern Pacific's president, to give formal word that Sargent was the railroad's choice. But time passed and

Stanford unaccountably failed to act. Sargent, still confident but beginning to show signs of nervousness, pondered the meaning of the continued silence in the clapboard mansion at Palo Alto. After a time he dropped his friend a note:

" Dear Governor: It is very necessary that you come out soon. . . . I have a good majority of those elected and can see success ahead. But your presence here and your strong influential words will make assurance doubly sure. I know your personal friendship for me will induce you to comply with my request. . . ."

To this letter Stanford made no reply. More days slipped by. By the time the new legislature gathered at Sacramento, rumors were circulating that Sargent had lost the all-powerful railroad support. For once even the politicians were mystified. That Stanford wanted the office for himself seems at first to have occurred to no one. His friendship for Sargent, the latter's lifelong support of the railroad's interests, and the road's habit of rewarding the faithful with political office were all against the possibility. Stanford, however, was planning just that; he had convinced himself that a term in the Senate would be a fitting climax to his public career.

The Governor had succeeded in getting himself into a difficult position. Besides his widely known friendship for Sargent, there was the fact that the latter was generally known to be the railroad's candidate. There was, too, his definite, though secret, promise to support Sargent — and there was Huntington, who had been present when his word had been given. But against this stood a still more potent factor: Stanford himself was determined to take the office. To that end, he had allied himself with a group of Sargent's political enemies, among them Frank Pixley, Creed Haymond, and Henry Vrooman, and these were pressing him to announce his candidacy. This, however, he could not quite bring himself to do. While he hesitated, the legislature convened and the date of the balloting drew near. Sargent — now thoroughly alarmed and more than a little suspicious — grew daily more insistent. To his letters and telegrams Stanford at length brought himself to reply. But his effort was a feeble one. While he personally continued to support Sargent, he stated, the situation had grown complicated. There were many factors that must be considered very carefully. . . .

Sargent was too old a hand at politics not to realize what was taking place. On January 13, 1885, a week before the scheduled election, he wrote to Stanford pointing out that two of the latter's friends were in Sacramento " trying to pull away my votes in the legislature." He continued: " As this is so inconsistent with your letter of yesterday, I call your attention to it directly that you may stop it. . . . I appreciate the friendship these men have for you and that their zeal for you is the cause of their acts. But they should not trifle with your honor. . . ." Sargent added that he had the election by a majority of twenty " if these gentlemen would speak a word of encouragement for me, instead of opposing me; and I would have a fair majority if they would be neutral." His earlier letters had begun: " My dear Governor "; in this the salutation was more formal, perhaps a trifle ironical: " Hon. Leland Stanford."

245

At the same time the remnants of another friendship were disappearing. Sargent did not fail to inform Huntington of how events were shaping themselves at Sacramento. An ominous wire presently reached Palo Alto: " It is reported that you are in the field against Sargent. I cannot believe it. Please telegraph me at once."

Stanford could no longer evade the issue. Soon after Huntington's telegram reached him, he issued a statement confirming what California's political writers had been prophesying for days. On the insistence of his friends and for the sake of concord within the party, Stanford had decided with much reluctance to enter the race. . . . The Republicans met in caucus on January 20. Stanford received the nomination on the second ballot. He got 47 votes. Sargent was able to hold but 16 of the " fair majority " he had expected a week earlier. On January 28 the predominantly Republican state senate voted Stanford into the office.

His motives were variously explained. To mitigate the charge of betrayal, one California politician, Henry Vrooman, announced that Stanford had allowed his name to be presented " only when I told him plainly that I and his friends were bound to make him senator in spite of everything he could do for Sargent." But Sargent, after thirty years in California politics, had made other enemies, and these were unwilling to let credit for his defeat go to others. Frank Pixley, who had been state treasurer when Stanford was Governor, and whose weekly *Argonaut* had for years been singing Stanford's praises, later laid claim to whatever glory there might have been in having in-

stigated the coup. But it remained for Stephen T. Gage
to put forth the most original claim to the honor. It was
his argument, he stated, that had finally won over his
chief, then vacillating between personal vanity and loy-
alty to a friend. A period of residence at Washington,
Gage had informed Stanford, might prove beneficial to
Mrs. Stanford, whose health had not been robust. The
theory that not political ambition but regard for his wife's
health had prompted Stanford's decision was not widely
accepted. California papers commented in ironic vein on
Washington's rise to prominence as a health center.
Others pointed out that if a man wished to live in Washington for his wife's health he might go as a private citizen
and avoid the necessity of breaking his word to an old
friend. The railroad papers, of course, approved whole-
heartedly, while others, following their natural bent,
straddled the issue. The Los Angeles *Times* commented:
" The result is now known. We accept it, without dis-
pleasure, as the best choice, all things considered, that
could have been made. . . ." With unconscious cyn-
icism the paper went on to develop the theory that since
the state was fated to be represented in the Senate by a
man pledged to serve the railroad, the road's president
was better than a subordinate. Stanford was a man of
wealth and therefore presumably able to resist the temptation to sell his vote.

During the ensuing days numbers of prominent citizens were persuaded to state their opinions of the episode
in the press, but no statement was forthcoming from
Huntington. Stanford took his seat on March 4, 1885,

the day of Cleveland's inauguration, and Huntington was not in the gallery to witness this new Stanford triumph. Nor was he ever a guest at the new Senator's apartment in the Arlington Hotel or in the pretentious house he later leased on Farragut Square.

Throughout the uproar and later the New Englander maintained in public a discreet silence, but those who knew him well — including Stanford himself — were not convinced that he had forgotten the episode. Their doubts proved well founded. Privately Huntington had decided that Stanford's vanity had passed the limit of tolerance. Even his concern for public policy was no longer a permanently restraining influence. He had definitely decided to give himself the pleasure of deflating the Stanford balloon. It was only a matter of choosing the right time.

7

CHARACTERISTICALLY, Huntington was in no hurry to take his revenge. He laid his plans with patience and care, and five years passed before he was ready to act. The annual meeting of Southern Pacific stockholders was held at San Francisco on April 9, 1890. So far as advance information went, it was to be a regular meeting given over to routine business. A few, however, knew that matters of more importance were to take place, for Huntington had partially shown his hand at a preliminary meeting at New

York five weeks earlier. Present were Huntington and Stanford, the two survivors of the original four, Charles F. Crocker, son of the original Charles, who had died in 1888, and two attorneys representing the interests of Mrs. Edward T. Searles, Mark Hopkins's widow.

Into the midst of this group Huntington had casually dropped his bombshell. At the forthcoming annual meeting, he announced, Stanford was to be dropped as president of the road and Huntington himself was to succeed him. An agreement embodying this and other matters was presented, and all present — Stanford included — signed it. The reason the latter agreed without a struggle to give up an office he had held for nearly three decades is partly explained by these excerpts from the document:

" Fourth: That the papers in possession of C. P. Huntington in reference to the Sargent matters be either destroyed or delivered sealed to the undersigned for disposal as they shall see fit.

" Fifth: That all parties owning or representing interests in the property of the Pacific Improvement Company shall in good faith refrain from hostile or injurious expressions concerning each other, and shall in good faith cooperate for the election of Leland Stanford to the next term of the United States Senate."

Stanford was to be allowed to return to the Senate, but this time he was to pay for the privilege. The price would have been high even had Huntington carried out his part of the agreement — which, as events proved, he had no intention of doing.

The Southern Pacific's annual meeting was held at San

Francisco the following April, and the ready-made program was duly put through. Stanford rose from his accustomed place at the head of the directors' table and Huntington took his place. The latter had prepared a statement; his first act as president was to rise and read it. He began by thanking his associates for the honor they had conferred on him, and by promising to continue to serve the best interests of the corporation.

The new president's remarks so far had been both conventional and expected. What followed was neither:

" I can promise you nothing more, for at all times my personal interest has been second to that of the company. It shall be so in the future, and in no case will I use this great corporation to advance my personal ambition at the expense of its owners, or put my hands in the treasury to defeat the people's choice and thereby put myself in positions that should be filled by others, but to the best of my ability I will work for the interests of the shareholders of the company and the people whom it should serve."

This was a typical example of the Huntington method of attack. He had waited more than five years, perfecting his campaign, maneuvering his less skillful opponent into a position from which there was no possibility of escape. It was also one of the few occasions when Huntington exhibited the slightest talent for showmanship or allowed himself the luxury of satisfying a personal grudge at the expense of business expediency; but having decided to settle an old score, he was not content until he had made a thorough job of it.

The blow fell at a time when Stanford's prestige was at

its height. The doors of his new university had been thrown open only a few months earlier and the magnificence of the gift had for three years been a favorite topic throughout the West. Moreover, he had been for a generation the nominal head of the Republican party in California; he was then a Senator and had been Governor. And since its organization he had been president of incomparably the largest corporation in the West.

Unquestionably, it was Stanford's darkest day. For his removal from the presidency of the road he had been prepared. The rest was a complete surprise. That Huntington, having got what he wanted, would ignore the other provisions of their agreement had evidently not occurred to him. Years later a member of the Stanford household recalled that when the Governor returned to Palo Alto that evening he appeared to have grown years older since the morning.

Huntington's unexpected revival of the Sargent incident and his public admission that Stanford's election had been bought with railroad money received attention beyond the walls of the directors' room at Fourth and Townsend streets. For years, opposition papers in California had been stating that much railroad money had been spent at Sacramento in the campaign of 1885. To have the charge confirmed, and by Huntington himself, was a wholly unlooked-for piece of good fortune and editors made the most of it.

Newspaper readers of the Coast were presently enjoying an unusual privilege: that of witnessing a public airing of their mutual dislike by the two surviving members of the Big Four. For Stanford, always hospitable to the press and concerned for his standing in the eyes of the public, turned to the newspapers in an effort to counteract Huntington's deplorable frankness; this was to be expected. That Huntington would overcome his aversion for publicity and fight vigorously, was not. The successive interviews grew in frankness as the angry partners reached the stage of personal abuse. Thus the literate West learned that Stanford had so little regard for the honesty of his associate that he would trust him only so far as he could " throw Trinity Church up the side of Mt. Shasta," and Huntington was goaded to the length of calling the estimable founder of the new university " a damned old fool."

The battle was brief and uneven. Stanford was normally able to hold his own in an exchange of invective, but this time it was his bad luck to be on the defensive. Hostile newspapers were asking not merely for abuse of Huntington, but for proof that the latter's charges were untrue. The quarrel put the railroad-controlled press in a difficult position. Its editors were in doubt as to which side of the controversy they were expected to take. Most of them played safe and either ignored the situation or quoted minor railroad officials as deprecating the unfortunate misunderstanding. Creed Haymond, the current chief of the railroad's legal staff, spoke soothingly to reporters: " The facts of the election are not known to Mr. Huntington in their true light." Others followed his lead. Frank Pixley's *Argonaut,* usually shrill in its support of Stanford's interests, was singularly temperate. The reason was known to many; Pixley believed himself responsible for persuading Stanford to run against Sargent, whom he heartily disliked. The editor was sulking because he could not claim credit for a personal victory over Sargent, but must help maintain the fiction that the latter had been reluctantly sacrificed because Stanford alone could have won for the Republicans.

After interest in the controversy had begun to die down, Stanford accommodatingly added more fuel by a demand that the new board of the Southern Pacific investigate Huntington's charge that railroad money had been used to buy his election. Opposition journals pointed out that the investigation might better be conducted by a less biased body. In Washington the matter of appointing a Senate committee to look into Stanford's fitness to remain a member of that body was seriously discussed.

Neither investigation materialized. The Senate took no official notice of Huntington's charges, and the railroad's directors prudently refused to render a decision that must win them the enmity of either Stanford or Huntington. Meantime the advice of conciliation began to make headway. Stanford was prevailed on to temper his demands for an immediate investigation, and Huntington agreed to write a letter of apology. The latter proved to be a curious document. The degree of sincerity with which it was written may be judged from the following excerpts:

Dear Governor:
So many items mentioning your name and mine have lately appeared in the daily papers that some of our friends think

it would be well for me to write you a letter. Hence this communication; although I do not apprehend any danger that you and I will be put in a hostile attitude in our business — or for that matter, in our personal relations; but the intervention of others who do not altogether understand our difference may tend to separate our friends. Our views when at variance have been freely expressed and it is needless to allude to them further than that we have each of us agreed to disagree. . . .

The remarks that I recently made at the Southern Pacific board meeting were intended only as a seasonable expression of my views on these subjects. . . . My words, and especially the phrase which relates to campaign uses of the Company's funds, or, as it expressed it, " putting hands into the treasury of the Company to defeat the people's choice " have been construed in some quarters as a personal attack on you. Allow me to say that I greatly regret this impression since I did not intend to make such an attack or to charge that you had used the Company's money to advance your personal interests or in any improper manner, and I am satisfied that you have not done so. Allow me also to express the wish that our relations may continue as friendly hereafter as they have been heretofore.

C. P. Huntington.

This was not the complete vindication Stanford had been demanding daily; but he must have realized that it was the best he could get, for he prudently let the matter drop. Huntington was agreeable; he was already tired of his unaccustomed place in the limelight. Moreover, he had accomplished what he had set out to do. Why ask more? To carry the quarrel further might in truth hurt business. The principals granted no further interviews; Creed Haymond again became spokesman for the company. The feud had burned itself out. Both principals were heartily glad that it had settled one point; it would no longer be necessary for them to maintain the pretense of friendship. Thereafter they met only when business affairs made it unavoidable; their conversation was monosyllabic and their infrequent letters severely formal. Only once did Huntington interject what might be termed a personal note; a year later he brought himself to state, with perhaps unconscious irony: " I certainly have no reason to complain of you, or of any of my co-directors in the past, for I have usually had my own way."

8

ONE of the minor results of this public airing of the Huntington-Stanford feud was that certain Coast journalists propounded this question: which of the two men had played the most important part in the creation of the road? One weekly, reviewing the years when the Central Pacific was being built, pictured the Governor carrying the main burden of the enterprise, meeting and overcoming a succession of crises: financial, legislative, administrative. While Stanford was in the midst of the tumult, fighting, conciliating, driving the great inert machine toward success, where was Huntington? Huntington, remarked the editor, was in the East buying supplies, spending money that had been raised by Stanford, and

writing petulant letters demanding why more rapid progress was not being made. For the rest, this critic claimed
that Huntington lacked many of the qualities necessary
in a successful promoter. Unlike the affable Stanford, his
attitude in business was formal and direct; he had neither
the ability nor the desire to place himself on a friendly
footing with those with whom he dealt. He lacked, too,
eloquence in argument, the power of winning the support
of others by firing them with his own enthusiasm — a gift
that Theodore Judah had possessed in a high degree.

That there was much truth in this estimate of Huntington cannot be denied. Unquestionably there were phases
of the enterprise in which he was the opposite of an asset.
Until late in life he uniformly refused to make speeches,
whatever the occasion. His manner toward interviews,
when he could be persuaded to grant them at all, showed
clearly his hope of getting the nonsense over as quickly
as possible.

The chief reason for his failure as a herald of goodwill
for railroad ambitions was a constitutional dislike of asking a favor of any man. He was proud to announce, in
season and out, his ability and willingness to pay for what
he wanted. Consequently, when it was not a question of
buying, he was ill at ease, and his attitude usually became
one of combined defiance and arrogance. From this standpoint Huntington's value to the railroad was less than
nothing. He was hardly more helpful when it came to the
practical details of construction and operation. There
is no evidence that he had any grasp of engineering problems or, except in their relation to costs, any interest in

them. During the entire construction period it was said that he contributed but one suggestion. When the problem of how best to scale the final steep rise to the Sierra summit was furrowing the brows of company engineers, he proposed the building of a huge elevator in which whole trains could be lifted up and down the troublesome thousand-foot cliff.

Huntington had obvious limitations as a railroad engineer and as an ambassador of goodwill, but he was of course far more than a mere purchasing agent for the road. It was, however, years before the full extent of his other activities became generally known. Much of this information reached the public against Huntington's wishes and over the objections of railroad attorneys. The rest he told voluntarily when, in later years, he adopted one of the weaknesses of old age, that of boasting of past triumphs. A favorite narrative concerned his clash with Secretary of the Treasury McCullough over the delivery of $2,400,000 in subsidy bonds.

This was in the late '60s when the rival roads were reaching ahead to grasp as large a share as possible of the government's subsidy. After a slow start the Union Pacific had by 1867 begun to hit full stride, and its owners became ambitious to build as far west as the California border. This would have given their Western rival only the costly section over the Sierra, leaving the Union Pacific in control of the traffic to the Nevada silver mines.

Alarmed letters went east to Huntington reporting Union Pacific advance-construction crews in central Nevada, five hundred miles west of Salt Lake and less than half that distance from the California line. Every mile of desert construction taken over by the rival company meant the loss of twenty thousand dollars' clear profit from the government subsidy, and of course the loss of a mile of completed road. Couldn't something be done to make the Union Pacific stay on their own side of the Rockies?

Huntington read these worried appeals with unconcern and promptly one of his awkwardly phrased, hastily scrawled letters was dispatched west. Let the partners stop worrying about the Union Pacific. Let them attend to their own sufficient job, which was to construct their railroad — as much of it as they could and as fast as they could. The cars of Tom Scott's Pennsylvania Railroad saw much of Huntington during the ensuing weeks as he shuttled between New York and Washington. At the capital he visited department heads, talked with important figures on the Congressional railroad committees. Word was sent west outlining a plan of counter-warfare, and soon Central Pacific crews were playing the same game as their Eastern rivals. If the Union Pacific sent advance parties five hundred miles ahead of their tracks, the Central Pacific could, and would, send theirs a thousand. Before their line was complete even to the California border, company engineers were in Salt Lake City, letting contracts to Brigham Young to grade Central Pacific roadbed *east* of Ogden. Huntington's strategy soon became obvious. Had both companies built as far as their lines were surveyed, the rails would have paralleled each other for more than fifteen hundred miles — and the government was granting only one subsidy. Both sides were frankly bluffing; both were playing for an advantage when the inevitable compromise was made.

The question, as Huntington had foreseen, would ultimately be settled, not by surveying crews in Utah and Nevada, but by Congress. And there the Central Pacific had a decided advantage. Huntington, then as always, knew very clearly what he wanted for the company, and he had been long enough in Washington to know how to go about getting it. In this instance he wanted to maneuver the government into paying over to the Central Pacific the subsidy bonds for part of this debated section of the line. With an innocent air of attending to a routine detail, he filed with the Secretary of the Interior a map of a projected new section of the line — one extending as far east as Echo, well up toward the summit of the Rockies. The map was accepted by the department. Next Huntington applied for bonds covering two thirds of the subsidy on this section. All this was in accordance with the Pacific Railroad Act, as amended, which specified that in certain emergencies bonds in that proportion could be paid in advance of actual construction. The sum involved was $2,400,000.

With what one writer called his "remarkable persistence in presenting an argument," Huntington succeeded in convincing not only the Secretary of the Interior but the Attorney General, the federal railroad commissioners, and finally President Johnson that an emergency existed and that the bonds should be delivered. Accordingly, they were ordered paid. Huntington was on the point of receiving them when astonished officials of the Union Pacific learned what was happening and Oakes Ames reached Washington in time to arouse official doubts as to the justice of the transaction. Secretary of the Treasury McCullough was prevailed upon to delay turning over the bonds while Congress investigated.

But to withhold a sum of that size from Huntington, once it had been promised to him, proved a greater task than McCullough had imagined. In his curious anecdotal style Huntington later gave his version of what happened next:

" I went to McCullough and said I: ' Here's a report I want you to have.' He had heard we were working there — meaning among the departments — and he had a talk with Ames. I knew he had agreed not to show me the bonds; but I was determined to have them if I could.

" I got a report from the Attorney General that I was entitled under the law to those bonds. I got one from the Solicitor of the Treasury; he asked for that, I was legally entitled to them. I got two cabinet meetings in one week outside of the regular day. The majority of them voted that I should have the bonds. Then he would not let me have them. I went there nearly a week. I wanted to get them the day the administration closed. . . . I called at McCullough's office; I sent in my card. McCullough would let me know the next morning. . . . I said, never mind, I will go and see him. I did not know McCullough. I wanted those $2,400,000 bonds. ' Well,' said he, ' you seem entitled to them.' I answered: ' That is right; give me the reasons, Mr. Secretary, why you won't let me have them? ' ' Well,' he said: ' You seem entitled to them under the law.' I said: ' That is all right; give me the bonds.' ' Well,' he replied, ' No, I can't do it.' ' Well,' I said, ' I want your reasons. I have men in New York who are interested with me; when I go back, if I don't have the bonds I want the reason why. You can see for yourself.' Finally he remarked, ' You do seem entitled to them.'

" Well, I was nearly a week. I went in there every day and asked him to give me the bonds and asked for the reasons. One day there was a score of men right behind me. ' Now,' said he, ' if you do not let these gentlemen see me, I will decide this thing against you.' ' Now,' I replied, ' Mr. Secretary, rather than have the Secretary of the United States do so foolish a thing as that, I will sit here for a fortnight.' For half an hour or so I sat down. ' Now,' said he, ' Mr. Jordan (he came up just then) , Mr. Huntington is worrying me to death. He says he wants those bonds; what do you think of it? ' Jordan said: ' I have given you a written opinion, Mr. Secretary, that he is entitled to the bonds under the law.' ' Well,' said he, ' he shall have the bonds. . . .' A little after eight o'clock I went out, and found the bonds in my room."

The full amount was not delivered. Huntington's persistence had succeeded, however, in adding a million and a third dollars to the Central Pacific's treasury.

9

CONSIDERING the size of his fortune and the number of years he remained in possession of it, Huntington's benefactions were notably few. Moreover, what he gave was seldom given carelessly. He was not the type of rich man who, recalling from time to time that a certain degree of philanthropy is expected of him, arrogantly tosses a few dollars into whatever palms happen to be extended. On occasion he passed out trifling sums for unknown or dubious purposes, as when he gave a hundred dollars to a solicitor for a home for disabled miners and when he endowed the famous waterfall in San Francisco's Golden Gate Park. But usually when he parted from his dollars, he wanted to know in detail how they were to be spent and by whom.

Several years of Huntington's money-grubbing youth had been spent in the South, where the condition and prospects of the Negro had engaged his interest. More than fifty years later, the scant group at his funeral included J. R. Frizzel of the Hampton Industrial School and Booker T. Washington of Tuskegee, visible evidence of the dead man's long but never extravagant support of the theory that young Negroes might sensibly be taught blacksmithing and simple arithmetic. In 1896 his secretary, George E. Miles, recalled a visit to Huntington's office by the Negro principal of the Salisbury School, in North Carolina. Huntington that morning had denied himself to all callers, but when he heard the Negro's voice in the outer room, his door flew open. " Come in, Price," he called. " I have given orders to keep out everybody this morning, but you can walk in at any time."

The philanthropist took the trouble to point out that his sympathy for the black men did not spring from the fact that they were required to work hard; Huntington had never been of the opinion that hard work was anything but a privilege. But by his code, honest effort should be coupled with at least a hope for advancement, and it was the lack of such hope that made the Negro's plight deplorable.

By the middle '70s, efforts to train young Negroes in the manual trades, which had been advocated by many since the close of the Civil War, had begun to make headway. Huntington grew interested in one such venture: General S. C. Armstrong's Hampton Institute. He investigated the work and ended by giving financial support, but in moderation. His first contribution was fifty dollars. Later he established a trust fund of a thousand dollars, the income from which would pay tuition for one student. Other minor benefactions followed, always after careful consideration and always with explicit instructions as to how the money was to be spent. Blacksmithing, carpentry, and other forms of wood- and metal-working seemed to him proper fields for instruction. The building and equipping of the institute's shops became his particular interest.

Unlike most amateurs in this field, Huntington never allowed his enthusiasm to get out of hand. Training for the Negro could be a benefit only if it were kept within narrow limits. The brightest of them, he felt, could safely learn trades and thereby have a means of lifting themselves out of the ranks of unskilled labor. To attempt to go further, to give them even the beginnings of a formal education, was pernicious folly. Would someone please tell him what in hell the Negro was expected to do with his " education " after he had it? Let him learn how to do useful work with his hands. If he wanted more, teach him to read and write, to add and subtract. He let it be known that if General Armstrong yielded to the pleas of certain Northern backers of the school (who saw the institute turning out droves of black-skinned Ph.D.s) his support would be withdrawn immediately.

This was not philanthropy of a very spectacular sort, and other benefactions were on the same plan. In the middle '80s he presented a chapel, in memory of his mother, to the village of Harwinton, Connecticut. He returned there when he was sixty-six years old and spoke a few gruff sentences at the building's dedication. At about the same time he bought a house at Throgs Neck, at the edge of Long Island Sound, stocked the grounds with horses, cows, and dogs, and lived there summers, playing the country gentleman on an unextravagant scale.

In the near-by village of Westchester, now part of the Bronx, a group gathered one summer evening in 1891 to celebrate another Huntington gift: a small, church-like brick structure enclosed by a prim iron fence. The meeting came to order and the eyes of the villagers focused on the donor of Westchester's Library and Reading Room. Huntington talked with commendable brevity and listened to the speeches of five consecutive clergymen. His own remarks were packed with wholesome advice to the young. " Let me urge upon you the importance of choosing the right path early in life. . . . A wrong beginning is almost certain to result in a wrong ending. . . . Let me urge the careful use of your time."

Other speakers stressed the same virtues, at more length. One of the clergymen did not fail to point out that a few hours in Mr. Huntington's library was a better preparation for the morrow's work than an evening of roistering in the village saloons. He invited his listeners to consider what might happen to the renowned Huntington judgment should the latter take to frequenting bar-rooms. Lest the audience draw wrong inferences, the chairman interrupted to assure listeners that the philanthropist was a teetotaler — which was a mild exaggeration. The final speech ended, the group gave three cheers for Westchester's patron and filed out into the cool evening. A local account of the rites was headed: " Church and State Unite in Glowing Tribute to Young Men's Benefactor — Collis P. Huntington."

Those who expected little philanthropies to grow into big ones were disappointed; the trickle never came to resemble a flood. In the same issues that carried his obituary the nation's newspapers speculated on the possibility that death might have relaxed the famous tight fists. His will, however, revealed no posthumous generosity. Instead, the document provided that the stream of his assets flow through guarded channels into the hands of other Huntingtons, chiefly those of his wife and of his favorite nephew, Ed. There for nearly a quarter of a century longer his fortune remained intact. It was not until the 1920s that any considerable part of it was diverted into philanthropic channels.

The medium was this same nephew, Henry Edwards, son of Collis's elder brother Solon, co-owner of the Oneonta store in the '40s. When Collis left for California in 1849, Solon bore part of the cost of the shipment of whisky that went on ahead. Henry was born the year

Collis arrived in California. Twenty years later he called on his uncle at the Central Pacific's New York office, and the latter had him made manager of a little West Virginia sawmill. By a familiar Huntington transition, the young man presently owned the mill. Collis's interest, sharpened by this feat, caused him to take the young man into his organization. Thereafter, except for a brief period when he returned to the family store at Oneonta, he remained his uncle's aide, holding progressively more important railroad offices.

Childless himself, the elder Huntington developed a strong liking for his keen and acquisitive nephew. " No better boy than Ed ever lived," he once pronounced. In 1873 the young man solidified his position by marrying Mary Alice Prentice, niece of the first Mrs. Huntington and elder sister of Clara, whom Collis adopted. Thus entrenched, H. E.'s advance was rapid. By 1881 he was superintendent of construction for one of the Eastern lines his uncle was developing; five years later he was managing the Kentucky Central. By 1892 he had become the recognized Huntington representative at San Francisco, with an office at Post and Montgomery streets and a moderately elegant residence on a Jackson Street hillside. The newcomer had neither the support nor the admiration of the sons of his uncle's partners, and echoes of clashes with Charles F. Crocker and Timothy Hopkins found their way into the local press. But the elder Huntington was then solidly in the saddle and young H. E. uniformly had his way.

When Collis died, Henry was managing the railroad-owned streetcar system in San Francisco. The experience interested him. Later he was to demonstrate that local car lines could do in a limited area what his uncle's steam lines had done in whole states; that is, they could be made to shape the region's future by controlling both the rate and the direction of its growth. Soon after the century opened, H. E. moved to Los Angeles, at a time when that backward village was just beginning its startling rise in population and complexity. From his uncle he had inherited much real estate and to this he added a great deal more, buying numerous outlying parcels of valley and foothill lands.

The purchases were not made at random, though what plan he was following was not evident at the time. He began a network of fast interurban car lines, and when their routes were laid out it was found that they passed through miles of Huntington-owned land. Of course he profited enormously by the subsequent boom, some of the profits of which were put back into a variety of other local investments. His finger was presently in so many pies that the child in the classic Los Angeles dialogue, who had left the Huntington Hotel, traveled down Huntington Boulevard in a Huntington streetcar, and arrived at Huntington Beach, quite logically inquired if this ocean might also be Mr. Huntington's. The answer may have been that Mr. Huntington's uncle had once had control of the traffic on the ocean, but that his option had been allowed to lapse.

Thus far H. E. had conformed to the Huntington tradition: he had continued to make money and to hold on to it. He had even surpassed his uncle and evolved a new method of accumulating capital: that of marrying it. Divorced by his first wife in 1906, he seven years later, in Paris, unexpectedly married Collis's widow, thereby reuniting the bulk of his uncle's fortune. He was sixty-three, his bride a year or two younger.

Then at last the tide began to turn. From that time on, the business of adding superfluous millions to an already unwieldy total lost its fascination. After sixty years of remarkably persistent accumulation the stream of Huntington dollars began to flow outward. In their progress they cut through to an entirely unexpected channel.

About 1902 H. E. purchased the San Marino ranch, an area of foothill land, covered with brush and stunted oak trees, just beyond the Pasadena city limits. Eight years later he retired and went to live in a house he had built on one of its elevations. But the acquisitive instinct, well developed in all the clan, made a life of idleness out of the question. Like his uncle, he had earlier acquired a dilatory habit of buying pictures and books and had assembled a considerable though undistinguished collection of both. But it was not until after he had withdrawn to his San Marino hilltop that the fever set in in earnest. He continued, then and later, to purchase paintings, specializing in the eighteenth-century English school, but his main interest swung to books.

There followed a period of spending unique in book-collecting history. From 1910 until his death in 1927 the force and weight of his dollars dominated the markets of the world. When H. E. set out to buy a library he followed exactly the procedure his uncle had found most effective; he captured it by a direct assault, brushing aside obstacles and demolishing opposition. For over fifteen years he bought *en bloc* every important library that came on the market. Dealers everywhere gave him first choice of all worth-while books that came into their hands. His agents made clean sweeps of the auction houses here and abroad. They approached the owners of noted private libraries — in America, on the Continent, mostly in England — and made offers of such size that few dared to refuse. As a result, war-swollen taxes were paid on numerous English country seats, while their library shelves were swept clean of heriditary collections, and more truckloads of books ascended the California hillside to Huntington's new marble library.

While this fantastic buyer was in the market, rival collectors and the great public and state libraries had literally to be satisfied with what Huntington didn't want. When the disappointed ones complained of " the brute force of money," H. E. smiled and continued to take what he wished, and to pay for it liberally. He had a stock answer: " I am an old man. I haven't much time." Unlike his uncle, he was unable to convince himself that he would live forever. How many dollars were poured into the collection was never made public; probably it is not known. One estimate places the total at thirty million dollars. His method was admittedly ruthless, and admittedly his success was due to a bottomless purse. But the library and, incidentally, the art gallery he assembled and in 1919 placed in trust for public use (with an endowment

of eight million dollars) were one of the most princely
gifts in history. In fifteen years he had made his San
Marino ranch one of the world's important storehouses of
the literature and history of the English-speaking people,
a magnet that draws scholars and research workers from
every civilized country.

When the gift was consummated, Westerners reflected
not without irony that the dollars wrested from them by
a monopolistic railroad system had returned at last in the
form of canvases by Gainsborough and Sir Joshua Rey-
nolds, of incunabula, Elizabethan first editions, and literary and historical works of a bulk and value beyond esti-
mating.

10

". . . A TALL, well-built man, with a full beard tinged
with gray, a square, resolute jaw and keen, bluish-gray
eyes . . . sitting in his office chair, with a black skull-cap
which he usually wears in business hours, pushed back on
his head, he has an open, jolly, unassuming look. . . ."

This was Collis Huntington in lighter mood, as seen
in 1887 by Henry Clews, banker and co-tenant of the
handsome Mills Building on Board Street. Clews, who
saw him frequently, admired his active movements and
healthy appearance, qualities which he attributed to good
habits of his youth and good care in later years. At that
period Huntington himself found nothing wrong with
his health, although he had begun to observe that he tired

easily. " I would feel better if I didn't have to spend most of my life on trains," he once complained, and went on to outline his weekly schedule: two days in New York, one in Boston, four in Washington. That called for four nights of travel out of every seven. The situation was not improved by the fact that he had to commute between New York and Washington on Tom Scott's Pennsylvania, for he and Scott were fighting to control a second transcontinental line, then building across Texas and Arizona Territory. In the circumstances Huntington considered it unsound policy to accept passes on the Pennsylvania, and twice a week the old man reluctantly bought and paid for his ticket.

But he could not avoid going to Washington or occasionally to more distant points. In later years he made a number of trips to Europe, usually to quell incipient revolts of British holders of Central Pacific stock, who periodically needed to have explained to them why dividends had stopped the moment they made their investments. It was probably on one such visit to London that he crossed the Channel on a mere pleasure jaunt and took in the Paris Exposition of 1889. Paris journalists did not fail to interview the quaint American railroad baron. At home Huntington never hesitated to denounce American institutions, but abroad he proved as patriotic as a Rotarian. No, he was not much impressed by the exposition. Except, of course, the paintings, he had seen nothing that could not be better made in America, and at less cost. He even accomplished the prodigious feat of belittling the Eiffel Tower, at which the rest of the world was gaping in awe. It was 985 feet tall? Well, American engineers could build one " a mile high " if they wanted to. Besides, what was the use of the thing? The reporters withdrew in strained silence and Huntington and his wife remained a week longer, buying furniture by the dray-load for their Fifth Avenue house. No one pointed out that perhaps the latter too might have been better and less expensively made in America.

Travel for pleasure was an excellent thing if a man had leisure, but Huntington chanced to be busy. An interviewer asked if he intended to go abroad one summer in the '90s. " I have practically promised my wife to go," he replied, " but I have a bridge to build over the Ohio River at Cincinnati." Here was no senseless Eiffel Tower but something practical, something to shorten the haul of his trains and increase dividends. Europe would have to wait.

His twice-yearly trips to the Pacific Coast had the same practical excuse. His interests in the East grew in size and perplexity, but his major properties still centered in California and these needed periodical looking into. Had this not been so, it is doubtful if the old man would ever have returned to the Coast. His dislike for California and, in particular, for San Francisco, increased as he grew older. He had a theory that mild climate bred weaklings; a man who didn't have to fight the weather was unlikely to fight anything else. There were other reasons, less theoretical. Stanford's continued prestige on the Coast was persistently irritating, and the expense of preventing the passage or enforcement of anti-railroad legislation at

COLLAPSE OF COLLIS.

This is how Davenport views the knock-out of Huntington by Bierce. At the anti-funding jubilee last night the name of Mr. Bierce was frequently applauded, because of his vigorous efforts against the infamous refunding measure of the Pacific Railroads.

A cartoon by Davenport in the San Francisco Examiner,
June 30, 1896.

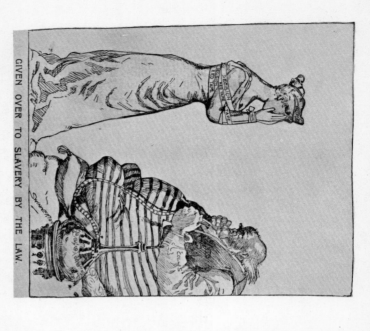

GIVEN OVER TO SLAVERY BY THE LAW.

Cartoon by James Swinnerton in the San Francisco Examiner, December 1, 1896.

Courtesy of the California State Library

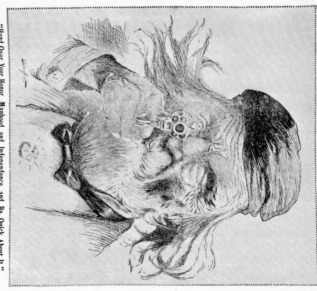

HIGHWAYMAN HUNTINGTON TO THE VOTERS OF CALIFORNIA:

"Hand Over Your Honor, Manhood and Independence, and Be Quick About It."

Cartoon by Davenport in the San Francisco Examiner, November 8, 1898.

Courtesy of the California State Library

Sacramento seemed to him far too high. There were also the sustained and bitter attacks on him by San Francisco newspapers, led by the *Examiner,* on the editorial page of which a then unknown cartoonist, one Homer Davenport, daily pictured him with his hands in the pockets of the common people, a design of dollar signs ornamenting his enormous paunch.

Huntington was never in agreement with the theory that the Coast had treated him and his partners with liberality and had been robbed for its pains. " We have served California," he announced, " better than any other set of men have ever served any other state in the Union." Again, of the metropolis: " We never had a dollar's worth from San Francisco, either in money or moral support." Of the state's lawmakers: " California has never had anybody in Washington that has done much of anything good."

On his San Francisco visits he had made his headquarters at the Palace Hotel, since its completion, and it was there he took his second wife in the winter of 1884. Nearly ten years had then passed since " Ralston's Folly," its serried rows of bay windows dominating the town, had providentially been finished in time to welcome General Sherman back to familiar scenes with a banquet still recalled by tottering citizens, and the Palace remained the wonder and pride of the Coast. The place was huge, ornately luxurious, and for thirty years it maintained its prestige without a sign of diminution. To live there was a badge of unquestioned eminence, for its two-acre roof sheltered positively everyone of consequence who reached the west coast. Local families that could afford the expense were known to exchange comfortable homes for the privilege of occupying two or three cubicles off one of its long, wide corridors, and humbler citizens frequently hired hacks, rode down Montgomery Street, crossed Market, and swung into the echoing Palm Court. There they descended in state, paid the cab fare, and contentedly walked out the nearest entrance.

But, for all its prestige, the Palace was far too big for its time and place, and whole floors of walnut and plush bedrooms remained untenanted. Moreover, the place was noisy from the passing cable-cars, the clatter of drays over the Market Street cobbles, and the procession of carriages around its central court. In the early '90s an ever interested city learned that Huntington would stop there no longer. He had purchased the austere Colton house on Nob Hill. It was directly across Taylor Street from the fantastic redwood mansion of the Crockers, and local critics regarded the circumstance as unfortunate, for that baroque structure, it was said, tended to " kill " its modest neighbor. There is no doubt that the complexity of the Crocker towers and gables and art glass, the incrustations of millwork and iron, caught and held the eye, and that by contrast Huntington's new property looked as unornamental as a Central Pacific way-station. The general opinion was that Huntington must have bought the place because he had got a tremendous bargain.

Huntington's purchase was surprising for another reason, for the house could hardly have held pleasant memories for him. It had been David Colton's residence — and

Huntington's association with that gentleman had a few years earlier been the means of exposing his business methods and ethics to an astonished and resentful public. The matter, however, disturbed him not at all. He had recently assumed the presidency of the Southern Pacific, the Palace Hotel was noisy, a residence on the Coast seemed desirable, and among the available houses this was the one he chanced to like best.

The deal was accordingly made, Colton's widow moved out, and for months the place stood vacant, for Huntington had meantime returned east. In the fall of 1892, however, signs of renewed activity aroused the interest of neighbors on the hill. Toward mid-November society columns broke out in excited paragraphs: " It is a satisfactory certainty that Mrs. C. P. Huntington will return here in early spring. She is having her residence on California Street redecorated and the reception rooms refurnished." Readers learned that while the furniture of the former occupant was " very rich and gorgeous " it was " rather old style " and that Mrs. Huntington was planning many changes. Cornices and curtains were to be removed, walls and ceilings refinished in lighter shades, and windows hung with something very new and smart: " orange-tinted brocade with a stripe in it." " The mansion," stated the society editor of *The Wave*, " will be very swell indeed."

11

DURING the next eight years Huntington spent perhaps six months in the San Francisco house, for at seventy and beyond he continued to extend his activities, and his complex interests prevented long absences from the home office.

By the middle '90s he was definitely a national figure, his name familiarly linked in the public mind with the Goulds, Vanderbilts, Hills, and other titans of transportation, and of course he shared with them the deference and the abuse of a money-conscious nation. How many dollars he had accumulated became a sort of national guessing game. When, toward the end of the century, one financial writer estimated his fortune at seventy million dollars, Huntington commented that this might be as good a guess as any. Asked to make an estimate of his own, he refused on the ground that guessing was a futile waste of time. But he then controlled enough miles of railroad to connect the North and South Poles, and he had recently traveled from Newport News to San Francisco riding every foot of the way over his own rails. He had, besides, the deciding voice in a score of other enterprises: steamship lines, coal mines, timber holdings in the Northwest, huge blocks of land in Southern California, great shipyards at Newport News.

All these were directed from his cramped and barren office on the seventh floor of the Mills Building, the glass door of which had no lettering but his name: C. P. Huntington. He worked at a long table-desk, perpetually piled with a mass of papers, one corner alone being kept clear for the transaction of current business. It has been said that across that desk corner business deals involving more than a billion dollars were worked out. " Over it have been drawn and studied carefully, inch by inch, profiles of thousands of miles of railroad. Plans and policies and combinations have been whispered around it. . . ." The desk with its faded red felt cover was once pronounced " comparatively new " by Huntington himself, who went on to say that it was less than twenty years old. The office floor was uncarpeted, the windows uncurtained, the few chairs so battered and angular that when Leland Stanford's widow ended the historic feud by calling on him in the late '90s, Huntington had to send out for a leather arm-chair in which the old lady might sit at ease.

He was less concerned for the comfort of other visitors. The latter filed through the anteroom on their way to or from the famous desk corner in a constant stream, its current accelerating year by year until, in 1896, his secretary wondered how a man past seventy-five could continue to carry the load. " He is the object," Miles wrote, " of continual solicitation on the part of promoters who are eager to secure the influence of his name in floating new enterprises. His anteroom is the rendezvous of a multitude of people who want something. He is almost momentarily the recipient of visitors' cards. His door is continually opening to let out one caller and admit another. His morning mail is supplemented hourly, and he is bound to finish it before he goes home. . . ."

This, in 1896, was the man who nearly twenty-five years earlier had convinced himself that overwork was ruining his health and so had made persistent attempts to sell out and retire. In the last year of the century, when preparations for building New York's first subway were begun, he recalled that he had planned just such a project as early as 1869 and had abandoned it for the opportunity to pick up, at a great bargain, an uncompleted railroad in Virginia: the Chesapeake & Ohio. " I don't work hard," he told one solicitous caller, " I work easy." He had .learned, he said, to keep troublesome business problems locked up in his office, and he carried home only those that required no concentration; sometimes he spent a pleasant hour or two of an evening scratching his signature on checks or scribbling a score or so of confidential letters. One of the last men to whom he granted an interview came away impressed at the old man's firm belief that there was virtue in work for work's sake. Sixty years had failed to shake a conviction formed in boyhood that there was something reprehensible in the enjoyment of leisure.

Yet there were moments when he confessed that a life less weighted by responsibilities might have been pleasant. He found time to recall his youthful tramps through the South when all he owned was carried on his back and, as Sherman was to do twenty years later, he lived off the country. Power and possessions were pleasant, but he thought it possible that one sometimes paid too much for them. He liked to reflect, too, on his infrequent trips out on the line when the Central Pacific was building. Once he had set off alone on horseback and had spent several nights under the stars. The memory of that brief touch of Arcadia remained with him to the end. A horse and a blanket and no other possessions; freedom to roam and loaf and be brazenly idle. " I could see how the Indians liked that kind of a life. . . ." But Huntington was not intended to be an Indian. On that same trip he came, one evening, on a group of teamsters hired by the railroad to haul ties from the Sierra foothills to the distant end of construction. He found the men reclining in the warmth of a huge bonfire. On the fire were a dozen ties. But he got no pleasure from the carefree scene, for the brightly crackling ties were costing him and his partners eight dollars each.

As he approached eighty he remained as vain as ever of his physical strength. When newspapers repeated some Connecticut ancient's boast that he had vanquished Huntington in a schoolyard fight, the latter made prompt and heated denial: " No boy in school ever licked me, or ever could! I could wipe up the floor with half the boys in school all together! " In San Francisco the *Examiner* suggested that the two fight over again, pointing out that the public would pay well for the privilege of looking on, and that Huntington's share of the profit might be used to maintain his lobby against the Nicaragua Canal.

Nothing came of the suggestion, and Huntington continued to keep competent watch over his involved affairs. But observers who saw him often began at last to detect signs that the old man was slowing up. For the first time in memory he began to arrive late at his desk and to allow employees to lock up at night. He gave over more time to such frivolities as billiards and whist, although he refused to play for stakes. Until he had passed middle life he had never smoked or used alcohol; in his seventies he became a fairly proficient cigar-smoker and admitted that he usually swallowed a slug of brandy before going to his early bed. But one drink a day was his limit; when he reached a hundred, he once said, he hoped to find time for serious drinking.

One by one other austere habits of his youth were shunted off. No longer insistent on doing as he pleased, he ended by doing whatever was conventionally expected of a multimillionaire. Thus his adopted daughter contracted an international marriage, he meekly dozed through interminable evenings in his Metropolitan box; he even conformed by wearing a Prince Albert coat during business hours. His belated taste for display found expression in a succession of " mansions," reaching its climax in the investment of two millions in a square, grim town house, suggestive of a country court-house, at Fifth Avenue and Fifty-seventh Street. But he disliked the place and rarely occupied it. He spent another quarter of a million for a marble mausoleum at Woodlawn and is said to have refused even to look at it after it was built.

By then most of his time was spent at Throgs Neck or in travel about the country; train travel became bearable in his old age because the motion and noise helped him to sleep. Among his last purchases was a summer camp in the Adirondacks, a log palace on Raquette Lake called Pine Knot Camp, bought from W. West Durant, a former president of the Union Pacific. So that he could reach it more conveniently, he had a twenty-six-mile railroad built. This passed through a strip of state-owned land, and newspapers had another opportunity to belabor him for disregarding the public's rights. The *World* inquired if this was not government for and by, not the people, but Huntington.

He was long past worrying about such attacks. Toward the beginning of August 1900 he left the Fifth Avenue house (where he was afraid he might die) for a month at Raquette Lake. There, early in the morning of the 14th, he awoke, announced: " I am very, very ill " — and died at once. The next morning his old California enemy, the *Examiner,* could not forbear brightening a conventional obituary with its famous remark that in life he had been " ruthless as a crocodile." Another local paper, the *Bulletin,* ran a front-page editorial sympathizing, not with Huntington's family, but with the *Examiner,* which had lost its dearest enemy. " Othello's occupation is gone."

Meantime, executives on the Coast hastened to send east a five-hundred-dollar bouquet of roses and lilies of the valley, and the San Francisco offices were ordered closed all the day of the funeral. In New York, crape was hung on the active door of the Mills Building office, while the favorite nephew, Henry E., hastened by special train from Texas, and after a day of hesitation Princess Hatzfeldt cabled from London that it would be impossible to cross the Atlantic in time for the funeral. For three days the nation's newspapers printed estimates of the

281

dead man's wealth and conjectures as to who would succeed him, and collected a disappointingly slender sheaf
of stories about his life and habits.

Six policemen were assigned to control the crowds before the Fifth Avenue mansion as the hour of the funeral
approached. But summer showers kept the curious away
and the policemen, with nothing else to do, stood in the
downpour, idly watching less than a score of invited guests
hurry through the stone columns of the gate.

COLTON

"I PROPOSE TO STAND OR
FALL WITH YOU ALL. . . ."

1

WHEN the last spike was driven at Promontory, the four
partners had already traveled far since the evening in 1861
when they had lent support to Judah's dubious gamble.
They had accomplished the most momentous engineering
and financial feat of their generation. They had emerged
rich and, to a degree, famous men. The completion of the
road was celebrated as a milestone in the nation's progress;
the names of the four were conspicuous in the chorus of
praise that issued from the newspapers and pulpits and
lecture platforms of the country.

With such laudation ringing in their ears, it is understandable that the group soon came to regard the operation of the railroad, with its variety of new problems and
its uncertain reward, as a dull business. There was a
natural reaction — a desire to rest on laurels already
won and to avail themselves of the ease their fortunes
had put within reach.

Thoughts of selling out were much on the minds of
all four during the early '70s. Crocker withdrew in 1871,
and returned again, not altogether willingly, two years
later. Huntington's letters of the period are full of refer-

ences to his desire to get out, and Hopkins, as usual, was willing to follow his lead. Only Stanford hung back; he was reluctant to surrender the distinction of his office as president and he had always had the faculty of taking his responsibilities lightly.

Negotiations for the sale of their interests to a group headed by D. O. Mills dragged on for months and finally came to nothing. Huntington, convinced that he was " losing his grip," cast about for other possible purchasers. But he had little real hope, for the financial skies were darkening steadily, and not many weeks later Black Friday ushered in the most severe money panic the country had ever known. All hope of a favorable sale was swept away. Instead of retiring with their profits, the partners faced the need of protecting their jeopardized fortunes. There was no further talk of letting go. The emergency not only kept the three partners together; it speedily brought Crocker back into the fold.

That the road was carried safely through this most critical phase of its existence was of course due mainly to Huntington. With a leader of only average resourcefulness and tenacity, disaster could hardly have been avoided. As it was, the issue for some weeks hung in the balance, while both on Wall Street and on the Coast rumors that the Central and Southern Pacific were going into receivership circulated almost daily. By his energy and stubbornness and a native adroitness in money matters, Huntington eventually carried them through. But the burden had been chiefly his own, a fact that he was never slow to point out to the others. His letters continued to harp on one theme: too much was falling on his shoulders, and his strength was not equal to it. The others were not doing their share. Stanford wasted his time on ranches and such nonsense. Crocker wandered aimlessly about the Coast and seldom went near his office; Hopkins was ill; " while I was working every day in the year almost, and about fourteen hours a day . . . I was not satisfied with the hours they put in."

Partly because of that dissatisfaction, partly because he needed someone in California who could be depended on not only to be on the job but to understand it, a fifth member was presently admitted to limited partnership.

The newcomer was General David Douty Colton. Forty-two years of age, a native of Maine, and a resident of California since gold-rush days, the General already had his finger in many local pies. He was red-haired, shrewd, industrious, and aggressive. These, and a driving desire to get ahead, to associate on terms of equality with the leading men of the Coast, were his chief characteristics. The type, a common one in early California, usually gravitated toward politics, and Colton was no exception. While he was still under twenty-five he became a useful cog in the political organization built up by David C. Broderick, the wily ex-fireman from New York. On the morning in 1859 when Senator Broderick and Judge Terry settled their differences on the sandhills south of San Francisco, Colton was one of his chief's seconds; later he helped keep the dead man's organization together. Colton's material prosperity, too, dated from that period. Certain parcels of San Francisco real estate owned by Broderick passed into his possession, and these later became quite valuable.

Like many another politician, Colton's interest lay in organization and manipulation; he had no strong wish for office. One term as sheriff in the mountain county of Siskiyou had ended his desire for public service. His liking for his military title, however, persisted. He was universally called " the General," not always without irony, for the title dated from an early connection with the state militia and he had never seen service. After the Civil War he went east, studied law at Albany, then returned and formed a partnership with an Albany classmate, Ralph C. Harrison.

The firm of Colton and Harrison remained in existence for years, but the General's talents lay in other directions and he soon gave up practice. " Why sit around waiting for a $50 fee when a smart trader can go out and make $500 in half the time? " He recognized that the judicious exercise of his political influence would most quickly gain his desires. Accordingly he set about widening his acquaintance and extending his party connections, always quite willing to make himself useful to anyone of importance who might need small favors at the city hall or in Sacramento. In return he was given the opportunity to participate in promising speculations in which the great men were involved.

Most of these ventures proved lucrative, and one seemed to be the opportunity of a lifetime. In 1871, gambling-mad San Francisco was stirred by news of immensely rich diamond fields in northern Colorado. A group of the Coast's shrewdest financiers formed a ten-

million-dollar corporation to exploit this greatest of bonanzas, and Colton was made its manager. Like everyone
else connected with the enterprise, the General believed
himself the owner of an incipient fortune of millions.
But presently came proof that the field had been salted
with a few thousand dollars' worth of low-quality dia-
monds bought in Antwerp and London; the two " honest
prospectors " disappeared with the $600,000 they had re-
ceived for their interests in the " discovery," and General
Manager Colton found his corporation dissolved before
he had completed fitting up its handsome offices. Along
with the other dupes, the General shared the ridicule of
the nation as he turned to more prosaic means of making
his fortune.

2

NOTWITHSTANDING this setback, the red-haired General
rapidly became a man of local prominence. By 1872, five
years after his return from Albany, he had gained the distinction of a house on Nob Hill, a ranch on the slopes of
Mount Diablo, and a three months' tour of Europe. The
activities of his wife and his pretty daughters were recorded in local society columns, and his advice on the more
practical phases of state politics was regularly sought by
men of the first importance.

But the General's ego grew with his prosperity, and
an acquaintance recalled that " he made money fast and
enemies faster." Even as late as the '70s, few of San Fran-

cisco's prominent men were distinguished for either their modesty or their good manners, and Colton was not one of them. The General's brashness and self-esteem alienated many who had to have dealings with him. When Alfred Cohen made his famous defense against the charge of embezzlement filed against him by the Big Four, the vitriolic attorney aimed some of his most telling blasts at Colton, then the Central Pacific's financial director:

" When I had business relations with the plaintiff and its officers and agents, I was compelled to come in constant contact with many men whose manners, whose habits, whose modes of thought and whose conversation were not calculated to advance me either in my own esteem or that of my fellow citizens, but I thank God . . . that I was not required to co-operate with ' General ' David D. Colton. . . ."

He sketched Colton's rise to local importance, hinted that he had made away with part of Broderick's estate, and continued:

" The inflation of his fortunes has brought with it inflation of vanity, until today there dwells on this peninsula no man so able or so important as is ' General ' David D. Colton — in his own estimation."

Cohen was not content to dwell merely on his victim's past and present; he also predicted his end:

" ' General ' David D. Colton will never go from among us by the ordinary processes of nature. When that dread hour arrives wherein a mourning community can hope to contain him no longer, it will only be necessary to cut the thread that binds him to this cold earth, when, like one of the painted,

DAVID D. COLTON
From a lithograph made from a photograph by Bradley &
Rulofson and published in the San Francisco News Letter,
October 12, 1878.
Courtesy of the California State Library

THE COLTON RESIDENCE AT CALIFORNIA AND TAYLOR STREETS, SAN FRANCISCO

After Colton's death this was purchased by Huntington and occupied on his periodical visits to San Francisco.

Courtesy of Edwin Grabhorn

transparent bags of gas sold by toy venders on the street corners, he will sail quietly away through the clouds and be seen no more."

Cohen's remarks, however, were not made until some years later, when the General was at the height of his career. He attained his greatest prominence through his connection with the railroad, and this was made possible mainly because of his friendship with Charles Crocker. Soon after he moved to San Francisco in 1873, Crocker, like the other two resident partners, began casting about for a suitable site for a new home. An area of land fronting on California Street, near the western edge of Nob Hill took his eye. The property was directly across Taylor Street from Colton's house, and the General did not fail to make himself agreeable to his wealthy future neighbor. Colton was in New York when, in December 1874, news reached him that the deal for the Nob Hill property had been consummated. He wrote Crocker at once: " I am delighted to learn that you have acquired those lots. I now feel . . . with you my next door neighbor my future good conduct is assured. . . ." The two were presently inseparable; they addressed each other as " Dave " and " Charley," exchanged advice on business deals, and traveled about the Coast looking over possible investments in mines and ranches. " To the House of Crocker the House of Colton sends love and greetings," wrote the General as the year 1875 opened. The Coltons enjoyed the privilege of yearly passes over the Central and Southern Pacific lines, and the General was permitted to invest moderately in one of the railroad-owned properties: the Rocky Mountain Coal and Iron Company, of which he was made manager.

This business association brought the General into closer contact with Stanford and Hopkins. The latter, however, failed to share their partner's enthusiasm for the newcomer, and Crocker's suggestion that he be given other railroad connections was coolly received. But the ambitious General was not easily discouraged. The Central Pacific had proved itself the most facile money-making machine ever seen in the West, and a place however inconspicuous at the same table with its owners was worth struggling for. Colton continued his intimacy with Crocker, remained agreeable through Stanford's sullen silences, and smilingly endured the inimical glances of tired Mark Hopkins. The matter could wait. Nothing needed to be settled in a day, and Huntington would soon be out on one of his visits. Meantime if the General's connections would permit him to be of any small service to the partners, they had but to ask.

Huntington duly arrived; Crocker presented his new friend, and the matter of his joining the Big Four was reopened. Huntington proved willing to listen. By then he had reached definite conclusions about his partners, and the chief of these was that they were not doing their share. A monopolistic railroad system produced not merely dollars but a complex variety of problems. No group of two-hour-a-day executives could cope with these, even had they been uniformly competent. By Huntington's code, subordinates were hired to carry out orders, not to give them, and he clung to his theory even though it often required that he remain at his desk until past midnight. He had given up hope for much help from the San Francisco trio, particularly from Stanford and Crocker. So Huntington listened while Colton, red-faced and self-assured, made his plea. The road needed a twelve-hour-a-day man on the Coast — but not any man. He must have a variety of qualifications and a variety of connections.

His face earnest, the General talked rapidly, persuasively. It grew clear that he knew the political ropes in California, that he understood what favors the railroad needed from legislatures and from city and county law-makers, and that he knew with certainty what steps were necessary to secure them. Huntington listened, hesitated — at length allowed himself to be convinced. Later he admitted that Colton had seemed " just the man we wanted."

The General was allowed to come in.

3

HE came in, however, with reservations. In return for the use of his talents in the interest of the railroad, he was permitted to share moderately in both its profits and its hazards. The General came in, but not all the way in, and the agreement he signed in the fall of 1874 bristled with clauses safeguarding the interests of the original four. The financial provisions were liberal enough so that the newcomer might, and did, enrich himself. But he also " put his head in a noose and gave Huntington the other end of the rope." From the General's standpoint, Huntington was not, as events proved, its best possible custodian.

Colton received twenty thousand shares each of Central Pacific and Southern Pacific stock. In return, he gave his note for a million dollars, payable in five years. During the first two years the agreement might be canceled at the will of either party and the stock and the note both returned. By this facile transaction the partners got the services of a politician skilled in the practical phases of his art, who could do on the Coast what Huntington was skillfully doing at Washington and who could be depended on to be on the job when he was needed. For his part, Colton became associated with the most powerful corporation in the West; he was able to speak publicly of the other four as " my partners " and to sprinkle his letters to Huntington with such phrases as " our interests " and " us five." To the ambitious General this was a privilege worth even the high price he was paying for it.

That the price was high grew clear not long before his two-year probationary period ended. Early in 1876 he received notice that the partners were terminating his connection with the company. The blow, reaching him out of a clear sky, proved a severe shock. In his plight he hunted up Crocker and threw himself on his friend's mercy. Crocker later stated that the General had shed tears as he pictured the ruin that would ensue to his personal fortunes. Colton had made it widely known that he was one of the associates; he had neglected to state that the arrangement might be only temporary. If he were dropped now, what would happen to his prestige? How could he face his friends? Possibly he thought also of his enemies, for the General's connection with the Big Four had not lessened his arrogance. He may have recalled an ironic reference in a local weekly to " the Big $4\frac{1}{2}$ ", and realized that if he were turned out on the street again it would hardly plunge the community into mourning.

There is some evidence that the dismissal had been engineered by Hopkins, whose dislike of the General dated from their first meeting. Perhaps the other partners, too, had become annoyed at the newcomer's mounting ego and had adopted this device only to remind him of the insecurity of his railroad connection. At any rate, the order was presently withdrawn, and the chastened General continued to bear his title of financial director. But the ground was less secure beneath his feet; he realized very clearly where he stood.

His plans were made accordingly. In less than four years his note would reach maturity. That it would have to be paid in full he no longer doubted; he could hardly hope for philanthropy from the partners. He therefore set himself with admirable earnestness to accumulate a million dollars by October 5, 1879. But the urgency of his need soon got him into new difficulties, for the General was playing a game in which his opponents held all the cards. He had put himself under the necessity of raising a million dollars in five years; the bulk of the money could come only from the railroad, which was controlled in every detail by the other four, two of whom regarded him with active distrust. He needed to exercise a high degree of diplomacy on one hand and a high degree of acquisitiveness on the other.

It was a difficult assignment, but he did his best. The original four then drew salaries of $10,000 a year as officials of the road. Colton received a like amount. It occurred to him that if the salaries were raised to $25,-000 he could pick up a few needed thousands. Accordingly he suggested that executives of so large a corporation should receive more than a paltry $10,000. The matter was unimportant to the other four, whose incomes were derived from other sources, and they thought it best not to make the change. He was blandly informed that moderate salaries for corporation executives are always pleasing to the stockholders.

Colton looked elsewhere for possible sources of new income. Before his admission to limited partnership he had been manager of the company's coal mines, and he had since continued to hold the position and to draw its $6,000 salary — evidently without the knowledge of the others. It was one of a number of ways by which he was storing up funds against the impending settlement. But while he made impressive progress, including some successful speculation in San Francisco real estate, it at length grew clear that he would still miss the goal by a wide margin. One unlucky factor was that his forty thousand shares of stock had not made expected advances; the market for railroad securities was still badly depressed. The outlook was dark.

4

In his dilemma the General hit on an ingenious scheme. By that time his duties as financial director had come to include oversight of the Western Development Company. This was the successor to the Big Four's famous " profit mill," the old Contract and Finance Company, by means of which the partners, as railroad officials, had awarded contracts on extremely liberal terms to themselves as railroad contractors. Colton had a one-ninth interest in this highly lucrative company. The value of his share, if it could be made available in time, would easily solve his troubles. The General pondered the situation; then, like all good tacticians, he decided that desperate situations demand drastic measures.

One afternoon in the summer of 1878 Huntington, Stanford, Crocker, and Hopkins were conferring in one of the rooms at Fourth and Townsend streets when the door opened and the affable General appeared. He was followed by two clerks loaded with bulky packages.

Colton announced pleasantly: " Gentlemen, here are your securities."

Under questioning, the partners were told that the Western Development Company had declared a dividend. General Colton had quietly arranged the matter. He had not troubled to tell the others, preferring to spare them the bother of discussing its details. In fact, he had planned the whole matter as a surprise. The faces of the four men must have convinced him that to that extent his coup had

been successful, for all later professed complete astonishment. The " dividend " proved to be a distribution of
the assets of the Western Development Company, chiefly
Central Pacific stock and Southern Pacific bonds. At par
their value was in excess of $21,000,000. Colton's one-
ninth interest had, therefore, a par value of two and a third
millions.

The ensuing half-hour was a difficult time for the General. The other men, none of whom had a million-dollar
note hanging over his head, accused him of an unwar-
ranted assumption of authority; more, they insisted that
the securities be returned at once. Again Colton was
forced to the extremity of throwing himself upon the
mercy of the four. To return the stocks and bonds would,
he pointed out, injure his standing with employees of his
department, many of whom had been busy for weeks working out the details of the transaction. He added a more
crafty argument: the Western Development Company
was entirely owned by the five of them; the transfer of its
assets to their personal accounts would injure no one; it
merely gave each the control of his share. The General
was not without a knowledge of human nature. As he
had foreseen, once his share of the handsome sum was in
his hands, each partner found himself reluctant to give
it up.

Colton won his point and the " dividend " remained
distributed. But again he was prevented from benefiting
by the move. He retained his one-ninth interest, but his
partners required him to sign an agreement that he would
not sell any part of it, and that he would turn the full

amount back whenever they demanded. He might have possession of the securities, but he must not use them to pay his debt; they were his, but they were not his. It was another of the General's empty victories.

Nonetheless, he remained hopeful. He had been nearly four years with the railroad, and the public, knowing nothing of the financial squirrel-cage in which his partners confined him, considered him almost as important as the Big Four themselves. He was known to be Huntington's political aide on the Coast, the man to be seen by all who wished to reach Huntington's ear or whose railroad business was of a nature that could not prudently be transacted through the usual channels. More, the prestige of his railroad connection had extended his acquaintance among leaders of the Coast who would otherwise have remained remote. In local papers his name was mentioned on equal terms with those of the lesser industrial and financial giants — the rising crop of bankers, promoters, merchants, and real-estate and mining speculators — and only a step below the half-legendary railroad and silver kings who constituted the city's gold-encrusted aristocracy.

Colton, indeed, rather frequently penetrated the rim of this charmed inner circle. With William Chapman Ralston, most spectacular of the Coast's bankers, he had (until the latter's death in 1875) been on terms approaching intimacy. As the railroad's representative, he usually joined in the excursions Ralston liked to arrange for groups of prominent visitors, and his name could always be found in printed lists of guests (sometimes occupying two columns of eight-point newspaper type) at the stupendous Ralston banquets at Belmont. Colton's family, too, became familiar to readers of social columns; their entertainments, their house guests, their travels, their summers at Mount Diablo, all were faithfully recorded. His two daughters, pretty and popular, were authentic belles of the city, and the marriage of the elder to Crittenden Thornton, son of a San Francisco judge, was a social event of importance.

The General was rising financially as well as socially. The incident of the Western Development Company dividend was comfortably forgotten. The partners, Huntington in particular, grew less cautious in extending him their confidence. He was even accorded the honor of having his name given to a crossroads station on the new Southern Pacific line east of Los Angeles — the town that sprang up beside the tracks now has a population of ten thousand.

As the General's sun approached its zenith, even the million-dollar note, then nearing maturity, seemed less formidable. The value of the railroad securities had been rising slowly above the financial swamps of 1871–3. The time was approaching when his stocks would realize enough to enable him to meet his note in full. But Colton had been using his limited opportunities to such advantage that there was no longer much likelihood that he would have to dump his securities on the still depressed market. For more than four years he had been drawing his moderate share of the railroad's profits. In 1878, when his note still had over a year to run, his assets were well above the three-quarter-million mark. Rents from his

San Francisco real estate averaged from $2,500 to $3,000 a month.

The former Sheriff of Siskiyou had not done badly from any standpoint. His Nob Hill residence, one of the most attractive in the city, had become surrounded by a dozen others, homes of the financial and industrial leaders of the West, with most of whom he was on terms of friendship. There were a few exceptions. Although Stanford's new mansion at Powell and California streets was but two blocks away, there is no evidence that he frequently made the short journey between them. Lists of guests at the Stanford receptions were printed in local papers, but the Coltons and their pretty daughters were seldom among them. On the other hand, they were invariably present at the Crocker parties and at most of the other large functions on the hill. Moreover, Colton's relations with Huntington were no longer entirely formal and business-like. In the middle '70s the General refurnished his residence, and one of his letters to Huntington turned aside from more important concerns to discuss a matter of art. One of the walls of his drawing-room needed to be properly covered: Huntington was sent five thousand dollars and given *carte blanche* to select a suitable painting. In April 1878 another message requested Huntington to have " his Mr. Phillips " purchase " 200 tube rose bulbs " and send them West. They were for Mrs. Colton's Mount Diablo ranch, and the General specified that they must be fresh and of the " very best quality."

There were some disturbing factors, perhaps some se-

cret doubts, but Colton must by 1878 have approached his
own definition of a leading citizen. His opinion was
shared by all to whom the appearance of wealth and power
was evidence not to be questioned. Even hostile editors
elevated the General above his station by according him
a full share of the abuse heaped on the Big Four. His correspondence of that period leaves little doubt that he then
considered himself secure. Early in 1878, with no visible
trace of irony, he wrote " My Dear Huntington " that " So
far as I am personally concerned, I propose to stand or fall
with you all." And a little later: " We have not got together enough and talked our plans over among ourselves.
It may not be boastful to say that we five men each in his
way has some strong points. . . ." Even his feud with
Hopkins seems to have been patched up, for on the latter's
death he sent this philosophical and prophetic note to
Huntington: " It was a terrible shock to us all . . . I
know how severely you will feel the blow, but it is only a
question of time with us all."

Colton was then enough in Huntington's confidence to
advise the elder man how to preserve his health, warning
him particularly not to overtax his strength. Nor did he
fail to add a compliment at the end: " I know, Huntington, I could not do half as well or half as much as you do
if I was in your place." The General had been engaged
because Huntington wanted a man on the Coast who was
not afraid to work hard, and his letters to Huntington (he
sometimes wrote three a day) contained frequent re-
minders that he was not loafing. " All my hair in front
has either dropped out or turned gray," he reported on

February 7, 1878. A month later he added: " Since November last I have not had 3 hours of sleep out of the
24. . . ."

A sense of humility had never been characteristic of
him, and success so increased his self-importance that he
could not hope for popularity. " D.D. had a way of strok-
ing the cat's fur the wrong way," recalled a one-time clerk
in the railroad's office. " He used to strut through the
building like a bantam rooster, looking neither to the left
or right." It was due, perhaps, to a desire to live up to his
military title. The red-haired General annoyed others besides the railroad employees. One morning early arrivals
on Montgomery Street found printed posters tacked to
walls and telegraph poles adjacent to the company's executive offices on the Market-Montgomery gore. Crowds
gathered before its not too cryptic warning:

A COLT- (ON) THE WRONG SCENT!

There is a Colt- (on) Montgomery Street, to be seen every
day, who needs a wholesome piece of advice. . . . Look out,
old SORRAL-TOP! Neither your PAID HOUNDS nor yourself, will
obtain the prey you seek for. There is a BLOOD HOUND on your
track you little dream so near, who will have justice, slow but
sure. Lawyer, Priest or Doctor, you cannot, shall not escape
calumny, and were you in any city but San Francisco, your
DAMNABLE LOOKS would hang you. Meddle no more with
business not your own, or you will reap a bitter but well-
merited punishment, fit for such scoundrels as yourself, for
you are known.   Justice

The poster aroused amusement, some curiosity, and
considerable speculation. It was presently forgotten — to

be recalled subsequent to October 8, 1878. At half past ten on that evening a carriage appeared before Colton's Nob Hill house; the General, inert and unmilitary for once, was lifted out, carried across the sidewalk, past the crouched lions of the steps, through the grilled door. Later the carriages of Doctors Lane and Keeney hurried up; their occupants hastened inside and remained for hours. Other men appeared: Charles E. Green, Colton's secretary; his law partner, Harrison; his daughter's father-in-law, Judge Thornton. Neighbors and late passers-by regarded the line of carriages with curiosity that did not abate, for lights on the ground floor and in upstairs rooms remained burning all night.

Downtown a startling rumor electrified the offices of morning papers: General Colton had been fatally stabbed. Reporters in hacks climbed the California Street hill, clattered up to the white house. They were refused both admittance and information. Hours later a statement was given out: some days before, the General had been injured by a fall from a horse at his Mount Diablo ranch. He was thought to be not seriously hurt. The newspapers printed the statement the following morning; they reprinted it word for word two days later when he died. Rumors persisted that the General had been murdered, but details of the mystery — if it was a mystery — never reached the public.

5

WHILE Colton's widow and his younger daughter were hurrying by special train from New York, and his former partners were composing messages of condolence, the public speculated on the General's rise to prominence and on the heights he might have reached had he not been cut off at the age of forty-seven. Like sentiments were expressed at the funeral, where banks of late autumn flowers cascaded about the altar of Grace Church, and wreaths from Stanford and Huntington were admired. Crocker, the dead man's closest friend, was prevented from placing his offering on the bier. He was in London with his family. " I loved Dave Colton," he later stated, " and when I heard of his death . . . I sat down and wept." In New York a few weeks later he paused to talk briefly with Huntington over their joint loss, then headed west, his private car attached to through trains.

Mrs. Colton was watching from one of her windows the evening of Crocker's return to Nob Hill. She saw his carriage arrive from the ferry and sent a servant across Taylor Street to ask that he call. Crocker appeared the next morning and the two shed tears while the dead man's virtues were recalled. But Mrs. Colton had been made sole heir in the will the General had dictated the night before he died, and at subsequent meetings matters of a practical nature had to be discussed. It was not long before the widow found Crocker's attitude growing less sympathetic, his visits infrequent.

Ellen Colton — she had been Ellen White, daughter of a Chicago physician — knew little of the General's business affairs, but she was a woman of energy and intelligence. By applying herself, she familiarized herself with the outlines of a complex situation. From Crocker, spokesman for the partners, she received reports that daily grew more disturbing. Men had been at work at the railroad offices. They had uncovered enough to show that the General's estate was in a deplorable condition. There was the famous Western Development Company dividend; Crocker stated gloomily that that would probably have to be returned. There were also the million-dollar note, soon to fall due, and the prospect of heavy assessments on the S.P. and C.P. stocks. Besides, the General had incurred obligations for the investment of funds in other railroad enterprises.

But that was not all. It became Crocker's duty to inform the widow that matters of a more disturbing nature had been disclosed. Irregularities had been found in the General's accounts. This had been a saddening surprise to all the partners. Crocker added: " I would have given $20,000 as quick as a penny to prove Dave Colton innocent." Despite all this, she was told that no attempt would be made to freeze her out. The Big Four were willing to carry their ex-partner's widow along with them; she was free to remain. To do so it was necessary only that she perform the obviously impossible feat of paying the General's obligations in full. In that event, the partners assured her, his defalcations (which, it was charged, amounted to $190,000) would be kept secret. There need be no scandal.

While the widow hesitated, the long-standing Colton-Crocker friendship cooled and evaporated. Crocker's visits across Taylor Street grew coldly business-like, then ceased entirely. " When I discovered what kind of a man Colton was," he explained, " I never went to see Mrs. Colton again. . . . I could not face her."

Thereafter negotiations were conducted through a third party, and Crocker's feelings were spared. One day he sent word that the partners had voted to return their shares of the Western Development Company dividend; Colton's share must be returned too. " You had better do it today — before night." The securities had been in the hands of the partners for many months, and Mrs. Colton failed to understand the sudden need for haste in restoring them. Crocker's emissary gave two reasons: the period during which claims against the estate might be filed would soon expire; besides, Huntington was about to return east and wished the matter settled before he left. But Huntington, as it proved, remained on the Coast for weeks longer.

S. M. Wilson, one of the railroad's staff attorneys, had been Colton's legal aide, and, like Crocker, a close friend. The widow turned to him for advice. His report, rendered in a few days, brought her no comfort. The estate owed the railroad a great deal of money, and the partners demanded a prompt settlement. If she hesitated, the four would file suit, and in that case Colton would be charged with stealing company funds.

To the widow, it had become a question of what could be salvaged from the wreckage and of shielding the General's reputation. She weighed the various considerations and decided to capitulate. The settlement was signed late in August 1879, ten months after Colton's death. By it the widow succeeded, temporarily, in preventing the embezzlement charge from becoming public, but that was about the extent of her victory. The securities the General had been at such pains to acquire were turned back. The list included half a million dollars in first-mortgage Southern Pacific bonds, the forty thousand shares of C.P. and S.P. stock, his shares in the Rocky Mountain Coal and Iron Company, ten thousand shares in the railroad-controlled Oriental and Occidental Steamship Company, and of course all the securities obtained in the Western Development Company dividend.

Other details were not overlooked. She was required to sign a release for nearly a third of a million dollars due Colton from his one-ninth interest in the Western Development Company. On one lot of bonds interest of about six thousand dollars was due; it was specified that these be turned back with the coupons unclipped. As a wedding present to his daughter, Colton had presented her with fifty shares of Southern Pacific stock; this, too, had to be returned. Of all the General's railroad property his widow was allowed to withhold only two hundred Southern Pacific bonds. These, however, she was not permitted to keep permanently. They were placed in trust; she was allowed to draw the interest on them for ten years, after which the bonds were to revert to the company.

The settlement did not leave the General's widow penniless, as was later picturesquely claimed by the Big Four's critics. Colton had made investments that had no connection with the railroad, and these yielded enough to support his widow and younger daughter in more than average comfort. But Ellen Colton believed the terms of the settlement had been more severe than circumstances warranted; that she had been made to part with far more of the General's assets than would have been the case had her knowledge of his affairs been more explicit. She was convinced, in short, that she had been dishonestly dealt with. But the agreement had been signed and its provisions carried out. There the matter rested for many months.

6

Meantime San Francisco newspapers published the inventory of the Hopkins estate — Uncle Mark had died a few months prior to Colton. With closer interest than most, the General's widow read the list of Hopkins's railroad securities and the values placed on them by the impartial court appraisers — values far higher than she had been allowed for identical issues she had turned back to the Big Four.

The information, of course, confirmed her suspicion that she had been defrauded, and she reached a decision to try to have her agreement set aside. Casting about for legal advice, she this time avoided attorneys with railroad affiliations. Her choice fell on J. Frank Smith, one of the few leading members of the local bar who were not inside the " railroad corral." Smith spent a week of investigation and came to share his client's belief that she had been cheated. Among the easily determined facts he uncovered were that the Western Development Company, which had been represented to her as insolvent at the time of the General's death, had in fact assets of more than ten million dollars; that Colton's share of the dividend had been turned back at much less than its market value; and that the embezzlement charges against Colton were unlikely to be sustained. Smith urged the widow to seek an annulment of the agreement and the return of her securities.

This step was not taken at once. From experience she knew that the surviving members of the Big Four would prove formidable opponents. In fifteen years the railroad had not lost an important case in the California courts, and she hesitated to institute suit until another out-of-court settlement had been attempted. The attitude of Crocker and Huntington during the earlier negotiations had been so hostile that this time she decided to approach Stanford. Smith accordingly wrote to him, outlining his client's claims and suggesting discussions leading to a friendly settlement. Stanford failed to make any reply, and Mrs. Colton thereupon commenced legal action.

The " Colton Trial " proved one of the longest and most sensational in the legal annals of the state. At the preliminary hearing, the defendants entered a general denial of the charges in the complaint and made a variety of counter-charges, including those accusing Colton of embezzlement. On motion of the railroad attorneys, headed by Hall McAllister (brother of New York's Ward McAllister, and himself a prominent social light), the case was removed to the superior court in Sonoma County, a farming community fifty miles north of San Francisco. The trial opened at Santa Rosa in November 1883, eighteen months after the filing of the complaint.

The case remained in the courts nearly eight years. Judge Temple, Sonoma County superior-court judge, presided over the original trial, which dragged on until October 1885. Meantime San Francisco newspapers kept correspondents at Santa Rosa, and daily reports of progress became staple reading for thousands. A stream of witnesses for both sides flowed from San Francisco to the valley town, and tons of company records were shipped north as the financial and political activities of the associates were probed and details long kept secret became available to an interested public.

The long trial told on the nerves of the participants, and clashes between opposing counsel increased in frequency and virulence. " The other side is ugly and nervous," McAllister wrote in the summer of 1884. " This is a good sign. . . . J. Frank Smith looked today like a ' damned soul.' " But the bad humor was not all between opposing lawyers. During the same month exasperation at one of his associates caused the normally urbane McAllister to burst out: " What a damned old bore Fullerton is! [Fullerton was also on the railroad's legal staff.] He has just come into my room (as he does every evening) to prevent me from working by going all through my trunk of papers. I requested him politely to leave, and he has just departed in a furious mood."

Correspondence between McAllister and Alfred Cohen — the latter was again devoting his talents to the service of the railroad — makes interesting reading. One of Cohen's duties was to round up San Francisco witnesses and to dispatch them to Santa Rosa as they were needed. There is evidence, however, that he was expected also to arrange for the convenient disappearance of persons who might have proved useful to the opposition. In a note from McAllister to Cohen, of July 1884, one reads this cautiously phrased suggestion, the first sentence carefully underscored: *" I understand that Colonel Gray was going to leave San Francisco, about Wednesday, and to be absent for a week or ten days.* If this should be so, the other side could not have him for a witness. . . ."

The testimony of certain railroad officials was a source of uneasiness, and McAllister's letters urged Cohen to coach them thoroughly before sending them north. Neither Crocker nor Stanford was ever an adroit witness; in the past both had caused railroad attorneys bad hours while they were under examination by opposing counsel. While a trip of Crocker's to Santa Rosa was impending, McAllister sent Cohen pages of careful instructions as to how he should answer questions expected to be fired at him during cross-examination. On the other hand, the railroad attorney on whose advice Mrs. Colton had made the original settlement proved a witness after McAllister's heart. " Wilson today was all that I could desire. He

showed just the right amount of non-eagerness and impar-
tiality which makes his evidence tell. . . . Hayes [Judge
Hayes was associated with Smith as counsel for the plain-
tiff] is preparing for a long X-ex. of Wilson, but I think
he can stand it on every point. . . ."

7

THE TRIAL dragged on and public interest began to wane
— then revived when the evidence took a new turn. One
afternoon Judge Hayes casually submitted a packet of letters, stating that by them he wished to show to what extent
Colton had participated in the inner councils of the Big
Four. The matter aroused no particular interest and
Hayes selected a letter and proceeded to read it. It proved
to be a rambling and gossipy message from Huntington to
Colton, written from Washington eight years earlier. In
a vein of complete frankness it dealt with the railroad's
control of state politics and of the California delegation in
Congress. The letter, and those that followed, were ample
proof of what Mrs. Colton's attorneys wished them to
prove: that the General and Huntington had been on very
confidential terms indeed.

It was the first public intimation of the existence of the
" Colton letters," which were soon to become notorious
not only in California but throughout the nation. For
their hastily scrawled pages exposed the railroad's political
methods with a thoroughness that a man of Huntington's

caution would have allowed only if he had had complete confidence in his correspondent. It was one of the few times the canny New Englander permitted himself the luxury of speaking his mind, and he and the railroad were to pay well for the privilege. Three years later, testifying before the Pacific Railroad Commission, the incriminating letters were read into the record and he was questioned in detail as to the meaning of various passages. The old man bore the ordeal for half a day, then burst out: " If I had known that this particular correspondence was to have gone into the national archives to go down to future generations, I would have tried to have it full in every way."

Hayes's reading of the letters brought forth vigorous objections from the railroad's attorneys, who foresaw that matters more important than Mrs. Colton's four-million-dollar suit were involved. But Judge Temple ruled that they were pertinent evidence and the plaintiff's counsel jubilantly read the entire six hundred into the record. From them the public learned not only the extent of the railroad's control over legislation but the by no means subtle methods by which its control was maintained. In his closely scrawled pages Huntington named scores of office-holders in California and at Washington who were taking orders from Colton and himself; he revealed the railroad's policy of promoting deserving politicians and summarily retiring to private life those who failed to " keep in line." The cost of getting a bill through a state legislature or through Congress was discussed as frankly as the establishment of a railroad tariff or the price of steel rails.

Opposition newspapers of course seized the opportunity with delight. The San Francisco *Chronicle* devoted solid pages of eight-point type to their publication, and others — notably the New York *World* — gave them almost as much space. Huntington's graphic picture of the railroad's control of legislation proved the real beginning of a fight to drive the corporation out of politics, a feat that was not accomplished, however, until a generation later.

Today the letters, and Colton's replies, are important chiefly because they present one of the few available portraits of the two men in informal moods, when the barriers were down and they felt safe to be completely themselves. Huntington's uniformly begin: " Friend Colton," and with no preliminaries plunge into the business at hand. That stated, they end with equal brusqueness, with " Yours truly " and the scrawled signature: " C. P. Huntington." The formalities of business correspondence are notably absent. When personal matters are mentioned they are passing references to a favorite theme: he is working too hard and overtaxing his strength; he is tired and wishes he could quit.

The letters mainly relate to two subjects: railroad finance and railroad politics, with the emphasis on the latter. Huntington devoted many pages to bitter condemnation of the California group in Congress. Nothing short of a hundred-per-cent railroad delegation was ever satisfactory or even tolerable to him. Colton's political connections plus the railroad's organization could never quite accomplish that, and at each election the opposition managed to put at least one man (usually a representative from San Francisco) into office. The rebel's appearance at Washington aroused Huntington to exasperated profanity. There were solid reasons for his discontent; from experience, he knew that a California delegation that would vote solidly for whatever the railroad wanted was a valuable asset; moreover he recognized that a shrewd politician who could get himself elected on an anti-railroad ticket was in a far better position to bargain profitably than one who had been committed to the railroad policies from the beginning.

Illustrative of this was the case of John King Luttrell, sent to Congress from San Francisco in 1874, without benefit of railroad backing. Soon after his election Huntington wrote to " Friend Colton ": ". . . I know he can be persuaded to do what is right in relation to the C.P. and S.P. but some political friend must see him, and not a railroad man, for if any of our men went to see him he would be sure to lie about it and say that money was offered him, but some friend must see him and give him solid reasons why he should help his friends." A note a week or two later indicates that Colton had attended to the matter: " Yours of the 12th is received and I am glad to learn that you have Luttrell under your charge, but you must be careful not to let him get anything to strike back with, as he is a cuss." What follows throws light on why Huntington felt the need of a discreet politician on the Coast: " I do not think it safe for Stanford to talk with him on our matters, as it would be just like him to get up in Congress and lie about what Stanford said to him."

Following the Luttrell references through the correspondence, one finds Huntington writing on December 1, 1874: " I will see Luttrell when he comes over and talk with him and maybe he and we can work together, but if we can brush him out it would have a good effect, and then we could, or at least would try, to get better timber to work with." The interview could not have been an entire success, for Huntington was presently convinced that better timber was necessary. " I notice what you say of Luttrell; he is a wild hog; don't let him come back to Washington, but as the house is to be largely Democratic and if he was to be defeated, likely it would be charged to us, hence I should think it would be well to beat him with a Democrat; but I would defeat him anyway and if he got the nomination, put up another Democrat and run against him, and in that way elect a Republican. Beat him."

By the following January, however, Luttrell was surprisingly in the good graces of the railroad. On the 29th, Huntington wrote: " I hope Luttrell will be sent back to Congress. I think it would be a misfortune if he was not." And a little later: " I hope Luttrell is elected and Piper defeated, as it is generally understood here that our hand is under one and over the other." From that time on, William A. Piper replaced Luttrell as Huntington's favorite aversion. Huntington was then opposing Tom Scott in his attempt to get governmental aid for his Texas and Pacific Railroad. That line seriously threatened the Big Four's monopoly of the Coast traffic, and the partners were rushing their own road to the Gulf in the hope of forestalling this potentially dangerous rival.

Both sides were courting the favors of Washington legislators, and the fact that the new San Francisco Congressman promptly joined forces with Scott infuriated Huntington. He wrote Colton: " All the members in the house from California are doing first rate except Piper, and he is a damned hog, anyway you can fix him." Again, three months later: " Scott got a large number of that drunken, worthless dog Piper's speeches printed and sent them broadcast over the country. He has flooded Texas with them. . . ." The wily Scott made capital of the anti-railroad newspapers in California, reprinting many of their more violent attacks and distributing them by the thousands, thereby seriously weakening Huntington's claim that California was solidly behind the Southern Pacific in the fight.

Colton's failure to win the unanimous support of the local press brought bitter complaints from Huntington. " The Sacramento *Union* hurts us very much. . . . If I owned the paper I would control it or burn it. . . ." Again, on May 2, 1876: " Is it not possible to control the agent for the Associated Press in San Francisco? The matters that hurt the C.P. and S.P. most here are the dispatches that come from S.F. . . ." In the summer of 1876, Huntington thus evaluated candidates in the coming state election: ". . . Wigginton has not always been right, but he is a good fellow and is growing every day. Page is always right and it would be a misfortune to California not to have him in Congress. Piper is a damned hog and should not come back. It is a shame for a great commercial city like S.F. to send a scavenger like him to Congress once. . . ." Fortunately for Huntington's blood-pressure, Piper failed of re-election and his place was taken by a man who more closely approximated the letter-writer's idea of a co-operative legislator.

When the Colton letters were published, railroad spokesmen on the Coast made valiant attempts to read harmless meanings into them. Huntington's concern over the caliber of men sent to Congress from California was, they cheerfully explained, merely the desire of a good citizen to see the most competent men elected. The theory fell short of conviction, for throughout the correspondence Huntington many times stated his opinion of the House and Senate in terms indicating a belief that those bodies were beyond redemption. " This Congress," he informed Colton early in 1878, " is the worst body of men ever gotten together in this country." Two months later he was definitely of the same opinion: " This Congress is, I think, the worst set of men that have ever been collected together since man was created." The subject fascinated him, and five days later he returned to it again: " I think in all the world's history never before was such a wild set of demagogues honored by the name of Congress. . . . We have been hurt some, but some of the worst bills have been defeated, but we cannot stand many such Congresses. . . ."

8

THE INTRODUCTION of the Colton letters was easily the most sensational episode of the Santa Rosa trial, one that caught the railroad forces completely by surprise. It was the opinion in legal circles on the Coast that the plaintiff's advisers had made a blunder in failing to put the letters to more effective use on behalf of their client. Huntington, of course, had assumed that Colton had destroyed the letters; he had given instructions that this be done. That his orders were not carried out is another indication of the General's astuteness; obviously he had not preserved the letters for sentimental reasons and he therefore must have foreseen that they might be useful in the future. It was claimed that had the fact that they still existed been revealed to Huntington in advance of the trial, the latter would have made any reasonable out-of-court settlement to get possession of them.

With their admission as evidence, however, the damage was done, and their only effect was to cause the Huntington group to contest the suit with greater vigor. The trial continued through 1884 and most of 1885, while its cost mounted to above over a hundred thousand dollars for each side. Judge Temple's decision, when it was eventually handed down, proved an almost complete victory for the defendants. Colton's name was cleared of embezzlement charges, but the plea for an annulment of the agreement was denied. The court held that the widow had entered into it with full knowledge of its terms, that the contract was sound and must be upheld. Mrs. Colton appealed to the state supreme court. After further long delays a second trial followed. The decision, rendered in January 1890, sustained the Santa Rosa judge. No further action was taken.

The long contest was an expensive one to General Colton's widow, but in the end it proved more so to the victors. Even journals friendly to the railroad and enjoying subsidies from the corporation did not claim that the Huntington-Stanford group had emerged with credit to themselves. Shrewdness, the ability to drive a close bargain, to press an advantage for all it was worth, were qualities still highly regarded among California businessmen, where there was no more coveted distinction than to be known as a " smart trader." But the application of such principles to the widow of a former partner proved distasteful even to those who were not sentimentalists. The victory cost Huntington and Stanford and Crocker far more in loss of respect than they gained in dollars.

More, Huntington's messages to " Friend Colton " focused attention on a situation that, even in the free and easy '80s, the general public found hard to accept. The outlines of the Big Four's political methods had been known long before the letters came to light, but it required their publication to dramatize the situation. It was Huntington's discussion of the cost of votes in the same terms and often in the same letters as the cost of other railroad necessities that first caused thousands to reflect on the possibility that the picturesque captains of industry who were building up the country would bear closer watching.

Huntington was not allowed to forget Colton's packet of letters; at each subsequent session of Congress they were regularly brought forth to hamper his plans and defeat his most cherished projects. Because of them, correspondents of hostile newspapers watched his every move when he came to Washington. By the middle '90s he had become a sort of symbol of predatory wealth bent on the corruption of the public's servants. It reached a point where Congressmen, fearing the effect on their constituents should they be seen talking with him, were known to dodge down Washington alleys at the old man's approach. Finally, nearly a quarter of a century after they were written, the Colton letters contributed largely to the defeat of Huntington's " funding bill," by which he had hoped to postpone for many years payment of both principle and interest on the original subsidy bonds — a piece of bad luck that cost the railroad and its owners many millions of dollars. To that extent the Sheriff of Siskiyou had his revenge.

IRON HORSE

"... WOULD YOU MIND
LEANING TOWARD THE CENTER ON
THE CURVES?"

1

A MORE sophisticated age is puzzled to understand the extent to which the sentimental '60s romanticized the iron horse. Railroads represented far more than mere transportation. The names of the little seventeen-ton locomotives first used on the Central Pacific were for years household words throughout California, and their comparative speed and power became the subject of countless debates among loafers congregated before frame stations at traintime. Not small boys alone but half the male population would have chosen to occupy the engineer's shelf of the " C. P. Huntington " rather than the Governor's chair. In the fall of 1866, the " Grizzly Bear," coasting one afternoon toward Dutch Flat, hit a cow and turned on its side. Crowds gathered from miles around to view the spectacle, and a Sacramento journalist wrote of the mighty cheer that arose when the engine was again on the rails. A speaker at a banquet celebrating the completion of the road assured his listeners that the accomplishment " completed the work of Columbus," and in 1868 Henry George, not yet engrossed in *Progress and Poverty,* wrote that " it will be the means of converting a wilderness into a populous empire in less time than many of the cathedrals of Europe were building."

Not only letters but every other form of art paid tribute to the new miracle, and gained popularity by so doing. Catalogues of the songs of the period regularly repeat the familiar theme, and any play during the '60s and '70s that introduced a locomotive into its third act or contrived to have its heroine throw the switch and save the night express was assured of success. Prosody followed the current fad, and as renowned a bard as Joaquin Miller wrote: "There is more poetry in the rush of a single railroad train across the continent than in all the gory story of burning Troy." When Bret Harte, in 1867, became editor of a new Western magazine, the device he chose for that speculative venture included, of course, the universal symbol of progress. But Harte was already looking back to the period he was to exploit, with varying success, for thirty-five years, and the *Overland's* trade-mark included not only a railroad track but a California grizzly, head down, legs braced against the ties, disputing the mechanical invasion of his realm.

Years before the road was finished, the wonders of George Pullman's new palaces on wheels had filled the imagination of Californians, who compared printed accounts of their luxuries with the bald day coaches in use in the West, and impatiently awaited the day when shining Pullmans might be seen on their side of the Sierra. The new cars were worth waiting for. It was the boast of the ex-cabinetmaker who built them that as much money and taste were expended in their decoration as in that of a rich man's parlor.

The millionaire of the period who found himself inside one of them might in truth have imagined himself at home. Scrollwork and gilt, in intricate patterns, velvet upholstery encrusted with braid and tassels, carpets with huge floral designs in raw primary colors — all these were obviously not for the poor. Yet thousands of impecunious Westerners cheerfully paid extra fees that they might see at first hand how luxury had been so combined with ingenuity that drawing-room, dining-room, and sleeping-quarters had all been compressed within the walls of a forty-foot coach.

At a period when the covered wagon was far from extinct, a crossing of the plains in one of Pullman's Golden Palace cars offered a study in contrast that impressed even the unimaginative. For one seeking a dramatic illustration of what his age had accomplished, an early guide book advised a passage on the overland out of Omaha. Let the passenger choose a warm day when the doors of all the coaches were open, and take his place on the platform of the last car. " On either side are the prairies, abode of the buffalo, where the eye sees naught but desolation . . . then, looking back through the long aisle, or avenue, one gazes on the supreme achievement of our civilization."

But it was a civilization often thickly coated with dust, and the car's luxury was not synonymous with comfort. An August crossing of the plains, at twenty-two miles an hour, over an uncommonly rough roadbed and through scenery unsurpassed in monotony, was an experience few

repeated from choice. To some extent the Pullmans mini-
mized the discomfort, for their innovations were not confined to opulent furnishings, potted ferns and rubber
plants, organs and hymnbooks, and towering wood-stoves.
Mechanically, George Pullman's masterpiece was a vast
improvement on the ordinary passenger coach of the period. Double, rattle-proof windows were already in use in
the early '70s; more important, the cars were equipped
with springs resilient enough to absorb part of the jolt
and sway that made early railroad travel an ordeal.

In general, the discomforts of the cross-country trip
were borne with fortitude by pioneer passengers, who
looked on them as a small price to pay for the privilege of
passing from ocean to ocean in eight days, a journey never
before possible in twice the time. The opening of the line
in 1869 made the transcontinental tour the world's pre-
mier novelty in travel. During the first year of its operation European steamers plied the Atlantic with empty
cabins while thousands overcame their fear of starvation,
derailment, and wild Indians and courageously set out
for the west coast.

Gathering at Council Bluffs over the three lines then
operating west from Chicago, daily crowds of adventurers
were ferried across the Missouri to the fifteen-year-old
metropolis of Omaha, eastern terminus of the Union Pacific. There they milled about the long station platform,
seeing to the checking of baggage and the purchase of
Pullman tickets, all the while beset by clamorous crowds:
peddlers of fruit, food, and remedies for car-sickness, so-
licitors of accident insurance (at disturbingly high rates),

newsboys, runners for hotels farther along the line, sales-
men offering lucrative investments in business property,
farmlands, and mines. Passengers forced their way
through the bedlam to the waiting train — often six hundred feet long — found the car and seats assigned them,
and sank down exhausted. There they thrilled with anticipation as the engineer applied the steam to the cyl-
inders and released long blasts from the whistle. A series
of rattling crashes ran down the train as couplings tight-
ened and cars jerked into motion.

2

ALMOST at once the train entered the uninhabited prairie,
and the adventurers were free to examine the flat landscape, to admire the trappings of the Pullmans, or, in the
words of *Williams' Guide,* merely to " sit and read, play
. . . games and indulge in social conversation and glee."
Narratives of early travelers throw no light on the nature
of the latter recreation, but all refer to the conversation,
if only to state that it must be conducted at the top of
one's voice to be audible above the clatter of the moving
train.

To the socially correct, cross-country travel presented
a variety of problems, not least of which was the question
of what to wear. The following is the recommendation
of one authority for a passage, in summer, between Omaha
and San Francisco: First day, light spring suit; second day

— for the approach to the Rockies — winter suit; third day, for Salt Lake and the Nevada desert, the summer suit (gentlemen should retain their coats) ; for the ascent of the Sierra, the winter suit again became *de rigueur,* with the addition of " all your underclothing "; the mountains behind, the traveler redonned his summer suit for the passage down the Sacramento Valley, and at the approach to the bay, made a final change to winter garments, to which he added, as he stepped on the ferry, his overcoat and scarf.

During moments when the sartorially correct passenger was not shifting from suit to suit, he was at liberty to consider the problem of whether he or his female companion should occupy the seat nearest the window. Most authorities agreed that she should be installed in the aisle seat, even though that subjected her to inconvenience from unsteady pedestrians and gave her a less than perfect view of the scenery. But on the other hand was the fact that the transcontinental line passed through an imperfectly civilized land, and Indians and Chinese were known to assume undignified postures beside the track in full view of scandalized passengers. Seated next to the window, the watchful escort in such emergencies had but to lean forward to shut off his lady's view.

Not etiquette but food was the early traveler's major interest. Three stops a day were made for meals, for overland trains did not regularly have diners until the late '70s. Long before the towns were reached, passengers aroused themselves to activity and crowded on the steps and open platforms, the less encumbered swinging to the ground

ACROSS THE CONTINENT

From a colored lithograph published by H. Schile, New York, about 1870.
Courtesy of Edwin Grabhorn

A CENTRAL PACIFIC PASSENGER COACH, 1869

One of the earliest type of passenger coaches used on Western railroads. This car came through from the East to Sacramento on May 10, 1869, being attached to Governor Stanford's special train following the ceremony at Promontory, Utah, when the "last spike" was driven in the first transcontinental railroad. Other cars of the same type were soon afterwards added to the equipment of the Central Pacific (now Southern Pacific). Bright paint, carved wood decorations, and gold-leaf trimmings gave an ornate appearance to the cars, but they were sadly lacking in many of the common comforts of modern coaches. The seats were straight-backed and thinly cushioned. A coal stove furnished the only heat. Light was provided by candles or oil lamps. Open vestibules offered little protection from the weather when going from one car to another.

Courtesy of the California State Library

while the cars were still in motion and leading a headlong dash toward the eating-houses. Frame structures with the depressing aspect common to nineteenth-century railroad architecture, they were filled with long tables, laden with thick crockery and steaming platters of food newly rushed in from the kitchen. The trains remained twenty minutes, the meals were *table d'hôte,* and the price, whether for breakfast, dinner, or supper, was uniformly a dollar greenback or, in California and Nevada, seventy-five cents in silver. Food was always abundant, and the meat excellent. Early tourists spoke well of the simple fare, for it filled both major requirements: it was substantial, and it could be hastily consumed. True, a few complained of the lack of fruit and green vegetables; these were seldom to be had at the prairie and desert stations.

Station eating-houses were operated by private individuals under contract to the railroads and subject to oversight by the latter. The supervision, however, was not so complete as to produce meals of uniform quality at all stations. The overland line had not been long in operation before certain stops became known for their specialties. Those who had been over the line were likely to advise travelers to be on the look-out for Laramie's beefsteaks, for antelope cuts at Sidney, for mountain trout at Evanston (where the westbound travelers first encountered Chinese cooks and waiters), for Green River's biscuits, and at Grand Island for " lots of everything."

But it was still an almost uninhabited land, and stations were infrequent and by no means evenly spaced. Eating-places were sometimes eight hours apart when the trains were on schedule — and they were often late. Guidebooks urged that travelers provide themselves with " a little lunch-basket nicely stowed with sweet and substantial bits of food " as insurance against too prolonged fasts. But the writer just quoted went on to issue a warning, phrased with an urgency that suggests a personal knowledge of the situation: let the lunch-baskets contain no boiled tongue. The journey from Omaha to the Coast required four days, and partly consumed boxes of food had a way of being stowed under seats and forgotten. A few slices of tongue that had passed their prime could make life unendurable for a carload of travelers.

Westward from Omaha, the trains maintained an average speed of a little more than twenty miles an hour, ample for the light equipment and uneven roadbed. From the velvet-hung windows of the Pullmans a highly scenery-conscious generation found even the prairies fascinating; the sunsets were highly spoken of by all. In the summer months tourists were likely to be treated to a more spectacular display, for sparks from the locomotives often ignited the dry grass and for hours thereafter the horizon was reddened by the glow of a prairie fire.

In the early years watchful passengers might still see an occasional telegraph pole shoved off the perpendicular, sure sign that some roving buffalo had used it for a scratching-post. During the daytime, amateur hunters kept watch ahead for sight of the still numerous herds of antelope. The animals soon grew accustomed to the trains, hardly bothering to glance up as they rattled past. Word that there were deer ahead was passed down the coaches, windows were thrown up, pistols were drawn from rear pockets and under-arm holsters, and soon a rattle of gunfire ran down the length of the train. Those inclined to deplore this useless slaughter of the graceful animals were presently reassured. To hit a deer with a pistol-shot fired from a swaying coach required more skill than the marksmen commonly possessed. Such " hunting " was a welcome break in the monotony of the trip; passengers looked forward to it just as those on the contemporary windjammers greeted the appearance of a school of porpoises and made equally futile attempts to bag them.

Diversions were few on the overland passage; bored passengers regarded an endless expanse of plain, broken at two or three hour intervals by a water-tank and a cluster of sod houses — " like islands in mid-ocean " — at which the train stopped briefly for water and fuel. At points where the railroad chanced to parallel one of the old stage routes, a dusty string of freight wagons might be met and passed, or a covered emigrant wagon crawling westward over rutted roads. In the plush seats of the Pullmans, passengers stared as long as the vehicles remained in sight, reflecting upon the rocket-like progress of their age.

When nightfall blackened the windows and the suspended kerosene lamps spread a yellow glow over the interiors, passengers were thrown on their own resources, and a more pronounced social atmosphere pervaded the cars. Those musically inclined clustered about the cabinet organ — a feature of the early through trains — song-books were distributed and the notes of *Oh, Susannah* or of popular hymns rose above the clank of the rails, the rattle of windows, and the eerie blasts of the locomotive's whistle. Elsewhere, travelers who had been over the road before told groups of the attractions in store for them ahead, or pioneers still under forty sent the timid uneasily to bed with tales of savages circling about embattled emigrant parties on these same prairies not twenty years before.

Meantime porters accomplished the ingenious conversion of the seats into comfortable, if not completely private, sleeping-quarters, and there were always a few who regarded the procedure with apprehension. For the American sleeping-car was for years under the suspicion that it might be a menace to public morals. As late as the middle '70s, sermons continued to be preached in advocacy of separate cars for males and females, and in innumerable conversations was weighed the question of whether it was moral for strangers of opposite sexes to occupy couches separated by only a foot or two of space and a pair of denim curtains. Companies operating the cars considered the matter important enough to justify counter-measures. Statements were accordingly issued arguing that railroad sleeping-cars were pervaded by a moral atmosphere no less lofty than that of the Christian homes of their patrons. Moreover, train officials nightly patrolled the curtain-lined corridors under orders to nip in the bud any attempt at breach of decorum.

Despite these precautions, thousands of Americans kept to the end their resolve never to go to bed on a railroad train. Other thousands, forced to that extremity by some emergency, lay broad awake until dawn, the ladies removing only their hats and gloves, and keeping foot-long hatpins, bought for the occasion, close at hand. On the cross-country journey, however, such measures were commonly followed the first night only, for even the strong-willed could hardly remain continuously awake through a ninety-hour journey. As the second evening approached, bodily fatigue, plus the sense of security induced by a personal knowledge of the situation, persuaded even the most resolute ladies to adopt a rational viewpoint. For, in the language of the guidebooks, " a restful night's sleep is the only wise preparation for the enjoyment of the wonders of the morrow."

3

DURING the early months after the line's completion, the novelty of cross-country travel made traffic brisk. It was not long, however, before the journey lost its flavor of adventure, and the number of through passengers fell far below what the companies had anticipated. For a decade one through passenger train daily was ample to accommodate the traffic. As late as 1879 one westward passenger found the train to consist of a combination mail and baggage car, one day coach, and an ancient sleeper. Even these accommodations seemed excessive, for he was the solitary through passenger, and for much of the journey the only passenger of any kind.

The failure of the road during its early years to attract a considerable number of passengers was variously explained. The discomforts of the journey, due to light equipment and uneven roadbed and to the heat and dust during summer, undoubtedly caused many to continue to patronize the Panama steamers. But a more important reason was that the same month the last spike was driven at Promontory, a French engineer completed another large construction job on the other side of the globe. The Suez Canal was opened and colonials of half the nations of Europe found steamer routes between the Orient and their home countries shortened by more than two weeks. This effectually ended a hope to which the railroad-owners had clung since Judah's day: that a heavy commerce between Europe and the Far East would flow over their line.

Reluctantly the Big Four were forced to give up their expectation of a large passenger traffic during the early years; this would come only by the slow process of increasing Pacific Coast population. Early travelers saw evidences that the company was making persistent efforts in that direction. At intervals, through trains slowed down and crept past sidings on which long lines of cars waited: combination freight and passenger trains, also westbound but on a slower schedule. Those in the Pullmans caught fleeting glimpses of the interiors of other passenger coaches, far less ornate than their own. These were the emigrant cars, in which less affluent citizens and hordes of settlers newly arrived from every country of

Europe were moving out to populate the railroad's lands from Omaha to the Pacific.

An excellent picture of life in the emigrant trains was preserved by a thin Scot who on an afternoon late in 1879 stood in a group on the station platform at Omaha. They faced a railroad official who read off their names, each in his turn gathering up his baggage and scurrying toward the shabby cars opposite. The amateur emigrant's name was presently shouted and Robert Louis Stevenson hurried toward the middle of the three dilapidated coaches at the end of a freight train.

Stevenson found himself examining the interior of a long, narrow box filled with unupholstered, traverse benches, a wood-stove at one end, a water-closet at the other, and a row of feeble lamps suspended from the ceiling. After a while the official who had checked the group on board joined them. Suddenly affable, he divided the men into pairs and introduced them, unconditionally guaranteeing the honesty and sociability of each. Stevenson was rejected on the ground of probable dishonesty by one hairy Yankee, then successfully teamed with an ex-sailor from Pennsylvania. When each man had been provided with a traveling companion, the reason for the company representative's solicitude became clear. To each pair he offered at a bargain price " the raw materials of a bed " — a board cut to fit the space between the facing benches, and three cotton bags leanly stuffed with straw. These were the mattress and pillows; the travelers were expected to provide their own blankets. The price of the outfit was $2.50. Before the train left — and long after Stevenson and his sailor bedmate had paid over their cash — the offering price fell to $1.50. A few stations beyond Omaha, peddlers besieged the cars offering identical outfits for 45 cents. The Scotsman recorded these details as his contribution to the economy of future travelers.

To the emigrants, as to those in the Pullmans, the long trip in time ceased to be a novelty and became routine. The domestic arrangements of the emigrants were ingenious. Passengers pooled their resources to buy not only beds but toilet articles, cooking utensils, and food. On the first morning out from Omaha, Stevenson invested in a tin washbasin, his bedmate in a towel; a third member was admitted to the corporation upon his purchase of a cake of soap. The railroad company, he pointed out, supplied the water. It supplied also fuel for the stove, in which, before the sun rose above the prairie horizon, a fire was crackling. Coffee-pots bubbled on its top, filling the car with an appetizing aroma, bread was toasted, and eggs broken into sizzling frying-pans. Soon the rising sun revealed the passengers crowded about their bed-boards, converted into breakfast tables, and an air of optimism and mild gaiety pervaded the company. It was, Stevenson recorded, the pleasantest part of the day.

But the emigrants had a variety of trials not shared by more prosperous tourists. The equipment of the emigrant trains was too ancient for further use by the regular passengers. Coaches were old and neglected, full of rattles and drafts and virtually springless. As late as the end of the '70s, one of the cars still carrying emigrants over the transcontinental line was the venerable coach which in 1865 had brought Lincoln's body from Washington to Springfield. Passengers on the low-fare trains were subjected to a variety of petty graft by the trainmen, who sometimes went to remarkable lengths. One account tells of a trip in which passengers had to take up a collection three times a day to bribe the crew to stop at eating-stations. If the bribe was not forthcoming, or if its amount was too small, the train stopped only at points where there were no restaurants.

Other forms of extortion, ranging from working agreements with gamblers, who set up faro games in the coaches, down to the admission of peddlers of fake jewelry, furs, and mining stocks, were common. Sometimes their methods descended to the outright theft of passengers' property while the latter slept or while they were at the station eating-houses. Victims naïve enough to complain at headquarters at the end of the journey received nothing more substantial than the promise of an " immediate investigation " from an incredulous clerk. Later, when the exploitation of travelers began to provide ammunition to journals opposing the railroad, some effort was made to clean up the situation, but such petty abuses were permitted for years. Leland Stanford, testifying before the Pacific Railroad Commission at San Francisco in the middle '80s, took occasion to deny that he had ever received a share of the profits of professional gamblers operating on the trains.

4

DURING the first years of the Central Pacific's operation, the running time between Omaha and Sacramento was four and a half days. The daily through train left Omaha at noon, made its first considerable stop at Grand Island, a hundred and fifty miles west, where passengers had a belated supper, and arrived the next morning at Cheyenne. The attractions of the second day included the approach to the Rockies, in the upper reaches of which sharp eyes could usually make out an occasional herd of mountain goats. Toward noon a stop was made at Sherman. The little wooden station bore a placard giving its elevation as eight thousand feet, and stating that it was the highest railroad station in the world. Passengers descended to inhale the light air, to withstand the cold gale that constantly blew through the pass, and to regard the bleak mountain scenery. The rest of the day the train wound down through the mountains, crossed the elevated Laramie plains, and, after a stop for supper at Green River, passed on toward the Utah line. At the village of Wasatch passengers descended to hear its citizens boast of a twenty-four-grave cemetery, in which twenty-three of the graves contained the bodies of persons who had died violently, and the twenty-fourth that of a prostitute who had poisoned herself.

The crossing of the Utah line aroused the heightened interest of tourists, few of whom failed to make the detour, over the forty-mile Utah Central road, to the publicized City of the Saints. There for a day or two they inspected the domed tabernacle, familiarized themselves with the exterior of Brigham Young's disappointingly modest " mansion," and speculated on the marital status of every woman they encountered on the shady, well-kept streets. Polygamy then held a lively fascination to the curious in every corner of the nation, and travelers who had been on the spot were assured of eager attention.

Those who saw Brigham Young commonly found the portly, seventy-year-old President of the Saints a disappointment. His appearance was that of a prosperous but harassed businessman. The ogre of legend, who divided his time between plotting insurrections against the Republic and his duties to his multiple wives, was not easily discernible. But the streets of Salt Lake City, then as now, revealed an uncommonly high average of pretty faces, and many male visitors left the city and abandoned thoughts of embracing its religion with a certain regret.

The fear of the Mormons themselves that the opening of the transcontinental line might mean the doom of their religion proved groundless, and Brigham Young's remark that " a religion that can't stand a railroad isn't worth its salt " (a common commodity there) was recalled with admiration. During the construction period Young obtained needed funds by making grading contracts with both companies. The completed line opened new markets for the fruits and grains of the valley, brought in settlers (many of whom became converts), provided funds for world-wide missionary efforts, and built up a lucrative tourist trade. As Young had shrewdly foreseen, the coming of the railroad prolonged the life of Mormonism rather than shortened it.

During the early months of operation the terminus of the two lines remained at Promontory. There westbound passengers bade farewell to the Pullmans, for the Central Pacific had not yet agreed to use the Pullman Company's cars. Until the terminus was moved to Ogden, the bleak village of Promontory enjoyed a season of prosperity, for there through passengers waited while mail and baggage were transferred. The process never occupied less than an hour; frequently, when one or another of the trains was late, the delay extended to half a day. The surroundings were as desolate as any in the country, and bored passengers had to look to the town for means of passing the time.

In the early months of 1870 a young Englishman named Rae became Promontory's unwilling guest during the two-hour wait between trains and strolled down its street to study the inhabitants at their work and play. He was struck by a certain incongruity between the street signs and the structures they advertised. A board shanty bore the name Pacific Hotel, a weather-beaten tent that of the Club House, and the false front of an unpainted frame hut, in large sun-bleached letters, the Continental House. Toward the lower end of the street, the Englishman's curiosity was doubly attracted by a line of tiny cottages, crowded close together, their doors opening directly on the board sidewalk. These bore no signs; moreover, their windows presented the novelty of " neatly arranged muslin curtains." But closer inspection revealed that the

338

doorway of the first framed " three smiling females," and the tourist hurried back past a huddle of saloons to the town's leading gambling hall.

Rae spent the rest of his stay on the edge of a crowd about a circular table, regarding the operation of a game that looked " as simple as thimblerig " and that bore an odd name: three-card monte. In fifteen minutes he saw a fellow-passenger part with every penny in his pockets and learned that the operators sometimes gave their victims a five-dollar gold piece to tide them over until they reached the Coast, and that the profits of a monte table often reached £300 a day. The Englishman picked his way back to his car, convinced that Promontory harbored as unsavory a nest of assassins as he was likely to encounter on the remainder of his way round the world.

Early travelers were usually disappointed in the Central Pacific's Silver Palace cars, which were inferior in appointments and comfort to the Pullmans. Their name was conceded to be the best thing about them, for they lacked not only the extremes of ornamentation that distinguished the Pullmans, but also the latter's mechanical excellences, including good springs. A further complaint was that the Central Pacific cars had no trained conductors such as the Pullman Company provided; instead, the coaches were under the management of Negro porters, with often unsatisfactory results.

Passengers were less comfortable on the run west from Promontory for still another reason — one that had nothing to do with the Central Pacific's equipment or service. The country traversed the first day out from Og-

339

den was barren and desolate. In summer, heat and alkali dust reduced whole trainloads of travelers to misery. Sweltering in their plush seats, they faced the alternative of keeping doors and windows closed and enduring semi-asphyxiation, or opening them to the clouds of alkali dust that swirled up from the unballasted roadbed — chemically impregnated particles that irritated the throat and lungs " as keenly as the steel-dust which cuts short the lives of Sheffield needle-grinders." One August afternoon east of Elko a group of passengers were not comforted when an optimist remarked that with congenial companions and sufficient water to keep the roadbed sprinkled the passage could be made tolerable. The reply was repeated by travelers for years: " With plenty of water and good company, hell would not be a bad place to pass through."

Despite its discomforts, a crossing of what was still called the Great American Desert did not lack interest. By the '70s Nevada had succeeded California as the bonanza state, and the rise of the Comstock millionaires had startled half the nation into the belief that a few dollars shrewdly placed in silver stocks might skyrocket the investor to wealth. Not only was the entire West playing the Comstock lottery; the fever had spread across the country, and few of the early tourists crossed the Nevada line without giving thought to the possibility of a lucrative speculation. Those who wished to try their luck never lacked an opportunity. If they descended at any one of half a dozen parched villages between the Nevada line and Reno they were confronted by a cluster of shed-like structures, all announcing themselves the headquarters of mining enterprises, and all bearing names connoting a high degree of solvency. Earnest individuals drew passengers aside and poured into their ears tales of treasure concealed in dry hillsides near by, needing only a few dollars for filing a claim or completing assays before it could be sold for a staggering sum to some waiting "syndicate."

One passenger in 1871 descended at Elko and in less than a quarter of an hour drove what he believed to be the best bargain of his career. He had hardly reached the ground when a stranger approached and offered him a half interest in the Fork and Spoon Mine for a thousand dollars, which he was assured was virtually a gift. " In five minutes, this very reasonable asking price had been halved, then quartered. By the time the engine was filled with water, the price had fallen to $50, then to $25. The whistle blew and the train began to move. I stepped from the platform, the philanthropist following, still offering me the certainty of wealth. ' Give me ten? ' he asked, and I shook my head once more. The train was moving faster. ' Hell,' he shouted, now running. ' I'm tired of mining. Give me a fiver and the claim's yours! ' In fifteen minutes I had made a clear gain of $995 — no, of $1000, for even his last offer I refused. With a look of entire good nature he let go of the rail, waved his hand in friendly farewell. I had saved $1000 — but had I let ten millions slip through my fingers? "

5

THE COMPILER of one guidebook warned westbound passengers that they might save themselves annoyance by making friendships during the early part of the journey and forming parties of four to occupy facing seats from Ogden west. The reason for this precaution, although it was delicately stated, was not to be mistaken. As the distance from the Atlantic Coast lengthened, a certain deterioration might be observed in the quality of passengers entering the cars. Between Omaha and Salt Lake, only those at least partly familiar with the social graces were likely to be encountered in the Pullmans. Farther west, that was not invariably the case. Unhappily, few of the passengers who entered the Silver Palace cars at Nevada sagebrush stations had the manners of a Chesterfield, the tact of a Machiavelli, or the respectability of one of Victoria's ladies-in-waiting. Nevada was then an uncommonly prosperous land and the railroad was still an intriguing novelty. Any one of the inhabitants of the state, excepting only Indians and Chinese, was likely to take it into his or her head to pay the extra fare and ride in the Silver Palace cars. Not a few did so from no other motive than vulgar curiosity — from a desire to verify by personal observation stories they had heard of the befringed and upholstered splendor of the coaches' interiors. In view of this, warnings to through passengers to choose their associates in advance become understandable. Without a seatmate of his own selection, the tourist from east of the Mississippi might find himself spending the last dozen hours of his journey in close proximity to some affable but unwashed prospector whose sole traveling equipment consisted of a plug of tobacco and a quart bottle of whisky and who hospitably insisted upon his companion sharing both. Worse, authenticated instances have been recorded where ladies of unblemished respectability were forced to share seats with perfumed madams of Virginia City's brothels, bound for San Francisco to look over a consignment of girls newly arrived from South America.

Tourists foresighted or adroit enough to avoid close contact with the natives found much to interest them in Nevada's parched towns. Even the singular persistence of the alkali dust, which in certain localities appeared in clouds when no breeze could be detected, and which was said to be present even in snowstorms, did not prevent passengers from an enjoyment of their transient contact with a frontier in the making. In outward appearance the new settlements were disappointing. Although maps of the Central Pacific route were dotted even in the desert section with the names of stations, most of them were merely barren sidings. Others boasted no more than a station house, the inevitable water-tank and piles of wood for the engines, and a low, cave-like warren where the Chinese section hands lived in waterless squalor. Usually no other habitations were visible, although from some the parallel lines of a wagon trail might be traced, wiggling off through the sagebrush toward some distant cluster of cabins.

Elko, about midway between Winnemucca and the

Utah line, was in the beginning '70s the liveliest of the desert towns, for it was the source of supply for the White Pine district, opened in 1868 and then booming. Through dusty windows passengers regarded the crowds milling about its sandy streets, elbowing into the packed stores and saloons, while scores of freight wagons took on machinery and supplies from the lines of cars on the sidings. There one afternoon a curious tourist saw a crated baby-carriage lifted to the top of a six-horse stage and, wandering on, paused to regard a circle of Indians on their haunches in the hot sand, oblivious of the surrounding tumult, while they dealt and redealt a pack of tattered cards, their squaws peering intently over their shoulders.

Farther west, at Winnemucca, the same tourist was privileged to see a far more resplendent redskin, Winnemucca, " the Napoleon of the Piutes." Above his bare feet and tattered trousers this Indian patrician wore a military tunic, with huge epaulets, its front encrusted with filth and faded gold braid, the whole surmounted by a feathered headpiece. It was Winnemucca's custom to meet every train and to stalk up and down the platform, one hand thrust between the buttons of his tunic in the pose that justified his title. A year or two after the line was finished, Winnemucca and his subjects were sent to a reservation in Oregon, and the town lost its most colorful citizen. By 1881 a Central Pacific guidebook listed its remaining features tersely: " a schoolhouse, two apartments, and no churches."

Throughout the '70s, Indians were to be seen at most of the Nevada stations; the braves loading wood on the locomotive tenders while their squaws and offspring besieged passengers with demands, not for the coppers of Eastern beggars, but for " two bits." They were mostly Shoshones, dirty and indolent, their cheeks smeared with paint, but their general demeanor unlike the redskins of fiction. Along with the Chinese, whom they regarded as social inferiors, the Indians were permitted to ride only in the emigrant cars, but many early gained a taste for hiding between the engine and the baggage car, or " riding the rods." Trainmen sometimes relieved the tedium of their run by hunting out the stowaways and tossing them from the moving cars. Some were killed as a result of this sport; others, of course, died in the frequent wrecks. For years Coast newspapers abounded in such items as this: " An eastbound freight train was wrecked Tuesday morning between Reno and Wadsworth. Fireman Riley sustained a fractured arm and three Indians were killed."

Wrecks were inevitable during the early period, for the roadbed was uneven, tracks had been hastily laid, and the iron rails, spiked to too-widely spaced crossties, frequently broke. Such safety devices as air brakes and automatic signals were still in the future. There was sometimes a large loss of life, but, in general, wrecks were more annoying than serious, for train speed seldom exceeded twenty miles an hour, and in Nevada and Utah the country was level or only slightly rolling. To the experienced traveler, a series of crashes ahead announced that the engine was off the rails; by the time the cars had jolted to a stop he had resigned himself to a half-day wait and the probability of missing a meal or two. Earlier, when one of the engines of California's first railroads left the rails, it had been necessary only to secure a fence-post from the roadside and pry it back on. The heavier locomotives of the Central Pacific required more formal equipment. Among the crew of each train was always someone with a knowledge of telegraphy; passengers saw him, iron spikes strapped to his shoes, climb the nearest telegraph pole and send news of the mishap to the nearest division point. After an hour or two the wrecking train appeared, either to lift the engine back on the track or, if it had been rendered *hors de combat,* to shove it aside for later salvaging and to draw the train to the next station.

6

IN the Sierra, wrecks were likely to be of more consequence. There a derailed engine, instead of plowing harmlessly into the sagebrush, might careen over a hundred-foot cliff, drawing half the train after it. The possibility was seldom absent from the thoughts of those making a first passage over the mountains. Not long after the line opened, a cartoon in a San Francisco weekly portrayed a nervous Englishman addressing a fat miner in the seat ahead: " I say, my man, would you mind leaning toward the *center* on the curves? " There were parts of the road, notably the passage about the famous Cape Horn, where the tracks skirted the sheer edge of vertical cliffs, and coaches overhung a thousand feet of thin air.

After that experience, over-imaginative travelers decided on the spot to return East by steamer, preferring to face the hazards of yellow fever at the Isthmus rather than that of being dashed to pieces in some Sierra canyon.

To those of steady nerves, however, the passage " over the hump " into California was easily the most interesting phase of the journey. When the train, drawn by two laboring engines, began the ascent of the winding Truckee River Canyon, bored tourists awoke to new animation. As the climb continued, it became possible to catch glimpses back over the heat-blurred Nevada plains. The cars wound upward through forests of pines, plunged abruptly into the snowsheds — long dim corridors filled with thunderous echoes and smoke from the wood-burning locomotives — and as abruptly emerged into the brilliant mountain sunshine. Presently faces were pressed to windows for a view, from a thousand feet above, of Donner Lake, forest-circled and peaceful, with no hint of its sinister past. The climb continued; a succession of tunnels and snowsheds followed, then a stop near the summit, where engines took on water and passengers stepped into a curious world of chilly sunshine and light, exhilarating air and, from a height of seven thousand feet, admired a panorama of mountains and canyons, dropping away to the east and west into the blue distance.

If the train was late, the run to Sacramento was seldom reassuring to the timid. At what must have seemed reckless speed, they coasted toward the lowlands, the light coaches swaying round the curves while wheel-flanges screamed against the rails, and the friction of the brakes heated the metal shoes until after dark they glowed red-hot, and passengers sniffed nervously at the smell of charring wood beneath the coaches. Yet accidents were infrequent in the mountain division, even during the first years before air brakes and proper signaling devices were installed. Passengers who expected the worst during the early part of the descent commonly regained their courage after the first score of curves had been successfully passed.

Other disturbing phases of the passage, however, were less quickly forgotten. In all except the midsummer months the task of keeping passengers warm during the Sierra crossing proved beyond the capabilities of the company's engineers. Later the installation of steam pipes and vestibule cars solved the problem, but neither was available in the '70s. At each opening of the doors the heat generated by the wood-stoves was swept out as though through a funnel. After a dozen such icy blasts one winter passenger set his chattering teeth and sketched a device that would have solved the problem. He proposed a long rod, to be suspended from the roof of the coach, bent to a right angle at each end, the angles facing in opposite directions, and the arc of each passing over the top of one of the doors. By a half turn of the rod, one door could be opened and the other locked; their simultaneous opening would thus be prevented and the terrors of frigid gusts sweeping through the car would be ended. The drawing was submitted to a skeptical trainman with the request that he turn it over to the company's engineers at Sacramento. With well-founded pessimism, the philanthropist commented in his diary: " My little invention is far too simple to interest them. They will find a hundred specious reasons why it cannot be adopted and future passengers will continue to suffer the same inconvenience."

California papers hostile to the railroad made much of the discomforts and dangers of the Sierra crossing. The failure of the company to operate Pullmans over the line in the early years and the delay in installing such safety devices as the Westinghouse air brake (invented in 1868), the Janney coupler, and automatic signals was soundly criticized. In the four San Francisco papers for which he successively wrote, Ambrose Bierce for years took pleasure in emphasizing what he called "the methods devised by the railroad company to punish the Demon Passenger." The following is typical: "The Overland arrived at midnight last night, more than nine hours late, and twenty passengers descended from the snow-covered cars. All were frozen and half-starved, but thankful they had escaped with their lives." When the Southern Pacific designated some of its trains "flyers," Bierce quoted figures showing the much superior speed of Eastern trains. To the list of dangers a patron of California railroads faced he added another: "the passenger is exposed to the perils of senility."

Details of wrecks were realistically recorded in the *Union* and *Bulletin* and later in the *Examiner,* despite protests by railroad officials. Such stories kept passengers away and lent point to demands that the road adopt effective safety measures. From the middle '80s onward, the *Examiner's* ridicule of Central and Southern Pacific trains and the manner of their operation was so damaging

349

that Huntington gave his personal attention to the matter of how the paper might be silenced. Nothing could be done, for the young man who owned the *Examiner* had the backing of a multimillionaire mother, and arguments that had proved effective elsewhere were there found to be useless. The *Examiner* continued to harp on the safety of Atlantic Coast railroads as compared with those in California. By the familiar journalistic strategy of giving slight mishaps an importance normally reserved for major catastrophes, the public was persuaded that a ride in one of the company's trains was a hazardous experience indeed. " Last week in Petaluma," stated an *Examiner* paragraph, " a man withdrew to his hay-loft, tied one end of a rope to a rafter and the other about his neck. He then stepped through a trap door. Petaluma is not on the line of the Southern Pacific Railroad. The citizens of towns that enjoy that privilege can commit suicide with far less fuss and bother."

In the late '80s a local train on the line out of Oakland jumped a switch, and the engine and two cars were derailed. No one was injured and little damage was done. The *Examiner,* however, was campaigning for what it termed the public's right to travel with a degree of safety " at least equal to that of a soldier on the battlefield." Reporters and artists rushed to the scene; pictures and lists of the " survivors " filled half a page, and an editorial pointed out that good luck and not good intentions on the part of the railroad management had prevented another wholesale slaughter of innocents. Bierce spent the summer of 1888 in the foothills near Auburn and his column,

" Prattle," regularly informed *Examiner* readers that the tracks of the overland line there were in the final stages of disrepair, its worn rails loosely spiked to rotting ties, and " over these rusted rails the company runs trains of ramshackle cars drawn by engines of antique design. . . ."

When Hearst sent Bierce to Washington in the middle '90s to fight the refunding bill, his attacks on the Southern Pacific first attracted national attention. But heaping ridicule on Huntington and his projects was no new job for the journalist. In California he had been engaged in that pleasant pursuit for two decades, beginning with his editorship of the *News-Letter* in 1868. On August 4, 1888 he wrote in " Prattle ": " The worst railroads in America are in the West. The worst railroads on the Pacific Coast are those operated by the Southern Pacific Company. The worst railroad operated by the Southern Pacific Company is the Central Pacific. It owes the government more millions of dollars than Leland Stanford has vanities; it will pay it fewer cents than Collis P. Huntington has virtues. It has always been managed by rapacity tempered by incompetence. Let Leland Stanford remove his dull face from the United States Senate and exert some of his boasted ' executive ability ' disentangling the complexities in which his frankly brainless subordinates have involved the movements of his trains."

7

DURING the early months after its completion the Central Pacific had no direct connection with San Francisco, and the transcontinental run ended at Sacramento. Passengers who stepped from the cars before the wooden station at the foot of K Street usually stopped overnight at the capital, and so were hauled off with their baggage in Tom May's bus to a local hotel: the affluent to the Capitol, Golden Eagle, or Grand, others to the more modest houses. Those who chose to continue on to the bay had a choice of two routes: they might transfer to the cars of the California Pacific, which operated a sixty-mile road down the valley to Vallejo, where connection was made twice daily with boats for San Francisco. The other and more popular alternative was the California Steam Navigation Company, the boats of which were the equals, in size and luxury, of any in the country. After days of travel through a bleak and largely uninhabited country, tourists stepped off the overland train and crossed the levee to the deck of the *Yo-Semite* with a sense of having returned to civilization at its most luxurious.

Dozens of early travelers exhausted their adjectives to describe the wonders of the *Yo-Semite*. The saloon was likened to the baronial hall of an English country seat; its furnishings to the most elegant drawing-rooms. Dining-room and staterooms were cool and spacious, and at night, with hundreds of deck and cabin lamps lighted, the pampered traveler must have looked back without regret to his passage of the Nevada desert only a few hours before.

One fact, however, marred the informed passenger's pleasure in the riverboats: their saloons were commonly more satisfactory than their engines, the boilers inferior to the berths. The first twenty years of steam navigation on the Sacramento presented a disconcerting record of founderings, wrecks, and explosions, with a list of victims mounting into the hundreds. But having survived the perils of the desert and of the Sierra crossing, overland passengers risked the hazards of the trip down the river for the opportunity it gave them for rest and relaxation. Even after the Central Pacific's trains reached Oakland, in 1870, experienced travelers preferred to descend at Sacramento and to spend a few restful hours on one of the river steamers before facing the noise and confusion of the Coast's metropolis.

MONOPOLY

1

FROM the first, San Franciscans viewed the Big Four's activities with marked and admirably maintained skepticism. The city's lack of enthusiasm for the railroad project dated from the evening in 1861 when Judah's most impassioned arguments had failed to secure enough stock subscriptions to permit the company to incorporate. For fifty years thereafter such opposition as the Big Four encountered was mainly centered in San Francisco. On the few occasions when the city, briefly sharing a general enthusiasm for the road, fell in line and authorized a concession, it invariably repented the bargain and went to extreme lengths to avoid going through with it.

The reasons behind San Francisco's coolness toward the road are easily explained. For a generation after the gold rush, the city's position as the financial and commercial center of the Coast was unquestioned. Virtually all commerce with the outer world flowed through the port; there were located the important mercantile houses, the leading banks and hotels and theaters, the largest population, and by far the most wealth. On the Coast, San Francisco's pre-eminence had never been questioned, least of all by its own citizens. The vast interior country, with its mines and cattle and agriculture, its towns and growing industries, was looked on merely as San Francisco's back yard: a profitable source of trade for San Francisco merchants, and of development by San Francisco capitalists.

Like the rest of the state, San Francisco had for years been advocating an overland railroad. But its citizens were confident that when the time arrived to build the road, San Francisco would put up the capital to make a start, San Francisco energy would carry it through, and of course San Franciscans would be in control. For the obscure corporation sponsored by a group of upstate merchants and without a single representative from the metropolis the citizens could see no hope; obviously the scheme would get nowhere.

But it presently grew clear that the scheme was getting much further than anyone had anticipated, and by 1863 San Franciscans proved willing to give it moderate support. That year the state legislature passed a bill authorizing the city to subscribe for stock to the amount of a million dollars in the Central Pacific and in another project, the Western Pacific. The latter road, which hoped to build from San Francisco to Sacramento, via Stockton, was absorbed by the Central Pacific in 1865. The act was one of a number enabling California counties to grant subsidies to the Central Pacific, which in two counties, Sacramento and Placer, overburdened the taxpayers for a generation. The legislation had to be confirmed by the voters. This was done readily enough in the interior counties, but San Francisco had already repented of its generosity, and violent opposition developed.

The opposition was based partly on the sound argument that the city had no business investing in so speculative an enterprise as a railroad. But a more potent factor was civic pride. Why should San Francisco, where hitherto every important enterprise on the Coast had originated, lend support to " Stanford's moonshine project "? Besides, construction work, after being vigorously pushed for a year, had begun to slow down, and the merchants in control were known to be hard-pressed for cash. San Franciscans were confirmed in their opinion that the project was headed for early failure. As the date for voting the stock subscription approached, all the city's newspapers and a large section of its citizens opposed it bitterly.

Railroad officials realized that only extraordinary efforts would save the measure from defeat. To them the matter was important enough to justify drastic steps. Their resources and their borrowing power had been strained to the limit to finance the first thirty-two-mile section, which needed to be completed before the federal subsidy would become available. Victory in the San Francisco election would mean that $600,000 cash would be immediately forthcoming: the sum was ample to rescue them from a critical situation.

It was the first time the future Big Four had had a vital stake in an election, but they proved to be anything but bungling amateurs. In Coast cities of the day, electioneering methods were without subtleties; those who needed votes and who could afford the expense followed the simple procedure of going out and buying them. San Francisco had thousands of voters who regarded their trips to the polls chiefly as an opportunity to pick up a few extra dollars. To those who knew the ropes any hotly contested election was good for a week's board and lodging.

Realists in politics as in everything else, the railroad group wasted no time in appeals to the logic of the voters. Instead their agents circulated among ward politicians, passing out liberally the only arguments they knew would be effective. But the issue was too important to leave anything to chance, and the railroad forces continued their persuasion before the very doors of the election booths. The election-day activities of the group were later reported in detail in *The Dutch Flat Swindle,* a thick pamphlet issued by the opposition and widely distributed at the time. Like much anti-railroad literature, however, the work soon disappeared from circulation, and it is now one of the prime rarities of Californiana. Its pages, given over to circumstantial accounts of activities of railroad agents at the polls, reveal that even at the beginning of their careers the partners knew how to protect their interests. The foreword comments:

". . . One of the largest stockholders of the company, the owner of 660 shares, the brother of its President, the agent of the Railroad Company for this purpose, with money procured from the Company, went through the polls, scattering money as inducements to vote in favor of the subscription; bought a large number of votes; and through the whole election day used his money profusely; now throwing it by the handful among the voters, who gathered around him in crowds; now making bargains with gangs of men to vote in a body for the subscription."

Typical of the score or more sworn statements of spectators is the affidavit of one William Kayser. On the morning of the election Kayser was at the polls of the fourth ward when the Governor's brother, Philip Stanford, drove up. ". . . He came there in a buggy and had a large crowd of men around him, and was handing money to them liberally; he held out money to all who offered to take; I didn't see him refuse anyone. He said to the persons standing by, ' Now go to work for the Railroad; do all you can.' " Kayser later saw Stanford at the sixth ward " handing out money liberally " and, passing on to the fifth ward, again encountered the industrious campaigner. ". . . The said Stanford came there in a buggy; he paid out money to persons standing around the polls, and then said to some persons, whom he had paid nothing to, that he had exhausted all the money he had brought with him, and that he would go back and get some more and come back in an hour. . . ."

The railroad forces carried the election, but their methods of persuasion proved a bit too open even for the time and place. Although it was then obligated to complete the transaction, the city stubbornly refused to pay a dollar. The question was accordingly thrown into the courts, and San Franciscans managed to keep it there for over two years. In the spring of 1864 a compromise was effected by which the $600,000 stock subscription was canceled and the city agreed instead to give the Central Pacific $400,000 in municipal bonds. But the thought of presenting the despised corporation with so large a sum proved no less revolting to civic pride than the stock subscription had been. When it came time to deliver the bonds, Mayor Coon refused to sign them, and the exasperated railroad officials had to resort again to the law. The state supreme court eventually ordered the Mayor to affix his signature to the documents. He did so — then pointed out that a city ordinance required that they must be countersigned by the city clerk. This time it was the latter, William Loewy, who refused to sign. Again the railroad went to the supreme court and again the city was able to delay the issue for months. Not until April 1865 was the last legal resource exhausted and the bonds reluctantly paid over. By that time the Big Four had no pressing need of the money. Although they were eventually defeated, San Franciscans had the satisfaction of knowing that it had cost the railroad group over $100,000 to collect their debt.

2

SAN FRANCISCO'S opposition to the Big Four was only partly because its citizens enjoyed a good fight. The railroad had not been long in operation before many came to realize that the interests of the corporation were opposed to those of the city.

Long before the Central Pacific was completed, the partners foresaw the possibility that they might control transportation of the Coast, and plans toward that end occupied their thoughts for years. A first step was to acquire local railroads in California: some already in operation, others building, others still in the paper stage. Before the end of the '60s, two lines adjacent to the Central Pacific's terminus at Sacramento had been bought: the California Central and the pioneer Sacramento Valley Railroad — the latter was the project that had first brought Theodore Judah west. At the same time the associates consolidated their control of transportation in the interior by beginning the construction of two new roads: the California & Oregon, extending north up the Sacramento Valley, and eventually on to Portland, and the San Joaquin Valley, which they built south. These two roads formed the nucleus of the corporation that became the Big Four's most valuable property, the Southern Pacific Railroad.

But control of the traffic of the interior was at first a minor aspect of the program. More important was the necessity for extending the transcontinental line from its original terminus at Sacramento to San Francisco and the elimination of competing roads between the two cities. From the beginning the Big Four had anticipated a large traffic of goods and passengers between Europe and the Far East, for the new railroad reduced the time required for passage between China and Japan and the countries of Western Europe by nearly half. They were accordingly eager for deep-water connections on the bay, where boats from the Orient could dock adjacent to the Central Pacific tracks.

During the late '60s the acquisition of such facilities in both Oakland and San Francisco received much attention. The associates went about the business with characteristic thoroughness, keeping in mind not only that their lines must have convenient terminal facilities on the bay, but that competing railroads must be prevented from having any at all. So skillfully did they play the game in Oakland that the railroad's "fence around the harbor" proved all but impenetrable. Not until nearly three decades had passed did any competitor manage to squeeze through.

When they tried to duplicate the feat in San Francisco, however, that city's suspicion of the Big Four's motives led to instant opposition, and another bitter quarrel ensued. Because San Francisco's waterfront was (and still is) under state control, the railroad first dealt with the legislature at Sacramento. In 1868 that body accommodatingly introduced a bill turning over to the Central Pacific and one of its recently acquired subsidiaries, the San Francisco & San Jose Railroad, title to a six-thousand-acre strip of land. The property extended eight miles along the city's bay frontage; its ownership by the Central Pacific would have prevented any competing line from entering the city.

Details of the bill reached San Francisco, and citizens and newspapers opposed the plan with their accustomed vigor. Citizens crowded halls at mass meetings, sent threats and recriminations to the Sacramento politicians, and in general made so much commotion that the bill was withdrawn. Defeated at this point, the group next sought control of Yerba Buena Island (popularly called Goat Island), midway between the Oakland and San Francisco shores. The legislature granted the company a block of submerged tideland north of the island for warehouses and docks, and a similar bill was introduced at Washington to permit use of the island itself, which was federal property. In this move San Franciscans again professed to see a threat to their independence. Again the irate citizens sprang to arms; again petitions were prepared and signed, orators addressed mass meetings, and delegations hurried to Washington to combat Huntington's lobbyists. After months of negotiation had failed to win a single concession from the city, the Big Four were forced to yield, and the Goat Island project was also abandoned. Meantime, by the purchase of two minor eastbay railroads and their trans-bay ferries, and by connecting these with its own road at Niles, the company obtained a reasonably direct route between Sacramento and the bay.

Control of the only transcontinental line and of the network of local railroads in California was, however, but part of the Big Four's strategy. Monopoly of the Coast was possible only if water transportation could also be brought into line. Such competition was of three sorts. Affecting the local situation were the river steamers operating between San Francisco, Sacramento, and Stockton, all of which had done a large business in freight and passengers since the early '50s. In addition there was a considerable coastwise trade between San Francisco and ports in the southern part of the state. Control of the river transportation was easy because the business was chiefly in the hands of one organization, the California Steam Navigation Company. The purchase of this company in 1869 put the Big Four in almost complete control of the traffic between San Francisco and the interior towns. During the early years the associates were unconcerned by the coastwise trade, since the boats did not come into direct competition with them until the Southern Pacific's Los Angeles branch was opened in 1876.

Of more immediate concern were the steamers and sailing ships plying between San Francisco and the East. Here, as in the case of river transportation, much of the business was controlled by one company, the pioneer Pacific Mail. The latter had entered the field before the discovery of gold, aided by a federal subsidy in the form of lucrative mail contracts. For more than twenty years, the company had done a huge business and made large profits for its owners. By the time the overland railroad was built, the Pacific Mail was not only a competitor for the coast-to-coast traffic but also controlled the trans-Pacific trade, operating a line of steamers between San Francisco and the Orient — a fact of importance to the Big Four, who were still hoping for a heavy traffic between the Far East and Europe.

The Big Four recognized the competition of the Pacific Mail as a formidable obstacle to their plans for monopoly. Obviously they would either have to control the company or find means of forcing it into a working agreement. As a first step in that direction the Central Pacific group joined the Union Pacific in establishing a competing line of trans-Pacific steamers, the Occidental and Oriental Steamship Company, and proceeded, by cutting rates below operating costs, to take virtually all the business away from the older company. This feat, together with the threat to put competing steamers on the run between San Francisco and Panama, was sufficient to bring the Pacific Mail into line. An agreement was presently signed by which the Big Four guaranteed that company a certain monthly profit from the operation of its Panama steamers, and in return the Pacific Mail agreed to raise its tariffs to approximately the same levels as those of the railroad. Their understanding with the Pacific Mail was important to the Big Four for another reason: the steamship company had long enjoyed an exclusive contract with the Panama Railroad for carrying its freight across the Isthmus, at rates so much below those charged others as to prevent any competitor from entering the field.

3

IN the early '90s a visiting Eastern journalist, after a week's close reading of Coast newspapers, remarked to Arthur McEwen: " Why are you all roaring, and roaring all the time, against the Southern Pacific? It's only one railroad. Can't you find anything else to complain of? "

The answer might have been that California's citizens feared the corporation because in one way or another they were all under its domination and because two decades of effort to break its control had accomplished nothing. The Big Four, having succeeded, in the early '70s, in their effort to control the movement of freight to and from California and within the borders of the state, established their rate-schedules on the basis of " all the traffic will bear," and they succeeded in maintaining that policy for more than thirty years. It was perhaps the nation's choicest example of a complete and sustained monopoly, an almost ideal demonstration of the power of a corporation to control for its own profit the economic resources of a region comprising one sixth of the area of the nation. That practically the entire population of the Coast realized what power the Big Four held over them, and for years fought stubbornly to break it, adds to the magnitude of the achievement. Although the citizens had on their side every important newspaper of the state save those frankly in the pay of the Southern Pacific, efforts to remedy the situation were uniformly unsuccessful because of the railroad's control of the legislature, of state regulatory bodies, of city and county governments, and, in many cases, of the courts.

The result was that from the middle '70s to 1910 the major share of the profit of virtually every business and industry on the Coast was diverted from its normal channel into the hands of the railroad and its controlling group. The merchant who brought in stock from the East paid freight bills so high that to sell his goods at all he had to cut his profit almost to the vanishing-point. The degree of prosperity of every business or industry was directly dependent upon the officials at Fourth and Townsend streets who fixed the railroad's freight rates. The latter performed their numerous and delicate duties with skill. They and their agents kept watch on the businesses of the railroad's customers; in San Francisco they even claimed — and were given — the right to make periodical inspections of shippers' books. If merchants were found to be growing prosperous, rates were raised; if too many went bankrupt, rates were lowered. The manufacturer was allowed to earn enough to keep his plant in operation; freight rates on the farmer's products were nicely calculated to enable him to clear enough to plant and harvest his next year's crop and to support himself, not too extravagantly, in the meantime.

San Francisco papers and those of the interior regularly printed letters from shippers relating their experiences with the Southern Pacific's freight agents. Rates on agricultural products were fixed on the basis of current market prices. A farmer who had grain to ship found that the grain rate was high when prices were high, low when they were low. The producer was usually allowed to clear enough to continue to produce, but in good years the profit went, not to him, but to the railroad. In the '80s a group of men began developing a gold mine near the town of Shasta, at the northern edge of the state, and started shipping quartz to a mill near San Francisco. The Southern Pacific was asked to fix a freight rate, and did so: $50 per car for the three-hundred-mile haul. The owners found that a profit was possible and soon were shipping an average of three cars a day. The railroad accordingly increased the rate to $73 per car and, when the miners continued to ship, raised it to $100. This brought the owners to the freight office at San Francisco, where they announced that the $100 rate would force them to shut down. The company official assured them that the railroad wished to put no one out of business. He then proposed that they produce the records of what they had received for their ore; railroad officials would then figure what profit they were making and the rate would be fixed accordingly. Scores of such incidents were recorded in local newspapers. In 1885 Northern California sheepraisers found that the cost of shipping wool east absorbed every dollar of their profit. Unable to obtain a reduced rate, the embattled ranchers loaded their product on wagons and sent it off on a three-hundred-mile haul to deep water on San Francisco Bay, from which point it was shipped by sail round the Horn to the Massachusetts mills.

One of the most celebrated of California's " rate cases " was that affecting Southern California's leading industry, the production of oranges. For years the rate for shipping oranges from California to points on the Atlantic Coast was $1.25 per hundred pounds — approximately $.90 a box. The growers proved that this charge left them an average profit of $.13 a box, a return that kept them perpetually on the borderline of bankruptcy. It required six years of concerted effort before the Interstate Commerce Commission, in 1905, forced a reduction from $1.25 to $1.15. The $.10 difference netted the growers in excess of $1,000,000 per year and literally elevated tens of thousands from poverty to a degree of comfort. Not so fortunate were the lemon-growers. The early producers had found a ready market and satisfactory prices, and in consequence the acreage devoted to lemons rapidly increased. However, the growers' prosperity came to the attention of the railroad tariff-fixing officials, who concluded that a larger freight return was possible from this source, and the rate was increased $.15 per box. It chanced that the company's experts here made a serious error, for the $.15 difference not only equaled the growers' net profit, but exceeded it. The growers hung on for several seasons while they attempted by persuasion and force to have the old rate restored. Then, tiring of producing lemons for the profit of the company that hauled them east, they began uprooting their orchards and planting other crops. Thereupon Southern Pacific officials, recognizing their error, restored the old rate — and the growers accommodatingly planted their acres with lemon trees again.

But the story was not yet ended. Even after the old rate was restored, it was found that the cost of delivering California lemons in Atlantic Coast cities was too high to enable producers to compete in price with Italian lemons, although there was a substantial tariff on the latter. California growers thereupon began a campaign for a higher tariff on lemons and at length succeeded in obtaining a fifty-per-cent increase. The growers of course foresaw a much wider market for California lemons and higher prices. But a few weeks after the new tariff went into effect the Southern Pacific again raised the rate on lemons from $1.00 to $1.15, and the growers' jubilation vanished. This, however, was in 1910, when the railroad's long period of immunity from government control was nearing its end. A few months later the Interstate Commerce Commission forced the company to restore the rate to $1.00 per box.

Instances of exorbitant and discriminatory freight charges could be cited endlessly. The Southern Pacific owned a twenty-one-mile railroad between Los Angeles and San Pedro. This line was the means by which the company discouraged merchants from having goods bought on the Atlantic Coast shipped west by sea. Including wharfage tolls, the rates were as high as $3.50 per ton for the forty-five-minute journey — practically half as much as it cost to carry goods on the five to seven months' journey from European or Oriental ports. A conversation between a Chinese merchant in Hankow and the captain of an American sailing ship was widely printed at the time. The vessel was loading pig iron at the Chinese port for shipment to Los Angeles. The merchant asked the freight rate and was told it would amount to $6.00 per ton. " How much of that goes to the owner of the ship? " " Four dollars," said the captain. " Ah, then Los Angeles must be far inland." The captain produced a map and the incredulous Oriental traced with his forefinger the 5,700-mile journey down the river to the ocean and across the Pacific to San Pedro, then the scarcely perceptible space between San Pedro and Los Angeles. Four dollars a ton for the first haul; $2 for the second. The Chinese regarded the other with polite disbelief. Only two explanations were possible: either Americans were all crazy or his friend the captain was an outrageous liar. Yet every shipper on the Coast could cite dozens of such rates. One Sacramento newspaper published the schedule of freight charges between that city and a number of points in Nevada, listing in an adjoining column the far lower rates charged by wagon-trains before the railroad was built. The editor called on Stanford to elaborate his frequent boast that the road had proved an unparalleled economic boon to the Coast.

4

OCCASIONALLY some reckless individual waged private warfare with the railroad and caused its owners restless days and nights before the insurrection could be put down.

One of the most picturesque of the rebels was John L. Davie, ex-cowpuncher, ex-opera-singer, ex-miner. When he came in conflict with the Southern Pacific, Davie was an Oakland storekeeper, selling — on the same premises — coal and books. One day in 1894 a salesman for a salt company persuaded him to add further variety to his stock; Davie placed an initial order for two schooner-loads of the salesman's product. Rather than have his coal and book business buried under a mountain of salt, he decided to build a warehouse on the Oakland waterfront. He selected a site on the estuary, a navigable arm of the bay that extended close to the town's business district, and submitted plans for his warehouse and wharf to the city

officials, who had control over this one small section of
the waterfront. Then his troubles began.

It must be explained that by a series of complicated
moves the Central Pacific had in the late '60s acquired
title to virtually the entire Oakland waterfront. By this
move its owners hoped not only to control the local traffic
between San Francisco and the growing eastbay communities, but also to prevent any rival railroad from acquiring a deep-water terminus and convenient access by
ferry to San Francisco. In both aims they met with more
than average success. Thirty years were to pass before the
completion of " Borax " Smith's Key Route provided the
first effective competition with the Southern Pacific's interurban system, and it was not until 1900 that the Santa
Fe's line to Point Richmond gave a rival transcontinental
line an outlet on the bay.

In Oakland the Central Pacific's " wall around the
waterfront " put the town at the mercy of the corporation
and, as population and civic ambitions grew, a struggle
to break the monopoly got under way. It was during this
period that Davie entered the picture, with his plan for a
warehouse on the estuary. The Southern Pacific was then
discouraging the development of the city's strip of waterfront, preferring that such industries as were established
be on Southern Pacific land where the shipping could be
controlled. According to its custom, the corporation had
made certain that its local interests would be protected by
the device of securing political control of the city and by
putting into office men pledged to support its policies.

Accordingly, when Davie's application reached the

ı board of public works, the board's president, a loyal railroad man named Tom Carrothers, succeeded in delaying
approval of it from week to week. Once Carrothers based
his objections on æsthetic grounds: he did not like the
design of the clock tower with which Davie proposed to
embellish his warehouse. Davie finally tired of waiting,
abandoned the original site, and leased two acres of tideland at the foot of Webster Street, owned by the Morgan
Oyster Company. This company held title under a state
law popularly known as the Oyster Bed Act; hence it was
not subject to control by either the railroad or the city.

The land was filled in and the warehouse and wharf
were erected. On one corner of the property stood a shack
used as headquarters by a group of hoodlums who called
themselves the oyster pirates; one of its members was a
lusty young rough named Jack London. Davie was careful not to disturb this group; he foresaw that they might
prove useful. Meantime he had decided to move his coal
business to the new site, and bunkers were built beside the
wharf. One day he went to San Francisco and ordered
three thousand tons of coal.

" Where are you going to land it? " he was asked.

Davie gave the location of his wharf.

" We can't send ships to Oakland," was the reply.
" The railroad has a fence around the city."

Davie stated that the matter of getting the coal landed
was his problem; it was duly sent and found its way without opposition into the new bunkers. Meanwhile word
reached Davie that the railroad was about to go into
action; he held a conference with the oyster pirates, then

went to a dealer in firearms and bought all the rifles he had in stock. These Davie loaned, with ammunition, to the gang. Incidentally, he never got any of his weapons back, nor had he expected to. The coal and salt business was ready to function.

A Sunday passed. On Monday morning Davie approached the foot of Webster Street and had some difficulty finding his new business establishment. Over the holiday a twelve-foot fence had been thrown up about the entire two acres. From inside issued the sound of hammers and axes. Davie found a crack in the fence and peered within. A gang of workmen were demolishing the warehouse and tossing the lumber into the estuary, where men and boys in rowboats were cheerfully towing it off. It was the railroad's wrecking crew, which had more than once discouraged those who tried to gain a foothold on the Oakland waterfront.

The angry coal merchant pried a board from the fence, squeezed through the aperture, and confronted the leader of the crew. The latter ordered him off the property, while others gathered about. Davie argued and threatened and carelessly neglected to watch a man who was circling behind him, a length of two-by-four in his hand. The timber descended, and Davie later awoke to find himself lying on his face in the street outside.

The former cowpuncher made his way to the nearest saloon, poured himself a drink, and went home to wash his wounds. An hour later he was on the street again, stalking back toward his disappearing warehouse. A group of citizens followed at a cautious distance, eying the two revolvers strapped to his waist, the shotgun across his arm. For the second time that morning he squeezed unnoticed through the fence. This time the company's wreckers were taken by surprise. With the muzzle of the shotgun close to their ribs, and Davie shouting profanity in their ears, half a dozen of the invaders were forced over the edge of the wharf into the estuary. A growing crowd of spectators cheered the exploit.

When the bloodless battle was over, Davie turned the enthusiasm of the onlookers to use. With the abandoned tools of the wreckers the crowd went to work on the fence, which disappeared in half an hour. Reporters for San Francisco papers had meantime reached the scene, and within a few hours Oakland's " waterfront war " was a major sensation. It was the first check the railroad had met during the years it had been maintaining its hold on the Oakland tidelands. The picturesque details of Davie's exploit stirred popular enthusiasm, and an interested public awaited the next phase of the battle.

It was not long delayed. In the emergency the railroad summoned its local political boss, Carrothers, and the latter summoned the Oakland police. Carrothers, the police chief, and a squad of patrolmen presently appeared at the estuary bearing a warrant for Davie's arrest. But the attention given the affair by anti-railroad papers had proved effective and the police were met by a belligerent mob of close to five hundred. They ignored the police chief's commands to disperse and at length the exasperated officer ordered his men to charge. The assault was met with enthusiasm by Davie's supporters, the oyster

374

pirates in the van. Police clubs were swung effectually for a few moments, then the superiority of numbers asserted itself and the invaders were forced off the property and into the street. A few scalps were laid open on both sides, a few eyes closed and noses broken, but there were no major casualties. The chief gathered his disorganized forces and withdrew, leaving Davie's army in possession.

This second successful skirmish solidified sentiment in favor of the embattled coal merchant. The use of the local police in fighting the railroad's battle was soundly condemned. The boss, Carrothers, found himself in a difficult position, with the railroad demanding that Davie be dispossessed forthwith and the public equally insistent that the police keep hands off. The logical alternative was resort to law, but the railroad was not anxious at the moment to submit to the courts the question of its title to the property.

According to Davie's later account, a less violent attempt to reach a settlement was next tried. Carrothers sought out the rebel and in a reasonable mood informed him that if he continued to hold the property it would jeopardize the railroad's title to the entire waterfront. He ended with a suggestion that Davie accept a blank check, fill it out for any amount his conscience dictated, and live at his ease in Paris for ten years. Davie had no supporting testimony for this charge, for no third person was present. In any event, he failed to take up residence in Paris, and warfare was resumed.

The contest by then had taken on the appearance of a siege. Davie and his oyster pirates remained on the property day and night, with rifles stacked in readiness and a sentry constantly on duty. The railroad's next move was an attempt to establish possession of a part of the land by landing a grain barge there at high tide. News of the coup leaked out and again crowds gathered to see the show. The implements of warfare were drawn up: two locomotives arrived on the adjacent tracks, and two flatcars loaded with chains. The chains were attached to the barge and the locomotives, and all waited for high tide. Crowding the barge was a group of men of the determined variety the railroad chose when work of this kind was in prospect. All were armed, as were many among the Davie force.

The situation began to assume a serious aspect, for the anti-railroad faction was determined to prevent the landing of the barge at any cost. Many of Davie's recruits were young roughs whose hatred of the railroad was based on encounters with brakemen in numerous freight-yards and lonely sidings, and the prospect of fighting it out now under the eyes of a sympathetic audience, and with the odds even, had so strong an appeal that Davie had difficulty keeping his forces in check. Meantime the water rose in the estuary, the crowd on the banks swelled, and verbal exchanges between the rival groups grew in frankness. At last the engines came to life, the slack of the chains was taken up, and the barge began to edge toward the shore.

What followed was in the same key as the melodramas unfolded nightly at Morosco's Theater across the bay. A skiff put out from shore carrying Davie and several helpers. While the gallery cheered and the railroad forces shouted threats and warnings, the skiff reached the tightening chains and the men attacked them furiously with hacksaws. On the barge and ashore loaded guns were held in readiness. Sanity, by some miracle, prevailed, however, and no shots were fired. In true Morosco style, the last chain parted just as the barge touched the edge of the disputed land. As it drifted out into the estuary the Davie force elected to follow up and complete the victory. Rowboats and planks formed a precarious bridge, over which passed an active file of Oakland youths intent on settling long-standing feuds with railroad policemen. Clubs and fists were swung for a few minutes, then the forces of the attackers turned the tide. The defenders were forced back and finally broke ranks; those still on their feet found dubious safety by jumping over the side.

But victory, as usual, went to the heads of the winners. The mob milled about, eager for further conquests, lacking only an objective. The latter was presently provided. The Southern Pacific had recently extended its interurban system by building a connecting link between its Oakland and Alameda tracks. In laying out this line the company, with permission of the city officials, had built directly through a city plaza at Fifth and Harrison streets, disregarding protests of the citizens. The battle on the barge recalled the incident, and the victors moved in a body to the plaza. On the way they broke into a railroad tool-house and armed themselves with sledges and crowbars. While the police, after another futile attempt to control the mob, stood by, the rails were ripped from the plaza, whereupon the wreckers, warmed to their work, continued to tear up the track for some distance in both directions, carrying off the ties for firewood and throwing the rails into the estuary.

As the evening progressed, the mob swelled and the destruction continued. The main-line tracks along First Street came in for attention, and track-wrecking continued until the hard work involved began to pall. More spectacular mischief then occurred to the ringleaders. The railroad's Oakland station, a small frame structure with a bell tower as its chief architectural ornament, stood near by. The suggestion that the crowd make off with the building was readily accepted. A dray was commandeered and drawn up beside the little structure, while half a hundred revelers lifted it bodily on board — the company's agent, badly frightened, still inside. With the bell ringing vigorously, the building was drawn up the street to a spot opposite the city hall, where the mob proposed to deposit it as an object lesson to the city officials.

At that point occurred the first real casualty of an afternoon and night of rioting. Too enthusiastic pulling of the rope loosened the station bell from its fastenings and it crashed to the ground, killing one unfortunate who failed to jump in time. The accident sobered the mob, which presently melted away.

5

THE IMPLICATIONS of the riot were recognized by the railroad officials; they abandoned force and resorted to law. On subsequent events of Oakland's waterfront war it is unnecessary to dwell in detail. The company's claim to complete control of the harbor was pressed in the state and federal courts and abandoned only after the Supreme Court rendered an adverse decision.

Meantime the company's efforts to maintain a monopoly on trans-bay passenger traffic brought on another series of picturesque incidents. Tiring of the high fares and inadequate service of the railroad's ferries, a group of Oaklanders, headed by the troublesome Davie, purchased a speedy steamer and set up a rival line. The fare was fixed at five cents, one third that charged on the Southern Pacific boats. The new "nickel ferry," the *Rosalie,* was both fast and luxurious and of course she was heavily patronized. On trips across the bay her captain occasionally amused himself and his passengers by overtaking the box-like company ferries and literally running rings around them.

Oakland patrons of the new boat soon discovered that they could ride to her dock on the railroad's interurban trains without cost; the road's franchise specified that no fares could be collected within the city limits. Hundreds of commuters accordingly crowded the trains for San Francisco, stepped off at the station nearest the new company's dock, and crossed the bay on the *Rosalie.* Acting as feeder for a rival ferry, without compensation, was naturally displeasing to the railroad officials, but for some time they were unable to find any way of preventing it. When stops convenient to the *Rosalie* were abandoned, the inconvenienced free passengers raised indignant outcries. Local public opinion was so strongly against the railroad that when it attempted to have its franchise amended to permit collection of local fares, the city officials, by then thoroughly intimidated, delayed for weeks before granting it.

Meantime, of course, the Southern Pacific was fighting the new line with all the considerable means at its command. The battle resolved itself into one of docking-facilities, the company doing all it could to hinder the arrival and departure of the *Rosalie* and the other boats that were added to the " nickel ferry " fleet.

The Southern Pacific then had far more influence at Sacramento than in Oakland or San Francisco. The state board of harbor commissioners, which controlled San Francisco's waterfront, in time discovered that it could not continue to give the " nickel ferries " regular docking-facilities. When the boats found a place at which to tie up on the San Francisco side, it was usually at the end of a pier that in some mysterious way was so closely packed with drays that it was next to impossible for passengers to make their way to the street. This difficulty was removed when Davie enlisted the aid of a San Francisco politician who organized a gang of longshoremen to clear the pier of the offending drays. This was not accomplished by peaceful means, for in the battle that followed, dozens were thrown into the water, but the nickel ferry's passengers suffered no further inconvenience from that source.

At the opposite end of the run they were not so fortunate. The approach to the Oakland terminus was through the narrow estuary. The Southern Pacific re-arranged its schedule so that its slower boats would reach the mouth of the channel ahead of the *Rosalie*. Once in the estuary, the railroad's boats pursued a leisurely zig-zag course, ignoring the speedier boat's signals that she wanted to pass. As on the San Francisco side, the new line could obtain no regular docking-facilities. When, as frequently happened, no other space was available, the *Rosalie's* captain entered the railroad's slip and there dis-charged and received passengers. The company discour-aged the practice by releasing half a ton of coal dust from a near-by bunker just as the *Rosalie's* patrons were crowd-ing the ferry apron, enveloping them in a dust-cloud from which they emerged stifled and unrecognizable.

About that time, Cleveland's Secretary of the Navy, Thomas Lamont, visited Oakland. The miniature naval war on the estuary aroused his professional interest, and he listened attentively while Davie gave his version of the strife. Davie was particularly disturbed by the refusal of the ferryboat captains to allow the *Rosalie* to pass. La-mont inquired about details of that vessel's construction. Was she soundly built? Could she withstand a consider-able blow on, say, her bow — such, for instance, as might be sustained in a severe collision? Davie replied in the affirmative, and Lamont suggested mildly that he might profitably consult a maritime attorney. Davie took the hint, posted himself on the legal aspects of the situation, and prepared for action.

On one of her trips a day or two later, the *Rosalie* lagged behind and allowed the railroad's ferry, the *Alameda,* to enter the estuary first. The *Rosalie* then drew astern and gave the signal for passing. The rival boat continued its course, weaving from side to side to prevent the other craft from slipping past. The *Rosalie* crept closer, repeating her signal several times. It was ignored, as usual. What happened next, however, was not. From the pilot house of the *Rosalie* orders were issued to clear the passengers from the bow; then the engine-room signal jingled for full speed ahead. The fast vessel gained momentum, rapidly closed the gap between her sharp bow and the stern of the *Alameda.* When the officers of the railroad boat realized what was impending, it was too late to avoid a collision. The ships met with a crash, the *Rosalie's* prow cutting fifteen feet into the *Alameda's* stern.

Passengers on both ships picked themselves up and rushed to the rails. The *Rosalie* backed off, little harmed, while the captain of the *Alameda,* fearing that his craft was about to sink, beached her at the edge of the estuary. The *Rosalie* stood by, her passengers hooting while the patrons of the *Alameda* climbed over the side and waded ashore through the mud. The railroad had previously met the competition of the nickel ferries by slashing their own rate to five cents for the round trip. Patrons who had been lured by this unquestioned bargain were contemptuously called " nickel-splitters " by the anti-railroad faction, and the sight of the economical ones wading ashore provided material for the humorists crowding the *Rosalie's* rails. Thereafter the laws of passing were observed by the company's ferries.

But warfare on the estuary was not at an end. The nickel ferries finally established their Oakland terminus at a point some distance beyond the railroad's slip. To reach the new dock, it was necessary to pass the railroad's wooden drawbridge at the foot of Webster Street, over which it operated trains, on an hourly schedule, between Oakland and Alameda. In its control of the bridge the company saw an opportunity to disrupt the schedule of its rival. Accordingly, the bridge-tender was instructed to keep the draw closed during the time its trains were on the Oakland side, and the tender thereupon became deaf to the signals of the rival ferries.

Half the population of the bay area awaited the next move of the nickel ferries expectantly. Again the public was not disappointed in its anticipation of prompt reprisals. The bridge-tender one day had a caller who explained to him the laws of right of way as they concerned the operation of drawbridges. The tender was unimpressed. He was a railroad employee and it seemed to him sound judgment to obey the orders of those who paid his wages. He continued to ignore the signals of the nickel ferries while the company's trains were on the Oakland side of the estuary.

One day the *Rosalie's* whistle was more persistent than usual; moreover, she continued to edge upstream until her bow was uncommonly close to the closed draw. A deckhand appeared at the ferry's bow with a coil of rope, which he tossed upward. A man who had been loitering on the bridge caught its end, drew in the slack, and hoisted up a hawser that was attached to its end. In an instant, the hawser was made fast to one of the wooden supports of the bridge. At the same time the *Rosalie,* her engines reversed, drew away from the bridge. The slack of the hawser was rapidly taken up and the loiterer raced to safety on shore. The bridge-tender did not act so promptly; instead he lost his head and ran about panic-stricken in the center of the draw. While this was going on, the hawser snapped taut and, with a crash of rending timbers, the draw tilted sharply and dropped into the estuary. The wreckage floated off with the drenched tender clinging to its top, and the ferry passed on to its dock.

The exploit caused Davie's arrest, but a friendly grand jury delayed issuing an indictment and he was never brought to trial. This episode marked the end of active warfare on the estuary. The railroad was then meeting successive defeats in its legal fight to maintain its Oakland waterfront monopoly, and it preferred to devote its energies to that more important issue. Moreover, the company realized that the nickel ferries were operating at a loss and that their backers would eventually tire of the game. This prediction proved correct. A few months later the rival line went out of existence and the Southern Pacific, again in control of the traffic across the bay, restored its former rates.

6

DURING the spring of 1880, half a hundred workmen put the finishing touches on Hopkins's Nob Hill mansion — which Uncle Mark had not lived quite long enough to occupy — and Leland Stanford and his wife and son set off on another of their protracted junkets to Europe.

Two hundred and forty miles to the south, events of another nature were taking place. The construction crews of the company's new southern route were pushing through the deserts of the Southwest to complete a second through line to the East, and the Southern Pacific's land office was busy populating the broad area of the lower San Joaquin Valley.

From the '70s onward, circulars setting forth the advantages of the region south of Fresno had been widely distributed through the East and Middle West. Settlers were urged to come west and buy railroad land, at extremely liberal terms, in the new Eden. The circulars were effective; the settlers came — long emigrant train-loads of them, complete communities that rolled westward as a unit, one family to a car that was jammed with household furniture, farm implements, horses, cows, children, young fruit trees, seed for the first season's problematical crops. The emigrants reached the new land of opportunity, dusty cars were shunted on sidings, and from their doors groups of travelers looked out at one or another of a dozen barren stations south of Fresno: Goshen, Tulare, Kingsburg, Tipton, Hanford. . . .

The Argonauts descended — and took up one of the most remarkable struggles for existence in the history of the pioneer West. Throughout the decade of the '70s the American farmer's instinct to hold on to his unproductive acres up to the point of actual starvation was demonstrated to perfection by these settlers in the Tulare basin. They were inhabiting a region potentially as fertile as any in the country, which, before the century was out, was to be transformed into a park-like district of vineyards and orange groves, traversed by well-kept roads and dotted with the mansard roofs and stable towers of a spacious era.

It was a different story in the '70s, when the board shacks of the pioneers were first thrown up in the parched valley. The seasons were a cycle of discomfort. In summer furnace-like winds swept down from the north, leaving burnt crops and fruit trees in their wake. Winter brought floods and washouts, spring frosts destroyed whatever young crops were above ground, and the sandstorms of autumn often completed the destruction. Homesickness for the green meadows of the East, and their common poverty, united the settlers into a group so compact that when a new obstacle presented itself, they surprised the West with their united opposition.

Having no property but their unproductive land, no working capital, and no resources except their labor, the group pooled the latter and set to work to build a system of water-distribution that would make their sterile acres productive. As the work progressed, it became in the literal sense a race against starvation. Foothill streams were dammed, miles of irrigation canals and tributary ditches were dug about the edges of rocky hillsides, all without proper tools or equipment. Because there was no money to hire engineers to run their lines, they twice bungled the job, and the relics of one of their abandoned canals, a slanting scar across the face of a Sierra foothill, is still to be seen. Motorists, streaking past on the paved highway below, regard it with curiosity.

The staple food of the construction gangs was corn, inadequately ground in household coffee-mills, supported by jackrabbit stew and varied by occasional feasts of trout from foothill streams. There were repeated setbacks and almost interminable delays. But the work was at last completed; the hoped-for streams of water reached the parched fields, and the fields responded with startling generosity. For the first time, except in the railroad's circulars, Starvation Valley began to belie its name. Figuratively, the farmers enjoyed the fruits of victory; actually, they set to work to learn, with more costly errors, the technique of irrigation farming. Nevertheless, life in the Tulare basin grew easier. The sack of corn and the coffee-mill were no longer mainstays in the farmhouse kitchens, and letters sent back to old communities beyond the Rockies began to strain credulity by boasts of the variety and quantity of crops. The hard-won victory over natural forces brought easier times to the valley.

Other forces remained to be dealt with. The Big Four were engaged in the huge scheme of expansion necessary to their plan for control of the traffic of the Coast. To the north, the costly road of the Oregon branch was pushing across the granite ridges of the Siskiyous, and many miles of unpopulated desert remained to be traversed on the long race to El Paso. Revenue had to be got where it was available, and little was allowed to escape officials at Fourth and Townsend streets. The new signs of prosperity in the Tulare basin were not overlooked.

The company's methods were characteristically direct. According to the circulars sent out by the land department, settlers were not to be required to pay for the property until the railroad could convey title to it. It could convey title only after the federal grants — of which this land was part — were accepted from the government. Hence the land the settlers had occupied during the early years and laboriously made profitable was owned, not by themselves or the railroad, but by the national government, and was reserved by the government until such time as the company wished to claim title to it. The latter had delayed taking over ownership for an understandable reason: ownership of property involves the obligation to pay taxes, and a company that was bending its resources to achieve a monopoly of Pacific Coast transportation had no money to spare for taxes. The settlers of the Fresno-Tulare district held their land by right of documents that proved less stable than deeds: by guarantees from the railroad that their claim to the property would be respected; that the sale price, when it was fixed, would be moderate. Ten dollars an acre was the highest price mentioned in the railroad's literature, and from $2.50 to $5.00 per acre was fixed as the " average " price. Moreover, the settlers' agreements stated that:

" In ascertaining the value, any improvement that a

settler or other person may have on the lands will not be taken into consideration: neither will the price be increased in consequence thereof. Settlers are thus assured that in addition to being accorded the first privilege of purchase, they will be protected in their improvements."

These were explicit promises, made in the name of the largest corporation in the West. They were made because the company wished to populate the country through which its new line passed without incurring the expense of taking over ownership of the land during the first unproductive years. It was an excellent piece of business for the railroad. Population meant not only traffic but enhanced values of the vast areas of government land it had received for building the road.

In 1877, the lean years in Starvation Valley having come to an end, the company began to assume title to the lands and, of course, immediately fixed prices for sale to the public. The settlers then learned three things:

That the land they were occupying was being placed on the open market for sale to the highest bidder.

That the sale price had been fixed, not at from $2.50 to $10.00 per acre, but at from $25.00 to $40.00 per acre, and that every improvement they had made — houses, roads, orchards, crops, and their irrigation system — had been considered and charged for in the company's sale price.

The settlers were not concerned when these facts reached them. The company, they recognized, was engaged in many activities; it had merely overlooked the earlier promises to them. To the railroad's local agents they presented copies of the papers which, they supposed, guaranteed their rights, and offered to begin purchasing the farms on the terms originally specified. The documents were forwarded to headquarters at San Francisco and the settlers went about their business while they awaited a reply. No reply was forthcoming. Weeks passed without an acknowledgment of their protest. Meantime, plans for the public sale of the property went forward.

It was not until advertisements appeared throughout the state offering the lands for public sale that the settlers began to grow apprehensive. Thereupon anger and determination took the place of confidence. The community that had fought through to success during the earlier period refused to give way before this new threat. Because they were accustomed to acting together in adversity, the group organized a Settlers' League, drew up a statement of their case, and sent it to the California representatives in Congress. Again nothing happened, and the League members realized that they were facing the expensive business of a resort to law. An assessment — the first of a series — was levied on members for attorneys' fees, and in due time a test case was filed in the federal court. Late in 1879 the case came to trial, the railroad marshaling its legal talent to the defense.

The decision was favorable to the railroad, and the settlers prepared to go back to their corn-meal diet while they carried an appeal to the Supreme Court.

7

EVENTS then followed one another rapidly. The rail-road's advertising campaign had begun to produce results. The offer of improved, irrigated lands for sale attracted groups of purchasers, and within a few weeks half a dozen new houses had been added to the settlers' community. New fields were laid out and new ditches were dug to tap the irrigation canal. For a time the settlers remained inactive; then one moonless night a crowd assembled, moved down dusty roads to one of the new houses. Its occupants were ordered to leave and, in silence, household possessions were removed beyond the danger area. New timbers were soaked with oil and for the next hour a prophetic red glow spread over the Tulare basin. News of the burning traveled. Prospective buyers of the land weighed its implications and decided to purchase elsewhere. The company's land boom collapsed.

Word of the midnight bonfire filtered upward through the railroad's organization and presently engaged the attention of the executives in San Francisco. One of the results was that a few days later an afternoon train from the north deposited two strangers at Hanford. These were prospective settlers, but of another variety than those who had preceded them. They had come into the valley, as it later developed, because the railroad had offered them free farms provided they were able to maintain possession of them against the settlers. The confident pair, Hartt and Crow, announced their ability to uphold their part of the bargain.

Their arrival completed the preparatory work. From the federal court the railroad had secured writs of eject-ment against several of the original settlers. These were put in the hands of the federal marshal of the district, with instructions to dispossess the farmers named and install Hartt and Crow in their places.

On May 10, 1880 the marshal arrived at Hanford to carry out his orders, and a feeling of expectancy gripped the valley. The League members were by then deter-mined to allow none of their number to be ejected until their case was passed on by the Supreme Court; public opinion of the entire countryside supported them. The president of the League, and its spokesman, was Major Thomas McQuiddy, one of the original settlers. Mc-Quiddy continued to advise moderation and sent an ap-peal to the marshal urging him not to serve the writs. But early the next morning, before his message had been de-livered, the official set off to carry them into effect.

The marshal traveled in a livery buggy, attended by the local land agent of the railroad. In a second buggy, close behind, rode Hartt and Crow, their vehicle supplied with shotguns, rifles, revolvers, and supplies of ammunition. The shotgun shells had been emptied of their original contents and reloaded with lead slugs. The two were tak-ing no avoidable chances.

For an hour the two vehicles rolled across the country-side, then came to a stop inside the gate of a settler named Branden. A meeting of the League was in progress down

THE CURSE OF CALIFORNIA.

Cartoon by Keller in the Wasp, *San Francisco, August 19, 1882.*
Courtesy of the Bancroft Library

THE OGRE OF MUSSEL SLOUGH

Cartoon by Keller in the Wasp, *San Francisco, March 12, 1881.*
The two heads are Stanford and Crocker.
Courtesy of the Bancroft Library

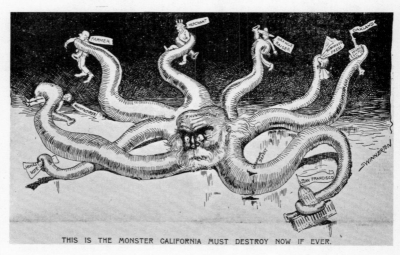

THIS IS THE MONSTER CALIFORNIA MUST DESTROY NOW IF EVER.

Cartoon by James Swinnerton in the San Francisco Examiner,
December 14, 1896.
Courtesy of the California State Library

the valley, and Branden was attending it. The four entered the farmhouse and stripped it of its possessions, depositing them at the roadside. The marshal thereupon declared Hartt lawfully in possession of the property. Four loaded rifle cartridges were left on the doorstep, a symbolical greeting to Branden on his return. The marshal, still attended by his escort, continued on to serve his second writ, this time on a farmer named Brewer, three miles and a half to the north.

Toward the middle of the morning the party arrived before Brewer's farm. Brewer was at work in his fields. With his three companions the marshal drove through the yard, past the farmhouse. He had progressed some distance into the field when a group of a dozen or more settlers came forward to meet them. The buggies drew to a stop, their occupants regarding the approaching group. They were League members, a serious-faced group of farmers who advanced slowly, several on horseback, the others on foot. They carried no visible weapons, though it developed that about half of them were armed with pistols.

The marshal descended from his buggy and went forward to meet the group. A spokesman for the farmers demanded that he delay dispossessing any of their number until the higher court had passed on the legality of the points at issue. The marshal replied that he had no choice in the matter and must obey orders. Thereupon the settlers insisted that they would not allow him to proceed. The group closed about him and demanded his surrender on the promise that he would be conducted to the railroad station and seen safely out of the county. The marshal, who had no taste for his role, submitted. Four settlers were assigned to conduct him and the railroad's agent to the nearest station.

Thirty yards away, Hartt and Crow sat in their buggy, interested spectators of what was going on. When it grew clear that the settlers were gaining control of the situation, Hartt reached to the floor of the buggy. His hand closed over the stock of his rifle.

" Let's shoot," said he.

His companion, the cooler head of the two, waved for him to be silent. It was not yet time for action. It became time a second or two later.

A man on horseback, James Harris, left the group and rode toward the buggy. He stopped a few feet distant and ordered the two to give up their weapons. Crow's shotgun, its hammers cocked, lay between his knees. He threw its stock to his shoulder, took deliberate aim, and pulled the trigger. Harris received the discharge full in the face. He was blown from the saddle.

The shot caused the group to spin around. As Harris's body fell, his neighbor, a farmer named Henderson, spurred forward, drawing his revolver. The sights were focused on Crow, the hammer descended, but the cartridge failed to explode. The narrow seat cramped the movements of the now active pair in the buggy. Hartt, gun in hand, started to spring to the ground. Henderson's revolver worked then, and Hartt pitched to the ground, shot in the stomach. The next second Crow's shotgun spoke again, killing Henderson. He tossed the empty gun away, seized a revolver, and leaped from the buggy, shooting into the group of farmers. He fired rapidly and accurately, wasting no ammunition. Daniel Kelly, urging his frightened horse forward, was shot three times in the body. Iver Kneutson fell dead as he drew his revolver. Edward Haymaker crumpled to the ground, shot in the head. Archibald McGregor, unarmed and on foot, received two bullets in his chest and ran screaming across the field. From a distance of a hundred and fifty feet Crow sent another bullet into his back and he pitched forward on his face in the grass.

An abrupt silence descended. The reek of black powder drifted over the field. For some seconds no one moved; dead and wounded lay unattended on the ground. Crow alone was busy; he had seized the opportunity to reload his guns. The spell of inaction was broken by the appearance, at a full gallop, of the League's leader, who had spent the morning trying to locate and overtake the marshal. McQuiddy assumed charge, directed the federal officer to forbid further shooting, then turned toward the still menacing Crow. The latter suddenly whirled about, bent low, and scurried toward the protection of the near-by barn. He gained the building, ran half around it, then turned and raced toward an adjacent field of standing wheat. Still stooping, he disappeared between the tall stalks, and Major McQuiddy issued an order:

" Don't let that man escape! "

One of the survivors, whose identity was persistently kept secret by his companions, took up the trampled trail through the wheat. For a mile and a half, across a series of wheatfields, the flight and pursuit continued. Mc-Quiddy meantime had guessed that the fugitive would try to reach the farm of his brother-in-law, one Hass. He sent two mounted men to watch there for his appearance. These waited beside a bridge over the irrigation canal near the Hass farm. There, a moment after their arrival, Hass himself appeared, driving a light farm wagon. In its bed were six additional guns and further supplies of ammunition.

" Where's Crow? " he shouted to the waiting pair.

At that instant Crow himself plunged into sight along the irrigation canal. He saw the two waiting at the bridge, leaped to cover, and raised his rifle. But the unknown who had followed him into the wheatfield was bringing the chase to a close. His rifle, not Crow's, spoke first. Crow spun about and fell dead beside the ditch.

Meanwhile on the field at Brewer's farm the survivors were carrying the fallen men to the farmhouse. Kneutson, Harris, and Henderson were placed on the porch; they were dead. The wounded — Kelly, McGregor, Haymaker, Hartt — were carried inside, crowding the floor of the hot little room. Two doctors, summoned from Hanford, found three of them mortally wounded. McGregor and Kelly died that night, Hartt the next day. Of the eight hit, seven died. Haymaker eventually recovered.

This ended what became known in California as the Battle of Mussel Slough. Its result was the rout of the settlers and the defeat of their cause. Even public sympathy was largely denied them, for as soon as news of the happenings on Brewer's field filtered into neighboring towns, railroad officials, in control of communication, clamped down a rigid censorship. At Goshen, the nearest telegraph office, a notice was posted that company telegrams only would be transmitted. At Hanford, railroad officials announced that the telegraph office there had been closed and its operator driven away by the outlaw farmers; that, because of "armed insurrection" in the district, the passage of all trains had been canceled.

In San Francisco a group of railroad officials, headed by Charles Crocker, made the rounds of the newspaper offices, where they convinced editors that their agents had been attacked by bands of ruffians. Other avenues of information being closed, the papers printed the version, and in that form the account of the fight was sent throughout the country. Later, other facts came to light. Reporters reached the spot and wired in their stories. Witnesses and survivors gave testimony. The railroad's telegraph operator at Hanford reached San Francisco and made it known that it was the company officials, not the farmers, who had ordered him from his instrument and closed the office.

The battle was a three-day sensation. The five dead farmers were buried on May 12 and a funeral queue two miles long followed the hearses to the cemetery. A few weeks later their families were evicted. Many arrests followed; five of the settlers received jail sentences, and the League recognized the futility of further resistance. From discouragement and from lack of funds to fight further, the pending test case was dropped.

Ironically, some years later the identical question between the railroad and settlers' rights was raised in another county of the state. This time the landowners succeeded in carrying their appeal to the Supreme Court. The decision upheld their agreements with the railroad.

Nearly twenty years later, a young Californian, Frank Norris, published a massive novel, *The Octopus,* and in one of its later chapters the morning on Brewer's farm was made to live again in one of the most impressive passages in the whole range of American literature.

May 10, 1880 was forgotten by the country at large before the week was out. California and the West remembered it a little longer. The railroad company, engaged in more far-reaching activities, gave the incident little further attention. For more than a score of years afterwards, Tulare County observed the day with public memorial services. But these too have been forgotten. Today in Hanford and Goshen, inquiry for the location of Brewer's farm awakens no glimmer of memory.

8

SECOND only to the railroad's resourcefulness in maintaining its monopoly was that of the Coast's shippers in devising means to evade it. Necessity forced the latter to a variety of ingenious but usually futile expedients. Sometimes, however, they managed to score a substantial if temporary victory.

Monopoly

In October 1891 the sailing ship *Armida* entered San Francisco Bay from her home port, Liverpool. In many quarters her arrival was looked on as a momentous event; some even regarded it as the beginning of the city's independence from the extortions of the Big Four's monopoly. The *Armida's* hold was jammed with goods manufactured in the Atlantic states and consigned to San Francisco wholesalers. They had been shipped from New York to Liverpool (where they were certified by American consular agents as of American manufacture and so not subject to duty upon re-entry into the country), then sent across the South Atlantic, round the Horn, up the west coast of South America, and thus at last to San Francisco. Despite this extremely roundabout course, the freight was delivered in San Francisco at rates ranging from three to five dollars per ton less than they would have been had it been sent overland across the continent.

Pleased at the success of their experiment, local merchants placed a volume of orders for delivery by the same circuitous route. Within a few weeks a fleet of vessels, mostly British, were at sea carrying goods from Atlantic Coast cities to European ports, then transshipping it for the long run to San Francisco and Los Angeles. This thriving trade was not allowed to continue long. While most of the fleet was still at sea on the first trip, the federal court declared the traffic illegal and ordered the confiscation of the cargoes. The action was taken on the ground that such shipments were an evasion of federal statutes providing that goods could be carried between American ports only in ships of American registry.

399

Their brief experience with substantially lower rates, however, had given California merchants a taste for more, and from that time on, the battle was waged in earnest. The attempt to break the monopoly with foreign ships having been pronounced illegal, the next step was to try it with those flying the American flag. Accordingly, early in 1892 the Atlantic & Pacific Steamship Company, chiefly backed by a firm of San Francisco wholesale merchants, began operating steamers in competition with the railroad-subsidized Pacific Mail. Because of the latter company's traffic agreement with the Panama Railroad, the new steamers were forced to make the long run round the Horn. Later, the Pacific Mail's contract with the Panama Railroad having expired, the rival line was able to make arrangements by which it, too, used the railroad across the Isthmus.

Because they at last saw the possibility of success ahead, San Francisco shippers began to act aggressively and as a unit. The next important step was the formation of a shippers' organization, the Traffic Association of California, the members of which bound themselves to make all shipments in vessels designated by the association. Although merchants of the interior, believing that the organization would chiefly benefit the metropolis, gave only qualified support, the association grew rapidly and was soon doing effective work. Its first objective was the further development of competition by water. Steamers in the coast-to-coast trade were then small, of limited freight capacity; the largest ship on the run between Panama and San Francisco was of less than 2,500 tons burden. For the

competition to be effective enough ships must be put in
service to handle a considerable volume of the traffic. The
Traffic Association therefore organized two new lines of
clipper ships, both of which began operating in 1892.

Meantime the Big Four had not been idle. To meet
the situation they resorted to methods that had been uniformly effective in the past. Shippers were warned that
the new lines would eventually be forced out of business,
and that those who patronized them might expect reprisals when they had to return to the older companies. The
railroad's means of eliminating rivals was the familiar device of a rate war. The procedure was to reduce its own
rates below operating costs, thus forcing similar reductions from its competitors, and maintaining the rates until
its less liberally financed rivals were forced into bank-
ruptcy. War was duly declared, and the result was an
immediate sharp drop in rates for transportation by water
between the two coasts. By arrangement with the railroad, the original lines of clipper ships had been charging
an average of $15.00 per ton for the run between New
York and San Francisco; by the end of 1892 they were
quoting rates as low as $3.50. Delighted Coast merchants
found that goods purchased not only in the East but as far
west as Kansas City could be shipped by rail to New York,
sent round the Horn, and delivered in San Francisco for
far less than they could be sent overland by rail.

As the volume of material shipped by water increased
— in the summer of 1893 above fifty thousand tons were
at sea — railroad officials regarded their falling receipts
and the lengthening lines of idle freight cars in their yards

and decided on sweeping reductions on the overland lines. By 1894, railroad rates had been slashed on an average by fifty per cent. The rate on California fruits remained at the old level, however, for in the days before refrigeration it was impossible to ship perishables via Panama or round the Horn. The railroad's reductions again equalized the cost of shipping by rail or water, and the bulk of the freight once more went overland, though on far less profitable terms to the transportation companies. Meantime railroad officials had hit on another device to bring the Coast merchants into line. This was the granting of preferential rates to Eastern wholesalers, on such favorable terms as to permit them to quote prices well below those of the local jobbers.

Despite formidable opposition, the shippers' revolt on the whole proved successful. One of its effects was the saving of millions of dollars in freight bills by Coast producers and businessmen. A more far-reaching effect was a growing conviction that the Big Four's transportation monopoly, which for twenty years had withstood all assaults, was after all not impregnable. All foresaw a long and hard struggle, for the contest had hardly begun, but at last there seemed a definite chance of victory. Meanwhile, for the sake of a temporary truce, the railroad had been willing to grant concessions. By an agreement reached in the middle '90s, San Francisco merchants withdrew their support from the new steamship and clipper lines (which had been operating at a loss), and so went out of the shipping business. But in return the railroad agreed to maintain the existing lower rates on through

shipments, to abandon the practice of granting secret reductions to Eastern wholesalers; and the promise was
given that no Coast shipper would be penalized for his
connection with the Traffic Association or his support of
competition by water.

9

THE FACT that the railroad after two decades of dictating
its terms to the public had at last agreed to bargain was a
significant and startling reversal of policy. That the company's conciliatory attitude may have been due to an
awakening sense of responsibility to the public was a theory no one bothered to put forth. The only logical explanation was that Huntington and his associates had recognized that the opposition was at last growing powerful
enough to be dangerous.

It was not the strength of the shipping public, however,
but their new methods that worried railroad officials.
With the scores of earlier attempts to break its monopoly
the corporation had not been much concerned. These
had all been resorts to legislation, and the company had
known how to cope with them. For years, anti-railroad
candidates had been put up at each state election; the
citizens had regularly voted them into office and just as
regularly bills empowering the state to fix railroad rates
had been introduced and duly written into the law. But
in no instance were they ever enforced. Somewhere along
the line the railroad had managed to head off every at-

tempt at regulation. Occasionally it was by the Governor's veto, more often by challenging the legality of the measures in the courts. If both these devices failed, the company had a final resource: that of controlling the agencies charged with putting the new measures into effect. It was by this means that the Big Four had defeated a statewide demand for railroad regulation in the early '80s. Outvoted in the legislature, and with an anti-railroad Governor, the company had managed to " influence " two of the three members of the state railroad commission (one by open bribery) , and the entire machinery of regulation had collapsed.

After a variety of such experiences the public saw no hope of relief through legislation; hence their resort to more direct measures. By instituting competition by water California shippers had forced down rates between the two coasts, and merchants and consumers in San Francisco and other bay and river towns had benefited. But the railroad's control of traffic with interior points had largely deprived them of the fruits of victory. For years local papers were full of protests not only against what citizens felt were excessive rates but against discrimination that had the effect of promoting business in certain localities and retarding it in others. Not the length of the haul but the presence or lack of competition was the determining factor in the fixing of rates, for both freight and passengers. In general, at all points served by boats, the railroad met the marine rates. Other localities, including most of the interior of the state and all of Nevada and Arizona, were charged rates skillfully calculated on what

the traffic would bear. Naturally, there were glaring in-
equalities. In many instances charges for goods shipped
through to San Francisco were much less than to interior
stations on the main line of the Central Pacific through
which the freight bound for San Francisco had passed on
the way west. In the Sacramento and San Joaquin valleys
the rates to Sacramento and Stockton (both served by
water) were low; to points beyond, where the railroad was
the only carrier, they were high.

Shippers early grew convinced that their only permanent relief lay in the building of competitive railroads.
Proposals for the construction of " people's railroads "
were advocated locally almost from the time the Central
Pacific was completed. Not until the Traffic Association's
successful campaign to reduce through rates by encouraging marine competition, however, were definite steps
taken. In the public enthusiasm for that victory, interest
in a rival transcontinental line revived and intensified.
Other projects were gradually abandoned and interest
centered on a proposed line from Stockton (connected
with San Francisco by water) down the San Joaquin Valley and eventually connecting with one or another of the
rival lines then building, or planning to build, to the
Coast. It was this project that the Traffic Association, toward the middle of 1893, took under its wing.

The story of the organization and building of the Valley Road is a striking illustration of how widespread was
the resentment in California against the monopoly. From
its inception, anti-railroad newspapers pictured the project as a means by which California was to free itself from

the extortions of the Big Four, and it is evident that the public shared the belief. To subscribe for stock in the enterprise became a patriotic obligation of every citizen. Newspapers devoted columns to each step in its organization, and the entire state looked to its completion in the expectation that the event would usher in a commercial millennium.

Despite these extravagant hopes and prophecies, the actual building of the railroad was a long time getting under way. The campaign for stock subscriptions had hardly begun when the business depression of 1893 struck San Francisco with particular force. Large mercantile firms that were expected to be subscribers were obliged to withhold their support and, failing to obtain pledges for the minimum sum required, the Traffic Association postponed action until the return of better times. The campaign was reopened in the fall of 1894 and pressed with renewed energy. Popular enthusiasm, encouraged by the anti-railroad faction of the press, brought in a substantial volume of subscriptions, and valley towns through which the line was to pass vied with one another in gifts of land for right of way and terminal purposes. The road's capitalization was $6,000,000. By February 1895, close to $2,-500,000 had been paid in, organization was completed, and a few weeks later the entire state celebrated the beginning of construction at Stockton.

The work was pushed with vigor. Because the route, extending down the center of the valley, presented few engineering difficulties, progress was rapid. The road reached Fresno before the end of 1896, and the following year was extended to Bakersfield. By 1898 the new company was operating close to three hundred miles of railroad and was pushing construction on its extension from Stockton to Point Richmond, which would give the line deep-water connections only ten miles from San Francisco. That year the company's gross business was approximately $500,000 — a highly satisfactory showing in view of the fact that its primary aim was not to make a profit but to force reductions in rates. As the road was built, new rates substantially lower than those of the older line were put into effect. The Southern Pacific, of course, met each reduction, and for three years merchants and producers enjoyed large savings on their transportation bills.

This favorable situation ended, however, just before the century closed, when the property was sold to the Santa Fe. The fact that the " People's Road," after so promising a start, was allowed to pass from local control was a shock to many of its supporters. Those who favored the sale argued that only by that means could California shippers assure themselves of the benefits of a rival transcontinental line and at the same time continue to enjoy competitive rates between San Francisco and San Joaquin Valley points. The Santa Fe, by purchase of the Atlantic & Pacific Railroad and by further construction, had at last managed to reach California and was then operating through trains to Los Angeles and San Diego. San Francisco business interests were naturally eager that the new company also have a local connection, and the sale of the Valley Road seemed the logical means of accomplishing that. The deal was accordingly completed. Control of the local road passed to the Santa Fe in December 1898. That company continued construction on the extension from Stockton to Point Richmond, which was completed sixteen months later, and the first transcontinental trains controlled by a rival of the Big Four reached San Francisco Bay.

10

BY 1900 the Big Four's domination was at last approaching its end. In California it was to maintain its hold for a decade longer, but the movement for more effective government control was steadily gaining force. By the late '90s it had grown clear that even the railroad's highly capable organization at Washington could not much longer hold back the flood. Huntington's stubborn fight to secure, first cancellation, then a drastic scaling down of the Central Pacific's debt to the government proved a turning-point, for the railroad forces had pressed the campaign with every means at their command. The amount involved had, by the end of 1898, reached approximately $59,000,000, including the original subsidy bonds (then past maturity) of some $28,000,000, with interest charges for thirty years, less certain minor payments that had been required by earlier legislation.

The aim of the Huntington lobby had been to persuade the government to refund the entire debt with new long-term bonds bearing very low interest — one proposal was for seventy-five years at two per cent. The negotiations brought forth countless proposals and counter-proposals and for some years engaged a major share of public attention on the Coast and elsewhere. The settlement, finally arrived at in 1899, was distinctly favorable to the government, and a corresponding defeat for the Huntington forces. It provided that the entire debt be refunded on a ten-year basis, with interest at three per cent. Although railroad officials had for years proclaimed the company's inability to pay except in small amounts spread over a long period, once the matter was settled, the debt was speedily liquidated. Payments of approximately $6,000,-000 were made annually for the next ten years, the final installment being paid in 1909.

Meantime profound changes had taken place in the structure and management of the Central and Southern Pacific. The summer of 1900 had marked the passing of the last survivor of the original Big Four. Among the group at Huntington's funeral was a dapper, silent little man of fifty-two, recently come to prominence in railroad circles: E. H. Harriman. Some years earlier, the panic of 1893 had forced the Union Pacific into receivership and, in 1895, Kuhn, Loeb & Company had undertaken its reorganization. Harriman, a stockbroker with a growing taste for railroad speculation, had participated in the refinancing and had been given a place on the new board of directors. By 1898 he was chairman of the Union Pacific's executive committee and actively pushing the road's physical rehabilitation. At the same time he was purchasing connecting roads as a means of building up a strong system. Control of the Central Pacific line to the Coast became a vital part of his plan, and immediately after Huntington's death he began negotiating with the heirs for their stock. The deal was concluded early in 1901, Harriman acquiring from the widow and Henry E. Huntington more than 400,000 shares of the stock. Other purchases brought the total to over 750,000 shares, sufficient to give him control, and the two links of the old transcontinental line were at last brought under single management.

Upon Harriman's brief and spectacular career as a railroad magnate it is unnecessary to dwell here. So far as California was concerned, the passing of the railroad's control to new hands brought no great change. Harriman improved the old road, virtually rebuilding it physically and improving service by providing modern equipment and faster train schedules. But rates remained as high as ever and attempts to secure relief by competition or through legislation were as effectually blocked by the new regime as they had been by the old. Regulation of transportation companies, however, and the breaking up of their political control had by then gained too much headway to enable even the railroad's well-intrenched local organization to hold out indefinitely. As the temper of public opinion changed, California newspapers and weeklies which for years had been accepting railroad subsidies found that their support of the corporation was costing them subscribers and prestige, whereas the anti-railroad journals reported mounting circulation and influence. As a consequence, many of the sheets cut themselves off from the Southern Pacific payroll and went over to the other side. In San Francisco, the success of Hearst's *Examiner* was attributed in no small part to its consistently violent attacks on the Big Four. Other journals began to find the same methods conducive to popularity; one afternoon paper, the *Report,* attained a large following although it apparently had no other purpose than to "fight the railroad."

Not long after the turn of the century the anti-monopoly faction in San Francisco gained a forceful ally when Fremont Older, managing editor of the *Bulletin,* persuaded the paper's owners to forfeit $250 monthly they had been receiving from the Southern Pacific and to go over to the opposition. Subsequent to the fire of 1906, Older and the *Bulletin* had been active in exposing municipal corruption and had taken a leading part in uncovering evidence for the prosecution. The "graft trials," after keeping the city in a turmoil for three years, came to an end in 1909, with very little accomplished. The trials had brought to prominence, however, a local attorney, Hiram W. Johnson, who had taken up the prosecution of the boss, Abe Ruef, after the regular prosecutor had been shot down in the courtroom.

Shortly after the graft trials ended, Johnson decided to run for Governor, and the *Bulletin* enthusiastically supported him. The campaign, one of the bitterest in the state's history, had but a single issue: that of ending the Southern Pacific's political domination. An industrious and eloquent candidate, Johnson visited every corner of the state, harping on his single theme and repeating his promise to "kick the Southern Pacific out of politics."

411

The railroad forces, realizing that they were making a last stand, fought back with every device and influence at their command. Nonetheless, Johnson was elected and the Southern Pacific's long-standing domination of state politics approached its end.

Johnson took office in January 1911. With him had been elected large majorities in both houses of the legislature, and all three members of the railroad commission. In his opening address to the new legislature Johnson stated: " Let us do our full duty, and now that at last we have a railroad commission that will do its full duty, let us give this commission all the power and aid and resources it requires." The power, aid, and resources were duly given; the commission set to work on a thorough overhauling of railroad tariffs throughout the state. During the first two years of its existence it ordered reductions of freight and passenger rates totaling six million dollars per year and, moreover, forced the transportation lines to put them into effect.

Johnson's inauguration as Governor thus terminated California's fifty-year battle to break the monopolistic control of its transportation. In a sense it marked the close of the era that had produced the Big Four.

BIBLIOGRAPHY

THE BIG FOUR were conspicuous figures on the Pacific Coast for well over a third of a century, and the contemporary record of their activities may be found in great bulk and variety in the files of California newspapers and weeklies, in numerous documents, pamphlets, and reports, and in several still-existing collections of correspondence by the four men and their associates. A great deal of this material is, in the nature of things, of little present-day importance, and much of the remainder was written from obviously biased viewpoints. Yet it is on these scattered, diffuse, and often prejudiced sources that any study of the group must be mainly based. Despite the great power they wielded and their by no means colorless personalities, the Big Four have received little attention from biographers, either during their lifetimes or later. Until 1931 no formal life of any of the associates had been published. Biographical material was confined to occasional sketches in newspapers and periodicals, to passing mention in histories or in books of reminiscences, or to brief and inadequate publications of the memorial-volume type.

The Central Pacific itself, and the region and period in which the Big Four chiefly operated, have received far more thorough treatment. In these fields Bancroft's massive *History of California* is a storehouse of pertinent detail, and the story of the Big Four's railroad activities in the West is told in such volumes as Sabin's *Building the Pacific Railway*, Daggett's *Chapters on the History of the Southern Pacific,* Russell's *Stories of Great American Railroads,* and others. But revealing biographical details are not frequently encountered in such factual records, and the author's main reliance has been on less formal narratives. The files of California newspapers and weeklies have yielded much of interest, in particular the Sacramento *Union* of the '50s and '60s, the San Francisco *Chronicle* and *Alta California* of the '70s, the weekly *Wasp, News-Letter,* and *Argonaut* in the '80s, and, in the '90s and later, the San Francisco *Examiner* and *Bulletin.* The manuscript statements by Huntington, Crocker, Stanford, and Anna Judah, obtained in the '80s by employees of the industrious Bancroft and now preserved in the Bancroft Library, are revelatory of the personalities and viewpoints of the men concerned. Hardly less valuable from the same standpoint is the testimony given, often unwillingly, by the surviving associates at hearings of the Pacific Railway Commission of 1887. Of the collections of correspondence examined, the most important for the light they throw on the characters of the group are the often published letters from Huntington to Colton, Colton's replies (recently brought to light), and the large and varied collection of Alfred Cohen, former Central Pacific attorney.

Use of the facilities and services of the Reference and Newspaper Departments of the San Francisco Public Library, the Bancroft Library, Berkeley, the California Section of the State Library, Sacramento, the Huntington Library, San Marino, and the Library of the Society of California Pioneers, San Francisco, is gratefully acknowledged. Among individuals, special thanks are due to Mr. Edwin Grabhorn for access to his comprehensive collection of Western railroad material, to Mr. Clarkson Crane for a reading of the manuscript, to Miss Caroline Wenzel, Mr. Francis P. Farquhar, and Mrs. Helen Putnam Van Sicklen for help in the selection of illustrations, and to numerous others who have responded generously to requests for information or for permission to examine material in their possession.

Following is a list of the more important books consulted:

BANCROFT, H. H.: *History of California.* San Francisco, Cal. The History Company, 1888.

—— : *Chronicles of the Builders of the Commonwealth.* San Francisco, Cal. The History Company, 1891.

BERNER, BERTHA: *Mrs. Leland Stanford.* Stanford University, Cal. Stanford University Press, 1935.

BOWLES, SAMUEL: *Across the Continent.* Springfield, Mass. Samuel Bowles & Company, 1865.

BURCH, JOHN C.: *Theodore D. Judah.* (In First Annual of the Territorial Pioneers of California.) San Francisco, Cal. W. M. Hinton & Company, 1877.

CARR, SARAH PRATT: *The Iron Way.* Chicago, Ill. A. C. McClurg & Company, 1907.

CLARK, GEORGE T.: *Leland Stanford.* Stanford University, Cal. Stanford University Press, 1931.

CLELAND, ROBERT GLASS: *A History of California: The American Period.* New York, N. Y. The Macmillan Company, 1923.

CLEWS, HENRY: *Fifty Years in Wall Street*. New York, N. Y. Irving Publishing Company, 1908.

COLE, CORNELIUS: *Memoirs*. New York, N. Y. (Privately printed) 1908.

DAGGETT, STUART: *Chapters on the History of the Southern Pacific*. New York, N. Y. The Ronald Press Company, 1922.

DAVIE, JOHN L.: *My Own Story*. Oakland, Cal. Post-Enquirer Publishing Company, 1931.

FULTON, ROBERT LARDIN: *Epic of the Overland*. San Francisco, Cal. A. M. Robertson, 1924.

GOODWIN, C. C.: *As I Remember Them*. Salt Lake City, Utah. 1913.

HARPENDING, ASBURY: *The Great Diamond Hoax*. San Francisco, Cal. The James H. Barry Company, 1913.

HITTELL, JOHN S.: *A History of the City of San Francisco*. San Francisco, Cal. H. L. Bancroft & Company, 1878.

In Memoriam: Leland Stanford, Jr. n.p., n.d.

JORDAN, DAVID STARR: *The Days of a Man*. Yonkers-on-Hudson, N. Y. The World Book Company, 1922.

LEACH, FRANK A.: *Recollections of a Newspaperman*. San Francisco, Cal. Samuel Levinson, 1917.

Memorial Addresses on the Life and Character of Leland Stanford. Washington, D. C. Government Printing Office, 1894.

MYERS, GUSTAVUS: *History of the Great American Fortunes*. Revised edition. New York, N. Y. The Modern Library, 1936.

MILES, GEORGE E.: *Collis P. Huntington*. n.p., n.d. (1896).

Bibliography

OLDER, FREMONT: *My Own Story*. New York, N. Y. The Macmillan Company, 1926.

PACIFIC RAILWAY COMMISSION: *Testimony Taken by the Commission*. Washington, D. C. Government Printing Office, 1887.

PERKINS, J. R.: *Trails, Rails and War*. Indianapolis, Ind. The Bobbs-Merrill Company, 1929.

POST, C. C.: *Driven from Sea to Sea*. Philadelphia, Pa. Elliot and Beezley, 1888.

QUIETT, GLENN CHESNEY: *They Built the West*. New York, N. Y. D. Appleton-Century Company, 1934.

RAE, W. F.: *Westward by Rail*. Second edition. London. Longmans, Green & Company, 1871.

REDDING, B. B.: *A Sketch of the Life of Mark Hopkins of California*. San Francisco, Cal. A. L. Bancroft & Company, 1881.

REED, G. WALTER (editor): *History of Sacramento County*. Los Angeles, Cal. Historic Record Company, 1923.

RENSCH, H. E. and E. G., and HOOVER, MILDRED BROOKE: *Historic Spots in California: Valley and Sierra Counties*. Stanford University, Cal. Stanford University Press, 1933.

ROOT, HENRY: *Personal History and Reminiscences*. San Francisco, Cal. (Privately printed) 1921.

RUSSELL, CHARLES EDWARD: *Stories of the Great Railroads*. Chicago, Ill. Charles H. Kerr & Company, 1912.

SABIN, EDWIN L.: *Building the Pacific Railway*. Philadelphia, Pa. J. B. Lippincott Company, 1919.

SHUCK, OSCAR T.: *Representative and Leading Men of the Pacific.* San Francisco, Cal. Bacon & Company, 1870.

STARR, JOHN W., JR.: *Lincoln and the Railroads.* New York, N. Y. Dodd, Mead & Company, 1927.

STEWART, WILLIAM M.: *Reminiscences.* Boston, Mass. The Neale Publishing Company, 1908.

TINKHAM, GEORGE H.: *California Men and Events.* Stockton, Cal. Record Publishing Company, 1931.

WALKER, DAVID H.: *Pioneers of Prosperity.* San Francisco, Cal. 1895.

WHEAT, CARL I.: " A Sketch of the Life of Theodore D. Judah." (In *California Historical Society Quarterly,* Vol. IV, No. 3.) San Francisco, Cal. California Historical Society, 1925.

WILLIAMS, HENRY T. (editor): *The Pacific Tourist.* New York, N. Y. Henry T. Williams, 1879.

YOUNG, JOHN P.: *San Francisco: A History of the Pacific Coast Metropolis.* Chicago, Ill. The S. J. Clarke Publishing Company, 1912.

INDEX

i

Index

A NOTE ON THE TYPE

THIS BOOK is set on the Linotype in Baskerville. The punches for this face were cut under the supervision of George W. Jones, the eminent English printer and the designer of Granjon and Estienne. Linotype Baskerville is a facsimile cutting from type cast from the original matrices of a face designed by John Baskerville, a writing-master of Birmingham, for his own private press. The original face was the forerunner of the " modern " group of type faces, known today as Scotch, Bodoni, etc. After his death in 1775, Baskerville's punches and matrices were sold in France and were used to produce the sumptuous Kehl edition of Voltaire's works.

This book was composed, printed, and bound by The Plimpton Press, Norwood, Mass. The illustrations were reproduced in aquatone by Edward Stern & Co., Philadelphia. The paper was made by S. D. Warren Co., Boston. Designed by W. A. Dwiggins.